The
Polar Regions
102

Russia
76

stern
urope
70

Central
Eurasia
78

theastern
ope

Central Eurasia
78

Eastern Asia
86

Japan
88

The Middle East
80

Southern Asia
82

Southeast Asia
84

Papua
New Guinea
98

uthern
Africa
94

Australia
98

New Zealand and the
Southwestern Pacific
100

Map Page
References

The
Polar Regions
102

THE READER'S DIGEST
Children's Atlas
of the World

THE READER'S DIGEST
Children's Atlas of the World

A Reader's Digest Children's Book
Published by Reader's Digest Children's Publishing, Inc.
Reader's Digest Road, Pleasantville, NY 10570–7000

Conceived and produced by Weldon Owen Pty Limited
59 Victoria Street, McMahons Point, NSW, 2060, Australia
A member of the Weldon Owen Group of Companies
Sydney • San Francisco

Copyright © 1998 Weldon Owen Pty Limited
Revised edition copyright © 2000 Weldon Owen Pty Limited

READER'S DIGEST CHILDREN'S PUBLISHING, INC.
President: Vivian Antonangeli
Creative Consultant: Michael J. Morris
Group Publisher: Rosanna Hansen
U.S. Editor: Sherry Gerstein
Creative Director: Ira Teichberg
U.S. Production Coordinator: Debbie Gagnon
Director of Sales and Marketing: Rosanne McManus
Director of U.S. Sales: Lola Valenciano
Marketing Director: Karen Herman
U.S. Consultant: Stephen F. Steiner

WELDON OWEN PTY LTD
Chief Executive Officer: John Owen
President: Terry Newell
Publisher: Sheena Coupe

Design Concept: John Bull
Managing Editor: Ariana Klepac
Art Director: Sue Burk

Project Editor: Scott Forbes
Consulting Editor: Colin Sale
Editorial Assistant: Anne Ferrier
Text: Scott Forbes

Senior Designer: Hilda Mendham
Designer, Thematic Spreads: Lena Lowe
Pre-press Co-ordinator: Jocelyne Best
Computer Production: Laura Sassin, Amanda Woodward
Computer Graphics: Stuart McVicar
Jacket Design: John Bull
Senior Picture Researcher: Anne Ferrier
Picture Researcher: Peter Barker
Archives: Rita Joseph

Illustrators: Susanna Addario, Andrew Beckett/illustration, André Boos, Anne Bowman, Greg Bridges, Danny Burke, Martin Camm, Fiammetta Dogi, Simone End, Giuliano Fornari, Chris Forsey, John Francis/Bernard Thornton Artists, U.K., Jon Gittoes, Ray Grinaway, Terry Hadler/Bernard Thornton Artists, U.K., Tim Hayward/Bernard Thornton Artists, U.K., David Kirshner, Frank Knight, Mike Lamble, James McKinnon, Peter Mennim, Nicola Oram, Tony Pyrzakowski, Oliver Rennert, Barbara Rodanska, Claudia Saraceni, Michael Saunders, Peter Schouten, Stephen Seymour/Bernard Thornton Artists, U.K., Marco Sparaciari, Sharif Tarabay/illustration, Steve Trevaskis, Thomas Trojer, Genevieve Wallace, Trevor Weekes, Rod Westblade, Ann Winterbotham

Maps: Digital Wisdom Publishing Ltd
Flags: Flag Society of Australia

Production Managers: Helen Creeke, Caroline Webber
Production Assistant: Kylie Lawson
Vice President International Sales: Stuart Laurence

Library of Congress Cataloging–in–Publication Data

The Reader's Digest children's atlas of the world / consulting editor, Colin Sale; [maps, Digital Wisdom Publishing Ltd.].—Rev. ed.
p.   cm.
"Copyright 2000 Weldon Owen Pty Ltd"—Prelim.p.[2].
Includes bibliographical references and index.
SUMMARY: Includes more than fifty maps; a fact file on each country and territory; illustrations of places, people, landscapes, and wildlife; an introduction to map making and map reading; projects; activities; and quizzes.
ISBN 1–57584–372–2 (trade hard cover : alk. paper).
ISBN 1–57584–378–1 (lib. ed. : alk. paper)
1. Children's atlases. [1. Atlases. 2. Geography.] I. Sale, Colin. II. Weldon Owen Pty Limited. III. Digital Wisdom Publishing Ltd. IV. Title: Children's atlas of the World.

G1021   .R563   2000   99-26619
                                                                                                                        CIP
912—dc21   MAPS

Color Reproduction by Colourscan Co Pte Ltd
Printed by Toppan Printing Co, (H.K.) Ltd
Printed in China

A WELDON OWEN PRODUCTION

The Reader's Digest
Children's Atlas
of the World

Consulting Editor: Colin Sale

Reader's Digest
Children's Books™

Pleasantville, New York/Montréal, Québec

CONTENTS

NORTH AMERICA 32

SOUTH AMERICA 48

How to Use This Atlas

THE READER'S DIGEST CHILDREN'S ATLAS OF THE WORLD takes you on a fascinating tour of our extraordinary world. Before you set off, read the sections called Maps and Mapmaking and How to Read a Map. There you will find out about different kinds of maps and how they are made, and learn how to read and use maps. The remaining introductory pages are a guide to our planet, Earth. They show you where it is located in space, what it is made of, how its landscapes have been shaped, and how weather, wildlife and peoples vary around the world. The atlas maps are divided into seven parts—one for each of the continents of North America, South America, Europe, Asia, Africa, and Australia and Oceania, and one for the polar regions. Each part begins with a continent map that includes country lists and shows the most important features of the landscape. The continent map is followed by a series of illustrated maps which are packed with facts, pictures and activities. The sample maps and notes on these two pages explain the features on both types of map. At the back of the atlas you will find the World Fact File. This provides useful information on all of the world's countries and major territories. Finally, there is a glossary of terms used in this book, as well as a gazetteer—a geographical index that helps you to find places on the maps.

ILLUSTRATED MAP

Country list This is a list of the countries or states on the map, their populations and capital cities.

THE READER'S DIGEST CHILDREN'S ATLAS OF THE WORLD

France

FRANCE, THE LARGEST COUNTRY in western Europe, has a varied climate and landscape. In the north, the weather is mild and wet, and much of the land is flat. As you travel south, the climate becomes warmer and the land more mountainous. Three-quarters of the population live in towns and cities, but most of the country is farmland, and France is Europe's leading farming country. The northern plains are covered in fields of wheat and sugar beets, and in central and southern France vineyards dot the hillsides—more wine is produced in France than in any other country except Italy. The area around Paris, the capital, is the most densely populated region. It is home to one-fifth of the country's population and most of its industries. Several great rivers, including the Seine and the Loire, cross France's northern and western plains. These waterways were once the country's main transportation routes, and their banks are lined with historic villages and magnificent castles known as châteaus. In the south, the mountains of the Pyrenees and the Alps separate France from Spain and Italy. Among their snow-capped peaks lie popular ski resorts and national parks that are home to eagles, marmots and goatlike antelopes called chamois. Along the Mediterranean coast there are many busy beach resorts. Near the Italian border lies Monaco, the second-smallest country in the world. Monaco is famous for its casinos and its annual Grand Prix motor race.

FRANCE
POPULATION: 58,979,000 • CAPITAL: PARIS
MONACO
POPULATION: 32,200 • CAPITAL: MONACO

Amazing Fact This box contains fascinating facts about the area on the map.

• AMAZING FACT •

France is now connected to Great Britain by an undersea rail link known as the Channel Tunnel. The tunnel took seven years to build and includes two rail tracks. Trains take 35 minutes to pass through the tunnel. Travelers can journey from London to Paris in about three hours.

BOULES
Boules is a bowling game that is popular in France. It is played with metal balls on a hard dirt surface.

Continent Facts This includes the size of the continent, its population and the names of its countries.

CONTINENT MAP

Records This is a list of the tallest, longest and largest features of the continent.

Size comparison These pictures show how the continent's most important mountains and rivers would look if you could see them side by side.

Political map This map shows all the countries in the continent.

THE READER'S DIGEST CHILDREN'S ATLAS OF THE WORLD

North America

THE CONTINENT OF NORTH AMERICA extends from just south of the North Pole to just north of the equator. It includes almost every kind of environment, from ice caps to forests, mountains, deserts and jungles. In the west, an almost unbroken chain of mountains stretches from Alaska to Costa Rica and includes the Rocky Mountains, one of the world's most famous mountain ranges. The United States (often called the U.S.A. or America) and Canada are the largest of the continent's 23 countries. The United States is made up of 50 states. Canada is divided into ten provinces and two territories. North America includes some of the world's biggest cities, but also vast areas of wilderness. Most North Americans are the descendants of European immigrants, but there are also many people of African origin as well as groups of native peoples.

CONTINENT FACTS

MAJOR MOUNTAINS AND RIVERS

WORLD RECORDS

CONTINENT RECORDS

POLITICAL MAP

Physical map This map shows the main features of the landscape.

Physical map This map shows the main features of the landscape.

Colored border
Each part of the atlas has a different colored border.

Map reader's grid The letters and numbers on the border help you find places on the map. See page 10 to find out how to use the grid.

Projects By trying out these activities and experiments, you can learn more about a topic or a part of the world.

country border

regional (state) border

disputed border

CHANNEL ISLANDS (U.K.)

territory and country to which it belongs

Baltimore
◉ **ANNAPOLIS**
✪ **WASHINGTON, D.C.**

✪ national capital
◉ regional capital
● city or town

Arno

river

Lake Ontario

lake

▲ **Ben Nevis**
4,406 ft (1,343 m)

▲ major mountain

Ⓔ African elephants

Ⓔ endangered animal

France See World Fact File page 107

• PROJECT: *Cave Painting* •

The cave paintings at Lascaux were created about 15,000 years ago. Here's how you can create your own painting that will look thousands of years old.

❶ Stuff a strong paper bag with crumpled newspaper and then staple the bag closed.

❷ Mix some glue and sand and use this to paint the whole bag. When it dries it will look like a rock.

❸ Collect three or four different-colored soils. Sift out the lumps and then mix each color with glue to make earth paints (add water if the paints are too thick). Now you are ready to paint. Like the artists who created the Lascaux cave paintings, you can paint animals living in your area.

Look Again
To answer these questions, you'll need to take a close look at the information on the map.

• *L*OOK AGAIN •
● Which cathedral lies southwest of Paris?
● Name a horned animal found in the Pyrenees.
● What kind of food is produced in Dijon?
● Which small country is located east of Nice?

Locator globe
This globe shows where the area on the map is located.

LOCATION

FRANCE

SCALE
MILES
KILOMETERS

TOUR DE FRANCE
France's most famous sporting event, this cycle race around the entire country covers about 2,500 miles (4,000 km).

61

Illustrations These show the people, places, wildlife and activities in the area on the map.

Feature illustrations These pullout features provide extra information on some of the map illustrations.

Scale The scale bar helps you to calculate distances on the map. To find out how to do this, see page 10.

Compass The compass helps you find north. To find out how to use the compass, see page 10.

---

*K*EY TO MAP COLORS

Desert and semidesert   Forest and grassland   Tundra   Ice cap

Maps and Mapmaking

A MAP IS A PICTURE that shows you what an area of land looks like from above. Any area, no matter how large or small, can be drawn as a map. Some maps show small areas such as a town; others show the whole world. Because maps usually show areas that are much larger than the page they are printed on, objects have to be drawn much smaller than they really are. This is called drawing to scale. The bigger the area of a map, the smaller the real objects have to be drawn. Maps that show a small area and a large amount of detail are called large-scale maps. Maps that show a large area and a small amount of detail are called small-scale maps. On most maps, real objects are represented by lines, colors and symbols. For example, on a map of a town, black outlines may indicate streets, and colored shapes may show buildings. On a map of a country, towns may appear as simple black dots, and rivers as blue lines. A book of maps—like the one you are reading now—is called an atlas. An atlas usually contains maps of the whole world as well as maps of countries and continents.

MAPPING THE WORLD

Each of these maps shows the location of Riverford School, but each is drawn at a different scale.

In this map of Riverford School, lines, colored shapes and labels are used to show the school, nearby streets and other features. Maps of small areas like this are often called plans.

This is a map of Riverford town. Because the area of the map is larger, less detail can be shown. You can now see that the school is near houses, a park and a river, but you can no longer see the school parking area or playing field.

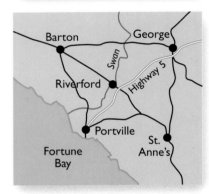

This map shows the region around Riverford. The town is now represented by a simple black dot, so you can no longer see the school or the streets. But you can see that Riverford is near water, and that it is linked to other towns by major and minor roads.

◆ AMAZING FACT ◆

In Greek mythology, Atlas was a man who led a rebellion against the gods. As a punishment for this act, he was made to support the world on his shoulders. When the first books of maps were published in the 16th century, many had an illustration of Atlas carrying a globe on their covers. As a result, a book of maps soon became known as an atlas.

◆ PROJECT: *Mapping Your Neighborhood* ◆

You can draw a map of your neighborhood. To do this you will have to think about where places are, how far apart they are, and what shape they are. You may need to go for a walk and make a list of the things you want to show on your map.

❶ Once you have decided what you are going to include, draw in the streets.

❷ Then add shapes to represent features such as buildings, parks and rivers. Label the streets.

❸ Now color your map. Use one color for houses, one for streets, and so on. Draw a key to show what the colors represent. Finally, add labels for important places such as your home and school.

MAKING MAPS

People who make maps are known as mapmakers or cartographers. Before airplanes and spacecraft were invented, mapmakers used information supplied by travelers and explorers to make maps. Nowadays, most maps are based on surveys and on photographs taken by satellites positioned in space, high above Earth. Mapmakers face one major problem: Earth is round, but most maps have to be flat. A globe is the most accurate kind of map because it is the same shape as Earth. But if you tried to create a flat map by simply peeling the surface of a globe, you would end up with a world map made up of pieces, or segments. You can test this for yourself by carefully peeling an orange and trying to flatten out the skin. You will find that it is impossible to make the peel lie flat without breaking it. In order to create a flat map, mapmakers have to stretch and squash the segments of the globe. The different ways in which they do this are known as projections. There are many types of projections, and each creates a slightly different map.

Arctic Circle (66.5°N)

Tropic of Cancer (23.5°N)

Equator (0°)

Tropic of Capricorn (23.5°S)

Antarctic Circle (66.5°S)

180°   Greenwich meridian (0°)   180°

A FLAT EARTH

As shown above, the surface of the globe can be divided into segments. To create a flat, rectangular map like the one on the left, mapmakers must fill in the gaps between the segments. To help them do this and plot locations, mapmakers use lines of latitude (horizontal lines) and longitude (vertical lines).

LINES AROUND THE WORLD

Mapmakers use a grid system to plot locations on the globe. Lines of longitude are drawn between the North Pole and the South Pole and are measured in degrees east or west of the Greenwich meridian (0°). Lines of latitude are drawn in a west-east direction and measured in degrees north or south of the equator (0°). The equator divides the world into the Northern and Southern hemispheres. The Greenwich meridian and the 180° line separate the Eastern and Western hemispheres.

How to Read a Map

MAPS ARE PACKED WITH INFORMATION. They tell you where places are, what size and shape they are, and how far and in what direction they lie from each other. Maps can also tell you about a region's climate, landscape, vegetation, towns and cities, and transportation routes. Once you have learned how to read maps, you can use an atlas to find out many things about countries all around the world.

FINDING PLACES

Most maps and atlases use a gazetteer and grid system to help you find places. You look for the place name in the gazetteer—an index of place names which usually appears at the back of the atlas—and then use the grid reference to find the location on the relevant map. Normally, a map grid consists of a series of letters along the top and bottom of the page and a series of numbers down the sides. Take a look at the map of Australia on the right. The grid reference for the city of Melbourne is H8. To find Melbourne, look at the letters on the top or bottom border and find H. Then find 8 on the left- or right-hand border. Imagine a line running down the page between the two Hs and another running across the page between the two 8s. (You can use a ruler to help you line up the numbers.) You will find Melbourne near the intersection of these lines.

USING THE MAP GRID

In the gazetteer of this book, each place name is followed by a grid reference. The grid reference for the city of Nashville, Tennessee, in the United States is 41 L4. To locate Nashville, turn to page 41 and find L and 4 on the grid. Trace a line down from L and another across from 4. Nashville is near the intersection of the two lines.

KEY
- City
- Capital cit
- River
- Lake
- Mountains
- Forest and grasslands
- Deserts

DESCRIBING DIRECTION

A map usually has a compass symbol, which indicates the direction of north (N) on the map. Sometimes, as on the map above, it also shows the directions of south (S), east (E) and west (W). You can use the points of a compass to describe where places are. For example, on the map above we can say that Sydney is east (E) of Adelaide and that Brisbane is north (N) of Sydney. Brisbane is both north and east of Adelaide, so we can use a combination of compass points and say that Brisbane is northeast (NE) of Adelaide. But Brisbane is farther to the east of Adelaide than it is to the north of it. So, if we want to be even more accurate, we can describe Brisbane as being east-northeast (ENE) of Adelaide. The compass above left shows all the combinations of compass points that you can use to describe direction.

G H I J

dry
land

river

forests and
grasslands

mountains

A L I A

Lake
Eyre
Cooper Creek
Brisbane

5

Darling

6

Lachlan

Adelaide
Sydney

7

Murray
CANBERRA

Melbourne

8

Hobart

9

G H I J K

COLOR KEYS

On this map of Australia, dark shading indicates mountains. Green represents forests and grasslands, and orange shows desert and other dry land. Areas of water such as oceans, lakes and rivers are all colored blue.

THE LAY OF THE LAND

The colors of a map may tell you something about a region's landscape, vegetation and climate. Often, shading is used to show mountain ranges, and colors are used to represent different kinds of vegetation. Green normally represents forests or grasslands, while yellow or orange indicates an area of dry land such as desert. On many maps, a special symbol, such as a square or star, is used to indicate a capital city. Most maps and atlases have a key that explains these features. In this atlas, you will find the key on page 7.

MEASURING DISTANCE

Most maps have a scale. This shows how distance on the map compares with real distance. Many scales appear as a bar that is divided into sections, as do the ones used in this book. In the scale shown on the map above, each section on the top part of the bar is equal to 250 miles, and each section on the bottom of the bar represents 400 kilometers. The project on this page shows you how to use this type of scale to measure distances on a map. Scales can also be written like this:

1:1,000,000

This shows that the map has been reduced 1,000,000 times. Distances on the ground are therefore 1,000,000 times greater than they are on the map. Thus 1 inch on the map is equal to 1,000,000 inches, or 15¾ miles, and 1 cm on the map is equal to 1,000,000 cm, or 10 km. Other scales are written like this:

1 inch = 10 miles

This shows that 1 inch on the map corresponds to 10 miles in real distance.

◆ PROJECT: *Using a Scale* ◆

To measure the distance between Perth and Sydney on the map at left, follow these steps:

❶ Place the straight edge of a piece of paper on the map so that it lines up the dots of the two cities. Mark their positions on the paper.

❷ Place the paper next to the scale so that one of the dots lines up with zero. The scale is shorter than the distance, so mark the paper where the scale ends and note the distance it represents.

Place the mark back at zero and repeat these steps as often as necessary. Add the figures to calculate the distance between the cities.

You can also use the scale to measure distances along curved lines.

❶ Place a piece of string on the map along the Darling River, bending it to match the course of the river.

❷ Grasp the string at each end of the river, then straighten it out and measure it against the scale. You can then calculate the length of the river.

N

Planet Earth

WE LIVE ON A SMALL PLANET in a tiny part of a vast universe. Our part of the universe is called the solar system. There are nine planets in the solar system, and they move around, or orbit, a star that we call the Sun. Enormous groups of stars are known as galaxies. Our galaxy is called the Milky Way and it is made up of at least 100 billion stars! There are many millions of galaxies in the universe and each one is surrounded by a vast, empty space. The solar system formed about five billion years ago from a large, swirling cloud of dust and gases. The hot, central part of the cloud became the Sun, while farther out, rocks and gases combined to form the planets. Other rock fragments became asteroids, or minor planets.

◆ AMAZING FACTS ◆

- Our galaxy looks like this. The faint, glowing arms of this galaxy are clouds of stars. Each of these stars is like our Sun and may have its own system of planets.
- Jupiter is bigger than all the other planets, moons, comets and asteroids put together. Yet, it is still only about a hundredth as large as the smallest star.

ROUND AND ROUND

As each planet orbits the Sun, it also spins, or rotates, on its axis—an imaginary line through its center. Earth rotates once every 24 hours, and takes one year to orbit the Sun. Planets near the Sun orbit more quickly than those farther away. Asteroids also orbit the Sun. Most are located between Mars and Jupiter, in an area known as the asteroid belt. The planets and asteroids are all held in their orbits by gravity, a powerful force that pulls them toward the Sun. Without this force, they would fly off into space.

THE PLANETS IN PERSPECTIVE

The illustration below shows the relative distances between the planets, as well as how long the planet takes to orbit the Sun (a year on that planet) and how long it takes to spin on its axis (a day on that planet).

Sun

Mercury Year: 88 Earth days. Day: 59 Earth days.

Venus Year: 225 Earth days. Day: 243 Earth days.

Earth Year: 365.25 days. Day: 24 hours.

Mars Year: 1.9 Earth years. Day: 24.6 hours.

Asteroid Belt

Jupiter Year: 11.9 Earth years. Day: 9.8 hours.

Saturn Year: 29.5 Earth years. Day: 10.2 hours.

Uranus Year: 84 Earth years. Day: 17.9 hours.

PROJECT: *Space Mobile*

You can make your own mobile of the solar system to hang up in your bedroom or in your classroom at school.

❶ First, collect some paper, colored pens, string or cotton thread, scissors and a coat hanger.

❷ Draw the Sun and each of the planets and color them. Make sure you copy the colors and relative sizes of the planets as shown in the illustrations on these pages.

❸ Carefully cut out each planet using a pair of scissors.

❹ Make a small hole in the top of each planet with the point of a pen or pencil and thread a length of string through the hole.

❺ Tie the Sun and the planets to the bottom of the coat hanger. Place the Sun in the middle and arrange the planets on either side of it in the order shown in the illustration on these pages. Don't forget that some planets are closer together than others.

❻ When all the planets are in place, the mobile is ready to hang.

WORLD IN MOTION

As Earth turns on its axis, we move in and out of the Sun's light. Day begins as we move into the light. As we turn away from the Sun, night falls. Because Earth is tilted at an angle, the amount of sunlight reaching different parts of the world varies throughout the year. When part of Earth is tilted toward the Sun, it is summer there. When it is tilted away from the Sun, it is winter.

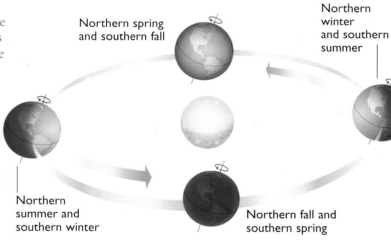

Northern spring and southern fall

Northern winter and southern summer

Northern summer and southern winter

Northern fall and southern spring

FIT FOR LIFE

Some planets are surrounded by a layer of gases called an atmosphere. As far as we know, Earth is the only planet in the solar system with an atmosphere that contains sufficient water and oxygen for life to flourish. Our atmosphere is so thin that if the planet were the size of an apple, the atmosphere would be only as thick as the peel.

Neptune Year: 165 Earth years. Day: 19.2 hours.

Pluto Year: 248 Earth years. Day: 6.4 Earth days.

An Ever-Changing Planet

EARTH IS SHAPED LIKE a large ball. Inside are several layers made of different materials. As Earth formed, heavy minerals such as iron and nickel sank to the center, while lighter materials rose to the middle and upper levels. At first, the upper levels consisted entirely of hot, liquid rock, but as Earth cooled, the outside solidified to form a thin, hard crust. This crust broke into several pieces, known as lithospheric plates. These plates float on the liquid, molten rock—or magma—underneath and are constantly moving, although you cannot feel the movement. Energy from Earth's core creates powerful convection currents that force the plates together and apart. This happens extremely slowly, but over millions of years these movements shape and shift the surface of Earth, causing earthquakes and volcanic eruptions and forming mountains and islands.

Inner core
Outer core
Lower mantle
Asthenosphere
Lithosphere
Upper mantle
Ocean crust
Continental crust
Convection currents

INSIDE EARTH

Our planet's solid iron inner core is surrounded by an outer core of liquid iron and nickel. Above this is a layer of solid rock called the lower mantle and a wide band of liquid rock known as the asthenosphere. Earth's outer layer is called the lithosphere. It consists of the solid rock of the upper mantle, and the crust. Crust under the land (continental crust) is usually thicker than crust under the sea (ocean crust). In Earth's core, temperatures reach an amazing 5,400°F (3,000°C). This heat creates strong convection currents that push the crust in different directions.

◆ PROJECTS: *Folding the Crust* ◆

❶ Cut a paper plate in half. These halves represent two of Earth's lithospheric plates.

❷ Using adhesive tape, attach a sheet of paper to the plate halves. The paper represents Earth's crust.

❸ If you slide one half of the plate under the other, the paper buckles. Similarly, when two of Earth's plates collide, their crusts fold, forming mountains.

❶ Take a sheet of paper, fold it in half and continue to fold it.

❷ After six folds, it becomes difficult to fold the paper any further. In the same way, the thicker Earth's crust, the greater the force required to fold it.

Spreading plates

Hot-spot volcanoes

Coastal collisions

Coastal Collisions

When thin ocean crust meets thick continental crust, the thin crust slides under the thicker crust. Magma rises to the surface and forms a line of volcanoes. This process formed Mount St. Helens in the United States.

Hot-Spot Volcanoes

Weaknesses in the middle of plates, known as hot spots, allow magma from the asthenosphere to burst through the crust and form volcanoes. The Hawaiian Islands were created by hot-spot volcanoes.

Spreading Plates

Circulating magma may force plates apart. Where the plates separate, magma rises through the gap and cools and hardens to form a ridge. Normally this happens under the sea, but in Iceland it can be seen on land.

WORLD IN MOTION

Convection currents cause Earth's plates to collide, separate and slide past each other. The effects of these movements are shown in the illustration above and in the photographs on the right.

200 million years ago

90 million years ago

Present

60 million years from now

PLATE MOVEMENTS
Earth's plates fit together like the pieces of a jigsaw puzzle, but the plates are constantly moving. This map shows the direction in which each plate moves. Most volcanoes and earthquakes occur where plates meet. This means that countries in the center of plates, such as Australia, have few earthquakes and volcanoes, whereas countries at the edges of plates, such as Japan, have many.

North American Plate

Eurasian Plate

Arabian Plate

Caribbean Plate

African Plate

Pacific Plate

Pacific Plate

Cocos Plate

South American Plate

Indo-Australian Plate

Nazca Plate

Scotia Plate

Antarctic Plate

Philippine Plate

→ Direction of movement

▲ Volcanoes

Earthquake zones

ON THE MOVE
Over millions of years, plate movements have joined and divided Earth's landmasses. Two hundred million years ago, there was a single "supercontinent." It split into two landmasses, which then broke up to form the continents we know today. Further changes to these landmasses will occur as Earth's plates continue to drift.

◆ AMAZING FACTS ◆
- When the volcano on the island of Krakatoa in Indonesia erupted on August 27, 1883, the explosion was heard 3,000 miles (4,800 km) away!
- More than 500,000 earthquakes occur every year. Fortunately, most of these are too weak to cause any damage.

Sliding plates

Folding crust

Undersea collisions

Sliding Plates
A fault line forms where two plates slide past each other. The friction between the plates creates earthquakes. These occur regularly along the San Andreas fault in California as part of the coastline slides northward.

Folding Crust
When two plates with crusts of similar thickness collide, the edge of one plate slides under the other, and the crusts buckle and fold to form mountains. This process created the massive Himalayas mountain range in Asia.

Undersea Collisions
When two plates with ocean crust collide, one may sink beneath the other, forming a deep trench. In places, magma bursts through the crust to form volcanic islands. The islands of Japan formed in this way.

◆ LOOK AGAIN ◆
- What is Earth's inner core made of?
- What kind of volcanoes formed the Hawaiian Islands?
- Where are earthquakes most likely to occur?

Weather and Climate

OUR WEATHER MAY CHANGE from day to day, but we usually experience the same kind of weather from year to year. The pattern of weather that occurs in a region over a long period is known as the climate. The climate of an area depends on three main factors: how far north or south of the equator it is (its latitude), how high it is (its altitude), and how close it is to the sea. As a result of Earth's orbit and its round shape, sunlight warms areas near the equator more than areas near the poles. Tropical regions are therefore hot year-round, and the poles are always cold. Areas between the tropics and the poles are temperate. This means that they have warm summers and cool winters. Mountains are colder than lowland areas because as you climb higher the atmosphere becomes thinner and retains less heat. In coastal regions, sea breezes and ocean currents prevent the weather from becoming too hot or too cold, so these areas have a milder climate than inland areas. Where winds blow inland from the sea, they are usually moist and bring high rainfall.

WIND PATTERNS

Because hot air rises and cold air sinks, the Sun's uneven heating of Earth's surface causes air to circulate as shown in the large diagram below. These patterns of air circulation are deflected by the planet's rotation, and form the major wind systems shown on the globe below right. These winds carry warm or cold, moist or dry air, and are an important influence on Earth's climates.

WORLD CLIMATES

The world can be divided into eight major climate zones, which are shown on this map and described on these pages. Ocean currents influence many of these climates. For example, northwestern Europe has a mild climate as a result of the warm waters of the Gulf Stream.

warm currents   cool currents

Cold Temperate
These regions have long, bitterly cold and snowy winters. Their summers are usually mild and damp

Mountain
Mountains are normally colder, wetter and windier than neighboring regions that lie nearer sea level.

Polar
The polar regions are extremely cold for most of the year. Although snow falls regularly, the poles are relatively dry.

Air Circulation

Warm and cold air meet, creating a belt of stormy, wet weather.

Cold easterly winds blow from the poles.

Upper air cools and sinks, creating dry conditions.

60°N

Air flows poleward from the southwest

30°N

Air flows toward the equator from the northeast

Warm, moist air rises at the equator, clouds form and rain falls.

Equator

Wind Systems

Polar easterlies

Westerlies

Trade winds

Westerlies

Polar easterlies

Wet Temperate
Wet temperate regions have four distinct seasons, with cool, wet winters and warm, wet summers.

Dry Temperate
Rainfall is relatively low in these regions. Most areas have mild, wet winters and hot, dry summers.

Desert and Semidesert
These are dry, barren areas with very low rainfall. They are usually hot by day, but may be cold, or even frosty, at night.

Subtropical
In summer, these regions are hot and wet like tropical areas. In winter, they are dry and mild like deserts.

Tropical
The tropics are hot and wet. In some areas, it rains all year round. In others, most of the rain falls in summer.

◆ AMAZING FACT ◆

Thunderstorms are most common in tropical areas, but occur all over the world. At least 20,000 storms occur each day, and at any one time about 2,000 may be taking place. Lightning from these storms strikes the ground as frequently as 100 times every second.

ENERGY FROM THE SUN
Because Earth is shaped like a ball, the Sun strikes it more directly near the equator than at the poles. This is why tropical areas are hot and the polar regions are cold.

◆ PROJECT: *Why the Poles Are Colder Than the Equator* ◆

❶ In a dark room, hold a lighted flashlight a few inches above, and at right angles to, a flat surface such as a tabletop. Observe the shape and brightness of the patch of light.

❷ Tilt the flashlight and note how the light changes. When the light strikes the surface from directly overhead, the patch of light is small and intense. When the light strikes the table at an angle, the patch is larger and weaker.

In a similar way, sunlight is most intense at the equator, where it strikes the ground from directly overhead. At the poles, the light strikes Earth at an angle and is spread across a wider area, making it much weaker.

The Living World

ALMOST EVERY PART OF OUR PLANET is inhabited by an amazing variety of living things. So far, scientists have named about two million kinds, or species, of plants and animals, but there may be between 10 and 100 million species on Earth! All living things inhabit the biosphere, which is made up of the land, oceans and atmosphere. Within the biosphere, there are many kinds of environments. Over millions of years, plants and animals have gradually altered their bodies and behavior to suit their particular environments. This process is known as adaptation. Together, an environment and its inhabitants form an ecosystem. The members of each ecosystem depend on each other for food and other resources. For example, vegetation provides food for plant-eating animals (herbivores) which may in turn be eaten by meat-eating animals (carnivores). These close relationships mean that damage to one part of an ecosystem is likely to affect every other part of it.

GLOBAL ECOSYSTEMS

Each of Earth's environments has its own community of plants and animals. This illustration shows how ecosystems change between the tropical rain forests (far left) and the polar ice caps (far right).

Oceans

The oceans contain a huge variety of species that have adapted to life under water. Marine plants include many kinds of seaweed. Animals include sea mammals such as seals and whales, coral, and thousands of fish species.

Tropical Rain Forests

The hot, humid weather of the tropics creates dense forests that are home to more species than any other environment. Monkeys and birds live high in the trees, while jaguars and other mammals prowl the forest floor.

Subtropical Savannas

With rain falling only in summer, subtropical areas have few trees. The African savanna grasslands support herds of herbivores such as zebras, which are hunted by lions and other carnivores. Vultures and other scavengers eat the leftovers.

Deserts and Semideserts

Desert species have adapted to drought. Some plants, such as cacti, store water in their stems. Others have long roots that reach water far underground. In hot deserts, many animals come out only at night, when it is cooler.

WORLD ENVIRONMENTS

Because the weather determines the types of plants that grow, Earth's environments are closely related to its climate zones.

- Tropical rain forests
- Subtropical savannas
- Deserts and semideserts
- Temperate grasslands and shrub woodlands
- Temperate forests
- Coniferous forests
- Mountains
- Polar ice caps and tundra

◆ AMAZING FACT ◆

The world's largest flower, the rafflesia, is found in the rain forests of southeast Asia and can measure up to three feet (1 m) in diameter. It gives off a smell like rotting flesh which attracts insects.

Mountains

The higher the land, the less vegetation there is and the colder and windier it gets. Thick fur coats keep many mountain animals warm. Some species, such as mountain goats, have special hooves that help them climb rocky slopes.

Polar Ice Caps and Tundra

The ice caps are bitterly cold and offer little shelter. Some animals have fur and a thick layer of fat to keep them warm. Tundra is treeless land that surrounds the Arctic ice cap. Its low shrubs feed hares, lemmings and other herbivores.

Temperate Grasslands and Shrub Woodlands

Moderate rainfall creates grasslands and shrub woodlands. Grasslands attract herbivores such as bison and are ideal hunting grounds for birds of prey. There is little shelter, so some animals live in burrows.

Temperate Forests

Trees grow well in wet temperate regions. In areas with cold winters, most of the trees are deciduous, which means that they shed their leaves in fall. Some animals migrate in winter; others survive on food stored during summer.

Coniferous Forests

Cold temperate regions are covered by forests of evergreen trees called conifers. Shaped so that snow slides off them, these trees are well adapted to the cold winters. Many animals have thick fur, and some hibernate for the winter.

◆ LOOK AGAIN ◆

- Name a plant-eating animal that lives on the African savanna.

- Which plants store water in their stems?

- How have animals adapted to mountain environments?

Our Natural Resources

EARTH PROVIDES US with everything that we need to live. Its atmosphere, rivers and lakes supply fresh water which, with sunshine and soil, enables plants to grow. In turn, plants produce vital supplies of oxygen and provide us and other animals with food. Animals supply humans with meat, wool and dairy products. Plants also provide timber, fuel, and textiles such as cotton. All these resources—water, plants, crops, animals—are renewable. This means that if we manage them carefully they will never run out. Other resources are nonrenewable. They do not regrow or replenish themselves and will eventually be used up. They include minerals, precious stones and fossil fuels (coal, oil and gas). Minerals—such as clay, chalk and many metals—and precious stones—such as diamonds and emeralds—have a wide range of uses, particularly in industry. Coal, oil and gas supply most of the energy we need for lighting and heating our homes and for fueling our cars. They are known as fossil fuels because they are the remains of animals and plants buried deep underground. Some of these nonrenewable resources may run out within the next 50 years. Because of this, and because burning fossil fuels creates pollution, scientists are trying to find ways of using renewable resources to supply more of the energy we need.

ENERGY SUPPLIES

The illustration below shows our principal sources of energy. As the chart on the right indicates, coal, oil and gas still supply most of our fuel. But alternative energy supplies such as wind and solar power are being developed in many parts of the world. As reserves of fossil fuels run out, these sources will become increasingly important.

Energy Use

- Hydroelectric 2.5%
- Alternative sources 0.5%
- Nuclear 7%
- Gas 23%
- Oil 40%
- Coal 27%

EARTH'S RESOURCES

The map above shows how land is used in different parts of the world, and where major fuel reserves are located.

- Major gas field
- Major coal field
- Major oil field
- Urban areas: towns, cities and industries
- Areas with large farms where people grow crops and raise animals for sale

Oil

Oil and gas are found together in rock layers in Earth's crust. They are extracted by drilling from sea- or land-based rigs.

Coal

Coal is more plentiful than other fossil fuels. It can be collected by digging at the surface or by mining deep underground.

Uranium

Radioactive elements such as uranium emit high-energy particles that are converted into electricity at nuclear power plants.

Geothermal Power

In some parts of the world, ground water is heated by hot volcanic rocks, creating steam that is used to generate power.

THE WATER CYCLE

A process known as the water cycle provides us with a regular supply of fresh water. Water in oceans, lakes and rivers is constantly evaporating into the air, where it exists as water vapor. The warmer the air, the more water vapor it can hold. When air cools, its ability to hold water decreases, and some of the water vapor turns, or condenses, into tiny water droplets or ice crystals. These droplets or crystals form clouds. If the droplets or crystals combine and become heavy enough, they fall as rain or snow. Water that falls on land drains into rivers, lakes and underground channels. It then flows into the sea, replenishing the oceans and completing the water cycle.

Areas with small farms where people grow crops and raise animals mainly for their own use

Deserts, dry grasslands and tundra used for grazing small numbers of animals

Areas that are too cold or dry for farming, but include some mining and hunting

Grassland areas used for grazing large numbers of animals

Forested areas with some farming, hunting and mining

Major fishing grounds

◆ PROJECT: *Create a Water Cycle* ◆

This simple experiment will show you how the water cycle works.

❶ Cool a long, metal spoon or ladle by placing it in a freezer for a few minutes. Choose a spoon with a wooden handle.

❷ Ask an adult to help you boil some water in a kettle or saucepan.

❸ As the water boils, the warm air above the water rises. As it starts to cool, it condenses and forms clouds of steam.

❹ Hold the cold spoon over the steam, being careful not to burn yourself. The cooling effect of the cold metal causes the water vapor to condense more quickly and form droplets of water on the underside of the spoon.

❺ The droplets grow in size until they become heavy enough to fall, just like rain. Some of the droplets may fall back into the kettle or saucepan, replenishing the water supply.

Hydroelectric Power
Hydroelectric power is created when water is passed through electricity-generating turbines at the bottom of a dam.

Wind Power
Windmills convert the power of the wind into electricity. The wind turns the windmills, which drive electrical generators.

Solar Power
Clusters of mirrorlike solar panels reflect the Sun's rays onto a solar furnace, where the intense heat is converted into electricity.

Sea Power
At a tidal dam or barrage, waves pass through narrow tunnels, driving huge turbines that produce power.

The Human Family

OUR PLANET IS HOME to about 6 billion people. This population is not spread evenly over Earth's landmasses. Instead, people are concentrated where resources are plentiful, or can be easily obtained by trade. Therefore, few people live in deserts or polar regions, but many live in fertile areas, close to energy sources, and near rivers and coasts. The world's population is now growing more quickly than ever before. In the time it takes you to read this sentence, more than 20 babies will have been born. Since 1950 the number of people on Earth has more than doubled. This growth is the result of a longer life expectancy due to improved medical services, and a high birth rate in some parts of the world. The most rapid population growth occurs in developing countries—poorer countries with little industry or technology. It is difficult for these countries to feed and take care of their growing populations, so many of them are urging their people to have fewer children.

NATIONAL POPULATIONS

This diagram shows the 10 countries with the world's largest populations. China has by far the biggest population—in fact, one in every five people in the world lives in China!

WHERE PEOPLE LIVE

The dots on this map show the world's most densely populated areas.

◼ Developed countrie
◼ Developing countrie

China	India	U.S.A.	Indonesia	Brazil	Russia	Pakistan	Bangladesh	Japan	Nigeria
1.25 billion	1 billion	274 million	216 million	172 million	146 million	138 million	127 million	126 million	114 million

CROWDED COUNTRIES

Some countries are densely populated—a large population lives in a small area. Others are sparsely populated—a small population occupies a large area.

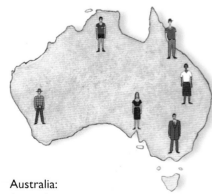

The Netherlands:
1,000 people per square mile
(400 per sq. km)

Australia:
6 people per square mile
(2 per sq. km)

GROWING CITIES

As countries develop, people move to cities to look for work in factories and businesses. As shown by this comparison of the populations of Paris, France, and Jakarta, Indonesia, cities in developing countries are now growing more rapidly than those in developed countries.

🗼 Paris   ⬆ Jakarta

1970	**1990**	**2010**
8.5 million 3.9 million	9.3 million 9.3 million	9.6 million 19.2 million

- Every second, three babies are born.
- If the world's population were spread out evenly over its landmasses, each person would occupy an area larger than four football fields.
- Standing side by side, everyone in the world could fit onto the island of Jamaica.

POPULATION GROWTH

Every four days, one million children are born. If the world's population continues to grow at this rate, it will have reached 10 billion by the year 2100. The populations of developing countries are expanding rapidly while those of developed countries are growing slowly or decreasing.

Developing countries

Developed countries

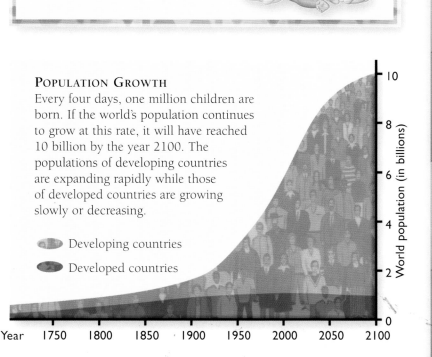

World population (in billions)

Year 1750 1800 1850 1900 1950 2000 2050 2100

RICH AND POOR

Countries with large industries and high levels of technology are called developed countries. People in these parts of the world are generally wealthy and have many possessions. In countries with little industry and technology, people are poorer and have few possessions. These countries are known as developing countries. Although they are home to far fewer people, developed countries are much richer and use a much larger proportion of the world's resources than developing countries.

More than 3,000 languages are spoken around the world, but more than one-third of the world's population speaks one of the following six languages. So you can learn to say "hello" to more than two billion people!

hello
English
(350 million speakers)

你好
ni hao
Chinese
(1 billion speakers)

mar-ha-**ban**
Arabic
(150 million speakers)

¡hola!
o-la
Spanish
(250 million speakers)

नमस्ते
na-ma-**stay**
Hindi
(200 million speakers)

привет!
pree-**vyet**
Russian
(150 million speakers)

Developed countries:
make up 20% of the world's population
own 80% of the world's wealth
use 70% of the world's energy

Developing countries:
make up 80% of the world's population
own 20% of the world's wealth
use 30% of the world's energy

A Shrinking World

IN 1850, THE JOURNEY BETWEEN London and New York took about three weeks. Now the same distance can be traveled in just over three hours. This dramatic difference has altered our view of the world. Countries now seem closer together than ever before—the world seems to be shrinking! Faster means of transportation, along with recently developed technologies, have greatly increased international trade and communication. Airplanes can carry goods to the other side of the world within a day. Fresh foods, such as meat, fruit and vegetables, which would previously have spoiled before they reached their destinations, can now be transported over long distances in refrigerated container ships. Modern telecommunications—telephone, fax and electronic mail services—allow businesses to deal directly with customers anywhere in the world. Telecommunications also enable us to increase our understanding of other places and peoples. We can watch television programs about other countries, speak to people on the other side of the world by telephone, and even make new friends on computer networks such as the Internet.

1860: Clipper ship, 3 weeks

1910: *Mauretania* steamship, 5 days

1939: Boeing 314 Clipper seaplane, 24 hours

Today: Concorde supersonic jet, 3½ hours

TRANSATLANTIC TRANSPORTATION

In the mid-19th century, a clipper ship was the fastest means of transportation between New York and London. The exact length of the journey depended on the weather, but the trip usually took about three weeks. By 1910, the steamship *Mauretania* had cut the Atlantic crossing to five days. In 1939, the Boeing 314 Clipper seaplane provided the first passenger aircraft service across the Atlantic, with a flight time of about 24 hours. Today, the Concorde supersonic jet can complete the same trip in three and a half hours.

SEA ROUTES

Today, few people travel by sea, but goods of all kinds are transported by container ships and tankers. This map shows the world's most important shipping routes and busiest ports. Rotterdam in the Netherlands handles more cargo than any other seaport.

AIR ROUTES

Flying is now the most popular form of international travel. This map shows the busiest international air routes and airports. Heathrow in London handles more international flights than any other airport, but Chicago's O'Hare Airport is the world's busiest, with more than 2,000 planes landing and taking off each day.

INTERNATIONAL TRADE

The countries of the world exchange a wide variety of goods. Countries that have more raw materials and produce more food and goods than they need export some of those materials to countries that have few resources. Other countries export little because they need all their own resources. In the diagram below, the arrows indicate the direction of trade in three categories of goods: food, raw materials (including minerals, fuels and timber), and manufactured goods (goods that are made in factories, such as cars and electrical equipment). The illustrations show the most important products in each region.

◆ *L*OOK AGAIN ◆

- If it is midday in England, what is the time in eastern Australia?
- Which is New Zealand's busiest port?
- What kinds of manufactured goods does Japan export?

→ Food
→ Raw materials
→ Manufactured goods

ASIA
Oil
Minerals
Timber
Cars
Cameras
Iron and steel
JAPAN
High-tech goods
Wheat
Iron and steel
Timber
High-tech goods
NORTH AMERICA
Cars
Iron and steel
Processed foods
EUROPE
Minerals
Beef
SOUTH AMERICA
Wheat
Wool
Coal
Wheat
Beef
Minerals
AFRICA
AUSTRALIA AND NEW ZEALAND

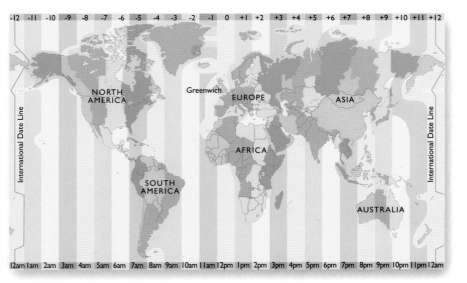

| -12 | -11 | -10 | -9 | -8 | -7 | -6 | -5 | -4 | -3 | -2 | -1 | 0 | +1 | +2 | +3 | +4 | +5 | +6 | +7 | +8 | +9 | +10 | +11 | +12 |

NORTH AMERICA
Greenwich
EUROPE
ASIA
AFRICA
SOUTH AMERICA
AUSTRALIA

12am 1am 2am 3am 4am 5am 6am 7am 8am 9am 10am 11am 12pm 1pm 2pm 3pm 4pm 5pm 6pm 7pm 8pm 9pm 10pm 11pm 12am

TIME ZONES

The world is divided into 24 time zones, and time is measured in hours ahead of or behind the time at Greenwich, England. The time is the same throughout each zone and is usually one hour ahead of or behind the neighboring time zones. The International Date Line marks where one day ends, and another begins.

A VIRTUAL WORLD

Computers are changing the ways in which we work, relax and communicate. You can now send electronic mail (e-mail) and other digital information from one computer to another almost anywhere in the world. You can also read magazines, hear music and even shop using information networks such as the Internet. Some networks allow you to speak directly to other people and even see them on your computer screen. This is called video conferencing. In the future, more and more people are likely to use computers for shopping, entertainment and business.

Planet in Peril

THE FUTURE OF OUR PLANET is at risk, now more than ever before. In the last 200 years, rapid population growth and the development of industry and technology have magnified the effect of our activities on the environment. Supplies of fossil fuels and other nonrenewable resources are running out. We are overusing the soil, forests and fishing grounds, and no longer giving these renewable resources a chance to recover. Waste from our homes and industries is poisoning water supplies, and gases from our cars and factories are polluting the air we breathe. Increasing air pollution may even be changing the climate. Scientists all over the world are trying to find ways to preserve resources and limit the damage we are doing to Earth. Through simple activities such as recycling, using our cars less and buying environmentally friendly products, we can all play a part in protecting Earth and preserving its resources for future generations.

A GLOBAL CRISIS

This map shows that environmental problems affect almost every part of Earth. The most serious problems are described and illustrated on these pages.

- Existing deserts
- Areas at risk of becoming deserts
- Existing rain forest
- Cleared rain forest
- Cities with severe air pollution
- Areas affected by acid rain
- Polluted waterways
- Heavy oil slicks created by shipping
- Light oil slicks created by shipping
- Major nuclear accidents
- Major oil tanker disasters
- Major oil rig explosions

• AMAZING FACTS •

- An acre (0.4 ha) of Brazilian rain forest is destroyed every nine seconds.
- Every day, more than 50 species become extinct. This is mainly the result of human activities such as forestry and hunting.

Holding Back the Desert

In dry parts of the world, overgrazing and clearing the land of its natural vegetation can turn fertile areas into desert. To keep deserts from spreading farther, we need to better manage the land we farm and replant trees and shrubs.

Saving the Forests

Vast areas of natural forest are being cleared to supply timber, fuel and paper, and to make way for towns and farms. You can help protect the world's forests and reduce the need for more wood by recycling paper. Replanting trees also helps.

Reducing Air Pollution

Cars and factories fill the air with grime and poisonous gases. Industries and car manufacturers are trying to reduce such pollution. You can also help by walking, cycling or using public transportation instead of traveling by car.

Oil Spills
Oil and other pollutants spilled by ships are a threat to wildlife. In 1989, oil spilled by the tanker *Exxon Valdez* off the coast of Alaska, in the United States, killed thousands of animals, including 350,000 seabirds.

Nuclear Accidents
Nuclear accidents occur rarely but can be devastating. In 1986, an accident at the Chernobyl nuclear power plant in the Ukraine released a cloud of radioactive gas across Europe, poisoning land, crops and people.

Oil Well Explosions
Accidents on oil and gas rigs can cause major environmental problems. During the Gulf War in Kuwait in 1992, hundreds of oil wells were set on fire, causing serious water and air pollution throughout the region.

Eliminating Acid Rain
Air pollution can turn rain into a strong acid. Acid rain kills trees, pollutes rivers and even damages buildings. The only way to stop acid rain is to reduce air pollution.

Saving the Ozone Layer
A layer of ozone in the upper atmosphere filters out harmful radiation from the Sun. This layer is being damaged by chlorofluorocarbons (CFCs)—chemicals found in some aerosols and refrigerators. Always buy CFC-free products.

Keeping Our Water Clean
The world's rivers and oceans are being poisoned by waste from factories and shipping, and sewage from homes and offices. To help protect water supplies, support local cleanup programs, and never dispose of garbage in or near waterways.

Sunlight passes through atmosphere and heats Earth.

Greenhouse gases retain heat close to Earth.

Earth

GLOBAL WARMING
Gases in the atmosphere, known as greenhouse gases, keep Earth warm by trapping some of the energy that comes from the Sun. But the burning of fossil fuels is raising the levels of these gases, causing the planet to warm too much. If this continues, some fertile land may turn into desert, and ice caps may melt, causing flooding in lowland areas. Most countries are trying to reduce greenhouse gas emissions.

> ### ◆ *L*OOK AGAIN ◆
>
> ● How can we prevent acid rain?
> ● What gases keep Earth warm?
> ● How can you help protect the ozone layer?

The Physical World

WE CALL OUR PLANET EARTH, but more than two-thirds of its surface is covered by salt water. Large areas of salt water are called oceans, and smaller areas are known as seas. There are four oceans—the Pacific, Atlantic, Indian and Arctic—and many seas. The Pacific Ocean alone is larger than all of Earth's landmasses combined. Land covers only 29 percent of our planet's surface. Its shape and the kind of soil and vegetation that cover it vary enormously from place to place. Throughout the world there are hills, mountains and areas of flat land called plains. Trees and other plants cover many parts of Earth, but some places have almost no vegetation. Deserts—very dry areas with sparse vegetation—cover about one-fifth of the world's land. The polar regions and many mountaintops are covered in ice and snow. The seas, too, have their mountains and valleys. Deep trenches are found in most oceans, and mountains on many islands are actually the tops of undersea mountains. For instance, Mauna Kea, on the island of Hawaii in the Pacific Ocean, is 33,480 feet (10,205 m) high, measured from the sea floor to its highest point. That's far taller than Mount Everest, the highest mountain on land.

PHYSICAL FACTS

Circumference of Earth around the equator: 24,902 miles (40,067 km)
Area of sea: 139,782,000 square miles (362,033,000 sq. km)
Area of land above sea level: 57,151,000 square miles (148,021,000 sq. km)
Largest ocean: Pacific Ocean, 64,186,300 square miles (166,241,700 sq. km)
Largest landmass: Eurasia (Europe and Asia), 20,733,000 square miles (53,698,000 sq. km)
Deepest ocean trench: Mariana Trench, Pacific Ocean, 35,797 feet (10,911 m)
Largest island: Greenland, 840,000 square miles (2,175,000 sq. km)

• AMAZING FACT •

Almost all of the water on Earth—97.3 percent—is salt water. Less than 3 percent is fresh water, and two-thirds of this is locked up in icecaps and glaciers. That leaves less than 1 percent in rivers, lakes and underground channels.

Countries of the World

APART FROM ANTARCTICA, which has no permanent population, all the land on Earth is divided into countries. There are almost 200 countries in the world, and each country has its own government and its own laws. The world's smallest country, the Vatican City, measures only one-fifth of a square mile (0.44 sq. km). That's about the size of 100 football fields. The largest country in the world, Russia, is 39 million times bigger! The lines that separate countries are called borders. On this world map, the countries are shown in different colors so that you can see the borders clearly. Borders may be straight or curved. Some are formed by rivers or mountain ranges; others cross lakes or seas. The sizes of countries and the shapes of their borders often change. Sometimes a large country divides into smaller countries because groups of people want to form separate countries. Neighboring countries often disagree about where a border ought to be. Such disputes have led to wars in many parts of the world. In this atlas, disputed borders are shown by a dotted line. Many countries govern areas of land in other parts of the world. These are called territories. On a map, the name of the governing country usually appears in parentheses after the name of the territory.

POLITICAL FACTS

Number of countries: 193
Number of territories: 65
Largest countries:
Russia, 6,592,812 square miles (17,075,383 sq. km)
Canada, 3,851,809 square miles (9,976,185 sq. km)
China, 3,700,000 square miles (9,583,000 sq. km)
Smallest country: Vatican City, 0.17 square miles (0.44 sq. km)
Longest border: U.S.-Canada, 3,987 miles (6,416 km)

• LOOK AGAIN •

The following shapes represent countries shown on the world map on the right. Can you find and name them?

KEY TO NUMBERED COUNTRIES

1 THE NETHERLANDS	9 CROATIA	16 YUGOSLAVIA
2 BELGIUM	■10 ANDORRA	17 ALBANIA
■3 LUXEMBOURG	■11 MONACO	18 MACEDONIA
4 CZECH REPUBLIC	■12 SAN MARINO	■19 GIBRALTAR (U.K.)
5 SLOVAKIA	■13 VATICAN CITY	20 ARMENIA
6 SWITZERLAND	14 BOSNIA-	21 AZERBAIJAN
■7 LIECHTENSTEIN	HERZEGOVINA	22 UNITED ARAB
8 SLOVENIA	15 MOLDOVA	EMIRATES

J K L M N O P Q

2
3
4
5
6
7
8
9
10
11

ARCTIC OCEAN

SVALBARD
(NORWAY)

JAN MAYEN ISLAND
(NORWAY)

ICELAND

FAEROE ISLANDS
(DENMARK)

SWEDEN
FINLAND

NORWAY

DENMARK

RUSSIA

UNITED
KINGDOM
IRELAND

RUSSIA

ESTONIA
LATVIA
LITHUANIA

POLAND
BELARUS

GERMANY

FRANCE

AUSTRIA
HUNGARY
ROMANIA

UKRAINE

KAZAKSTAN

MONGOLIA

ITALY
BULGARIA

PORTUGAL

SPAIN

GEORGIA

GREECE
TURKEY

MALTA
CYPRUS
SYRIA

UZBEKISTAN
KYRGYZSTAN

TURKMENISTAN
TAJIKISTAN

NORTH
KOREA

SOUTH KOREA
JAPAN

MADEIRA
(PORTUGAL)

TUNISIA

LEBANON

MOROCCO

ISRAEL
JORDAN

IRAQ

IRAN

AFGHANISTAN

CHINA

CANARY ISLANDS
(SPAIN)

WESTERN
SAHARA

ALGERIA
LIBYA
EGYPT

KUWAIT
BAHRAIN
QATAR

SAUDI
ARABIA

PAKISTAN

NEPAL
BHUTAN

TAIWAN

PACIFIC

OCEAN

MIDWAY ISLANDS
(U.S.A.)

MAURITANIA
MALI
NIGER
CHAD
SUDAN

OMAN
YEMEN

INDIA
BANGLADESH

MYANMAR
(BURMA)
LAOS

NORTHERN
MARIANA
ISLANDS
(U.S.A.)

WAKE ISLAND
(U.S.A.)

SENEGAL
GAMBIA
GUINEA-BISSAU
GUINEA
SIERRA
LEONE
LIBERIA

BURKINA
FASO

NIGERIA

ERITREA
DJIBOUTI

CENTRAL
AFRICAN
REPUBLIC

ETHIOPIA

LACCADIVE
ISLANDS
(INDIA)

SRI
LANKA

ANDAMAN
ISLANDS
(INDIA)

NICOBAR
ISLANDS
(INDIA)

THAILAND
CAMBODIA

VIETNAM

PHILIPPINES

GUAM (U.S.A.)

MARSHALL
ISLANDS

JOHNSTON
ATOLL (U.S.A.)

CÔTE D'IVOIRE
(IVORY COAST)

CAMEROON

EQUATORIAL
GUINEA
GABON

SÃO TOMÉ
AND PRÍNCIPE

ASCENSION
(U.K.)

CONGO

DEMOCRATIC
REPUBLIC
OF THE
CONGO
(ZAIRE)

UGANDA
RWANDA
BURUNDI

KENYA

SOMALIA

MALDIVES

BRITISH INDIAN
OCEAN TERRITORY (U.K.)

PALAU

BRUNEI
MALAYSIA
SINGAPORE

FEDERATED STATES
OF MICRONESIA

NAURU
KIRIBATI

INDONESIA

PAPUA
NEW
GUINEA

ST. HELENA AND DEPENDENCIES
(U.K.)

PAZ ISLANDS
(BRAZIL)

ANGOLA
ZAMBIA
MALAWI

TANZANIA

ZIMBABWE
MOZAMBIQUE

SEYCHELLES

COMOROS
MAYOTTE
(FRANCE)

MADAGASCAR

MAURITIUS
RÉUNION (FRANCE)

EAST TIMOR

SOLOMON
ISLANDS

TUVALU

VANUATU

NEW
CALEDONIA
(FRANCE)

WALLIS AND
FUTUNA
(FRANCE)

FIJI

TOKELAU
(N.Z.)

WESTERN
SAMOA
AMERICAN
SAMOA
(U.S.A.)

NIUE
(N.Z.)

TONGA

NAMIBIA
BOTSWANA

SWAZILAND
LESOTHO
SOUTH
AFRICA

INDIAN

OCEAN

AUSTRALIA

NORFOLK ISLAND
(AUSTRALIA)

KERMADEC ISLAND
(N.Z.)

ATLANTIC

OCEAN

TRISTAN DA CUNHA
(U.K.)

GOUGH ISLAND
(U.K.)

AMSTERDAM ISLAND
(FRANCE)

ST. PAUL ISLAND
(FRANCE)

NEW
ZEALAND

CHATHAM ISLANDS
(N.Z.)

PRINCE EDWARD ISLANDS
(SOUTH AFRICA)

CROZET ISLANDS
(FRANCE)

KERGUÉLEN ISLANDS
(FRANCE)

AUCKLAND ISLANDS
(N.Z.)

SOUTH
SANDWICH ISLANDS
(U.K.)

BOUVET ISLAND
(NORWAY)

HEARD AND McDONALD ISLANDS
(AUSTRALIA)

MACQUARIE ISLAND
(AUSTRALIA)

CAMPBELL ISLAND
(N.Z.)

PACIFIC

OCEAN

ANTARCTICA

North America

THE CONTINENT OF NORTH AMERICA extends from just south of the North Pole to just north of the equator. It includes almost every kind of environment, from ice caps to forests, mountains, deserts and jungles. In the west, an almost unbroken chain of mountains stretches from Alaska to Costa Rica and includes the Rocky Mountains, one of the world's most famous mountain ranges. The United States (often called the U.S.A. or America) and Canada are the largest of the continent's 23 countries. The United States is made up of 50 states. Canada is divided into ten provinces and three territories. North America includes some of the world's biggest cities, but also vast areas of wilderness. Most North Americans are the descendants of European immigrants, but there are also many people of African origin as well as groups of native peoples.

CONTINENT FACTS

Regional land area: 8,522,127 sq. miles (22,078,049 sq. km)
Regional population: 471,868,000
Independent countries: Antigua and Barbuda, The Bahamas, Barbados, Belize, Canada, Costa Rica, Cuba, Dominica, Dominican Republic, El Salvador, Grenada, Guatemala, Haiti, Honduras, Jamaica, Mexico, Nicaragua, Panama, St. Kitts–Nevis, St. Lucia, St. Vincent and the Grenadines, Trinidad and Tobago, United States of America

WORLD RECORDS

WORLD'S LARGEST GORGE
GRAND CANYON, U.S.A., 277 MILES (446 KM) LONG, 10 MILES (16 KM) WIDE, 1 MILE (1.6 KM) DEEP

WORLD'S LARGEST FRESHWATER LAKE
LAKE SUPERIOR, U.S.A.-CANADA, 31,800 SQ. MILES (82,350 SQ. KM)

WORLD'S LONGEST CAVE SYSTEM
MAMMOTH CAVES, U.S.A., 351 MILES (565 KM)

WORLD'S LARGEST ACTIVE VOLCANO
MAUNA LOA, HAWAII, U.S.A., 13,680 FT (4,170 M) HIGH, 75 MILES (120 KM) LONG, 31 MILES (50 KM) WIDE

WORLD'S LONGEST BORDER
U.S.-CANADIAN BORDER, 3,987 MILES (6,416 KM)

WORLD'S TALLEST ACTIVE GEYSER
STEAMBOAT GEYSER, YELLOWSTONE NATIONAL PARK, U.S.A., 380 FT (115 M)

WORLD'S LARGEST THEME PARK
WALT DISNEY WORLD, U.S.A., 47 SQ. MILES (122 SQ. KM)

CONTINENT RECORDS

HIGHEST MOUNTAIN
MOUNT MCKINLEY (DENALI), U.S.A., 20,320 FT (6,194 M)

LOWEST POINT
DEATH VALLEY, U.S.A., 282 FT (86 M) BELOW SEA LEVEL

LONGEST RIVER
MISSISSIPPI-MISSOURI, U.S.A., 3,740 MILES (6,020 KM)

LARGEST COUNTRY BY AREA
CANADA, 3,851,809 SQ. MILES (9,976,185 SQ. KM)

LARGEST COUNTRY BY POPULATION
UNITED STATES OF AMERICA, POPULATION 274,088,480

LARGEST CITY BY POPULATION
MEXICO CITY, MEXICO, POPULATION 15,048,000

MAJOR MOUNTAINS AND RIVERS

Mount McKinley (Denali), U.S.A. 20,320 ft (6,194 m)

Mount Logan, Canada 19,524 ft (5,951 m)

Orizaba, Mexico 18,700 ft (5,700 m)

Mount St. Elias, U.S.A.-Canada 18,008 ft (5,489 m)

Popocatépetl, Mexico 17,887 ft (5,450 m)

Mount Whitney, U.S.A. 14,495 ft (4,418 m)

Mississippi-Missouri 3,740 miles (6,020 km)
Mackenzie 2,630 miles (4,240 km)
Mississippi 2,350 miles (3,780 km)
Missouri 2,350 miles (3,780 km)
Yukon 1,980 miles (3,185 km)
Rio Grande 1,880 miles (3,030 km)

POLITICAL MAP

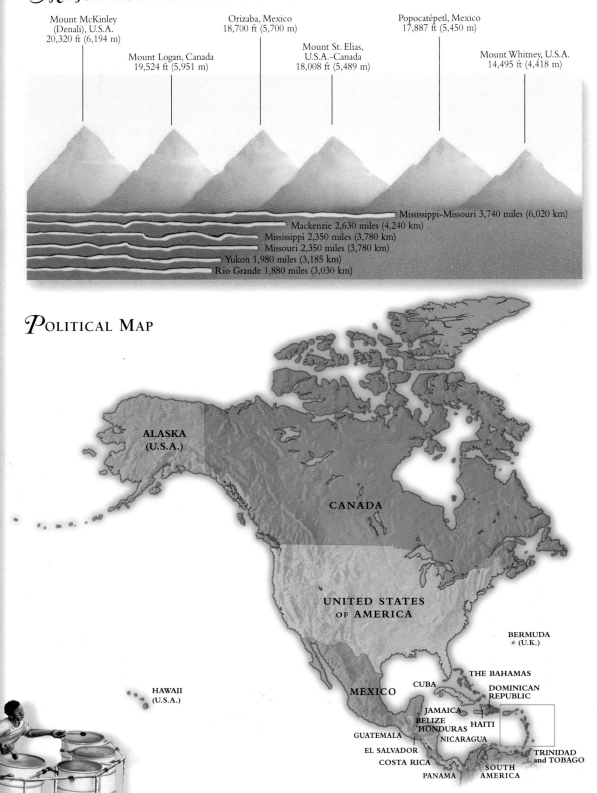

ALASKA (U.S.A.)

CANADA

HAWAII (U.S.A.)

UNITED STATES OF AMERICA

BERMUDA (U.K.)

THE BAHAMAS

CUBA

MEXICO

DOMINICAN REPUBLIC

JAMAICA
BELIZE
HONDURAS
HAITI

GUATEMALA

NICARAGUA

EL SALVADOR

COSTA RICA

PANAMA

SOUTH AMERICA

TRINIDAD and TOBAGO

VIRGIN ISLANDS (U.S.A./U.K.)

ANGUILLA (U.K.)

ANTIGUA and BARBUDA

ST. KITTS–NEVIS

GUADELOUPE (FRANCE)

PUERTO RICO (U.S.A.)

DOMINICA

MARTINIQUE (FRANCE)

ST. LUCIA

ST. VINCENT and THE GRENADINES

BARBADOS

GRENADA

PHYSICAL MAP

ASIA

ARCTIC OCEAN

× NORTH POLE

Chukchi Sea

Ellesmere Island

QUEEN ELIZABETH ISLANDS

Greenland

EUROPE

Beaufort Sea

Banks Island

Baffin Bay

Bering Sea

BROOKS RANGE

Yukon

▲ Mt. McKinley (Denali)

Victoria Island

Baffin Island

ALEUTIAN ISLANDS

▲ Mt. Logan
Mt. St. Elias ▲

Mackenzie

Great Bear Lake

Arctic Circle

Labrador Sea

Gulf of Alaska

C A N A D I A N

Great Slave Lake

Hudson Bay

LABRADOR

QUEEN CHARLOTTE ISLANDS

ROCKY MOUNTAINS

G R E A T

S H I E L D

Newfoundland

Vancouver Island

COAST MTS.

Lake Winnipeg

PACIFIC OCEAN

Missouri

Lake Nipigon

ATLANTIC OCEAN

Lake Superior

Lake Huron

P L A I N S

Mississippi

Lake Ontario

St. Lawrence

COAST RANGES

Great Salt Lake

GREAT BASIN

Lake Michigan

Lake Erie

HAWAIIAN ISLANDS

▲ Mt. Whitney

Colorado

Missouri

Ohio

APPALACHIAN MOUNTAINS

Bermuda

Mississippi

SIERRA MADRE OCCIDENTAL

SIERRA MADRE ORIENTAL

Rio Grande

Tropic of Cancer

Gulf of California

THE BAHAMAS

LESSER ANTILLES

Gulf of Mexico

GREATER ANTILLES

Popocatépetl ▲ ▲ Orizaba

Bay of Campeche

Caribbean Sea

Lake Nicaragua

SOUTH AMERICA

Equator

GALÁPAGOS ISLANDS

Western Canada and Alaska

CANADA, THE WORLD'S SECOND-LARGEST country, covers more than half of North America. Northern Canada is a vast wilderness where bears fish icy rivers for salmon, and wolves hunt caribou across snow-covered plains. The new Arctic territory of Nunavut, occupying the eastern mainland of the Northwest Territories and most of the Arctic islands, came into existence in 1999. Nunavut means "our land" in the language of its Inuit inhabitants. Few people live in this cold environment. Eighty percent of Canada's residents live within 185 miles (300 km) of the southern border, where the climate is milder and the land is more fertile. The prairie grassland that covers parts of Alberta, Manitoba and Saskatchewan is one of the world's most productive farming regions. These provinces also supply most of Canada's oil and gas. West of the towering Rocky Mountains is the Pacific coastline, a maze of islands and narrow waterways. In the Gulf of Alaska, glaciers creep down the mountains toward the shore, while seals and whales swim in the bays. Alaska is the biggest of the United States, but it is separated from the rest of the country by Canada. More than half of Alaska's lands are wildlife refuges, and the state contains some of North America's largest oil fields.

ALASKA (U.S.A.)
POPULATION: 614,100 * CAPITAL: JUNEAU

ALBERTA
POPULATION: 2,697,000 * CAPITAL: EDMONTON

BRITISH COLUMBIA
POPULATION: 3,724,500 * CAPITAL: VICTORIA

MANITOBA
POPULATION: 1,114,000 * CAPITAL: WINNIPEG

NORTHWEST TERRITORIES
POPULATION: 39,700 * CAPITAL: YELLOWKNIFE

NUNAVUT
POPULATION: 24,730 * CAPITAL: IQALUIT

SASKATCHEWAN
POPULATION: 990,200 * CAPITAL: REGINA

YUKON TERRITORY
POPULATION: 31,200 * CAPITAL: WHITEHORSE

• AMAZING FACT •

The United States bought Alaska from Russia in 1867 for $7.2 million. At the time, many people thought that this was a waste of money. But once the state's large reserves of gold and oil were discovered, the deal seemed like a bargain.

ALASKAN BROWN BEAR
At 9 ft (2.7 m) long, these huge bears are the largest meat-eaters living on land. They often fish for salmon in rivers and streams.

Map labels: Bering Strait · BROOKS RANGE · Beaufo... · Iditarod musher and dog team · Trans-Alaskan oil pipeline · Nome · Walrus · Yukon · Log cabin · ALASKA (U.S.A.) · Fairbanks · Caribou · MACKENZIE MTS. · Canada goose · Alaskan brown bear catching salmon · Mt. McKinley (Denali) 20,320 ft (6,194 m) · Gold · Dawson · Oil · Dall sheep · ALASKA RANGE · YUKON TERRITORY · Anchorage · Timber · Snowmobile · ALEUTIAN ISLANDS · Harbor seals · Mt. Logan 19,524 ft (5,951 m) · Mt. St. Elias 18,008 ft (5,489 m) · WHITEHORSE · Humpback whale · Kodiak Island · Gulf of Alaska · Zinc · Fishing boat · JUNEAU · BRITISH COLUMBIA · PACIFIC OCEAN · Grizzly bear · Salmon · Nat. gas · Tlingit totem pole · Williston Lake · ROCKY MOUNT... · Daw... Cr... · QUEEN CHARLOTTE ISLANDS · Prince Rupert · Timber · Prince George · COAST MOUNTAINS · Fraser · Bald eagle · Vancouver Island · Skiing · Kwakiutl ceremonial mask · Vancouver · VICTORIA

J K L M N O P Q

1 2 3 4 5 6 7 8 9 10

◆ PROJECT: *Inuit Finger Masks* ◆

In ceremonies and rituals, the Inuit (Eskimos) use tiny finger masks to represent their spirit ancestors. The masks are often carved from wood or stone, but you can make yours out of cardboard.

❶ Cut out a circle about four inches (10 cm) in diameter. Cut two small holes at the bottom of the circle large enough for your fingers to poke through.

❷ Draw a face in the center of the circle and color it. Cut a fringe in the cardboard or glue feathers or beads around the face.

❸ To perform with the mask, move your hand slowly from side to side to the beat of a drum.

Narwhal

ARCTIC OCEAN

Ellesmere Island

Musk ox

QUEEN ELIZABETH ISLANDS

Polar bears

PARRY ISLANDS

Arctic fox

Baffin Bay

GREENLAND

a

Banks Island

Snow goose

Prince of Wales Island

Somerset Island

Arctic hare

Inuit building igloo

Baffin Island

Davis Strait

Victoria Island

Traditional church

Inuit fishing through ice

Harp seals

Kittiwake

IQALUIT

t Bear ake

Silver

Wolf

NUNAVUT

Igloo-shaped houses

Southampton Island

Hudson Strait

Seaplane

LOCATION

ORTHWEST TERRITORIES

YELLOWKNIFE

Great Slave Lake

Gold

Gray jay

QUÉBEC

A N A D A

Slave

Moose

Hudson Bay

ⒺBeluga whale

Zinc and lead

Lake Athabasca

Uranium

Reindeer Lake

Churchill

Churchill

N

Edmontonia dinosaur fossils

LBERTA

Beaver

Nelson

Nickel and copper

W E

S

EDMONTON

Mountie

MANITOBA

ONTARIO

SCALE

Oil

Natural gas

SASKATCHEWAN

Wheat

Saskatchewan

Gold

MILES

0   100   200   300

0 100 200 300 400 500

KILOMETERS

Calgary

Saskatoon

Lake Winnipeg

REGINA

Grain elevators

Calgary Stampede

Legislative Building

WINNIPEG

ROYAL CANADIAN MOUNTED POLICE (MOUNTIES)

Canada's national police force was founded in 1873 to prevent disputes between native tribes and European traders.

UNITED STATES OF AMERICA

J K L M N O P

Eastern Canada

ABOUT 60 PERCENT OF THE POPULATION of Canada live along the shores of the St. Lawrence River and the Great Lakes, an area that occupies only 2 percent of the country's land area. From the early 17th century onward, European immigrants settled here because the land was fertile and the waterways provided transportation routes. Today, the region is home to many of Canada's biggest cities, including the two largest, Toronto and Montréal. Canada has two main languages—English and French. The majority of French speakers live in the province of Québec, which was once a French territory. The forests, lakes and rivers that cover most of Québec and Ontario provide a wealth of resources. Québec's forestry industry produces about 12 percent of the world's pulp and paper. Hydroelectric power stations create so much electricity that Québec and Ontario can export energy. The climate of eastern Canada ranges from temperate in the south to arctic in the north. For nine months of the year, Hudson Bay remains frozen, allowing polar bears to prowl the pack ice in search of food. Off Newfoundland's north shore float huge icebergs measuring up to 150 feet (45 m) high. Farther south, enormous tides surge in and out of the bays. In the Bay of Fundy, the sea can rise 50 feet (15 m) at high tide—high enough to cover a four-story building!

NEW BRUNSWICK
POPULATION: 738,000 ∗ CAPITAL: FREDERICTON

NEWFOUNDLAND
POPULATION: 551,800 ∗ CAPITAL: ST. JOHN'S

NOVA SCOTIA
POPULATION: 909,300 ∗ CAPITAL: HALIFAX

ONTARIO
POPULATION: 10,754,000 ∗ CAPITAL: TORONTO

PRINCE EDWARD ISLAND
POPULATION: 134,600 ∗ CAPITAL: CHARLOTTETOWN

QUÉBEC
POPULATION: 7,139,000 ∗ CAPITAL: QUÉBEC

◆ LOOK AGAIN ◆

- Which city is Canada's national capital?
- Which endangered sea mammal swims off the east coast of Newfoundland?
- What kind of mineral is mined in Newfoundland?

THE BIG NICKEL
The Sudbury, Ontario, area is rich in nickel. As a symbol of the metal's importance to the community, a giant Canadian five-cent piece, or nickel, stands outside the town.

ICE HOCKEY
This fast-moving game was first played in 1855 by British soldiers based in Ontario and Nova Scotia. It is now Canada's national sport.

Hudson Bay

Icebreaker ship

MANITOBA

Severn

Muskrat

Harbor seals

BELCHI ISLANL

Hiking

Kayaking

Lumberjack

James Bay

Timber

Common loons

Uranium

ONTARIO

Albany

Lake Nipigon

Moosonee

Freight train

Blue jay

Red foxes

Zinc

Nipigon

Hearst

Thunder Bay

Hydroelectricity

Silver

Lake Superior

Farmhouse

UNITED STATES OF AMERICA

Sault Ste. Marie

Ice hockey

Uranium

Lake Michigan

Sudbury

Maple f

Lake Huron

The Big Nickel

CN Tower

Parliament building, Ot

Pigs

TORONTO

London

Lake Ontario

Windsor

Lake Erie

Niagara Falls

J · K · L · M · N · O · P

Ivujivik

Hudson Strait

Polar bears

PÉNINSULE D'UNGAVA
(UNGAVA PENINSULA)

Wolverine

Snowy owl

Furs

Orca
(killer
whale)

Puffins

Iceberg

Ungava Bay

Labrador Sea

ATLANTIC OCEAN

Feuilles

Moose

Hooded seal

Nain

QUÉBEC

Beaver

Hydroelectricity

Réservoir de la
Grande Deux

Black bear

Iron
ore

Smallwood
Reservoir

LABRADOR

Gannet

Cross-country
skiing

NEWFOUNDLAND

Cross-country
skiing

Raccoon

Churchill

Happy Valley-
Goose Bay

Lac
Mistassini

Timber

Canada
geese

Blue whales

inc and
opper

Paper

Camping

Harp seals

Lac
Saint-Jean

Hydroelectricity

Cap-des-Rosiers
Lighthouse

Île d'Anticosti
(Anticosti Island)

Zinc

Statue of
De Maisonneuve,
founder of
Montréal

Château
Frontenac

Saguenay

PÉNINSULE
DE LA GASPÉSIE
(GASPÉ PENINSULA)

Gulf of St. Lawrence

Beaver

Traditional church

Newfoundland

St. Lawrence

QUÉBEC

Food processing

NEW
BRUNSWICK

PRINCE
EDWARD
ISLAND

Anne of Green
Gables's House

ST. JOHN'S

CAWA

Montréal

FREDERICTON

CHARLOTTETOWN

ST-PIERRE AND
MIQUELON (FRANCE)

Saint John

NOVA
SCOTIA

Hydroelectricity

UNITED STATES
OF AMERICA

HALIFAX

Lobster

N

W E

S

Bay of Fundy

Fishing
port

LOCATION

◆ AMAZING FACT ◆

The Canadian National (CN)
Tower in Toronto is the tallest
freestanding structure in the world.
Completed in 1976, it stands
1,816 feet (553 m) high—the
equivalent of a 150-story building!
On a clear day, you can see for
more than 75 miles (120 km)
from the top of the tower.

HARP SEALS
Each year in March, more than a
quarter of a million of these seals
travel to the islands in the Gulf
of St. Lawrence to give birth to
their young.

SCALE

MILES

0   50   100   150   200

0   100   200   300   400

KILOMETERS

J · K · L · M · N · O · P

Northeastern United States

THE NORTHEAST is home to 70 million people—more than one-quarter of the population of the United States. From Boston in the north to Washington, D.C. in the south, a line of great cities stretches for over 400 miles (640 km) along the Atlantic shore. Including its suburbs, New York City is home to almost 20 million people. It is the largest city in the U.S.A. and the third largest in the world. New York is one of the world's leading centers of trade, industry and culture. The heart of the city is the island of Manhattan, where giant skyscrapers, including some of the world's tallest, tower over long, straight streets packed with people and traffic.

The Appalachian Mountains separate the cities of the coast from the Great Lakes and the plains of the interior. They stretch for more than 1,600 miles (2,600 km) from northern Alabama, in the southern United States, to northern Maine. In the south, these mountains are rich in minerals—Kentucky produces more coal than any other state. Farms occupy many Appalachian valleys, but large areas of the mountains are covered by deciduous forests where black bears forage for blueberries and otters swim in the streams. In fall, these forests provide spectacular displays of color, as their leaves change from green to brilliant shades of orange, red and gold.

CONNECTICUT
POPULATION: 3,274,000 * CAPITAL: HARTFORD

DELAWARE
POPULATION: 743,600 * CAPITAL: DOVER

DISTRICT OF COLUMBIA
POPULATION: 523,100 * CAPITAL: WASHINGTON, D.C.

KENTUCKY
POPULATION: 3,937,000 * CAPITAL: FRANKFORT

MAINE
POPULATION: 1,244,000 * CAPITAL: AUGUSTA

MARYLAND
POPULATION: 5,135,000 * CAPITAL: ANNAPOLIS

MASSACHUSETTS
POPULATION: 6,147,000 * CAPITAL: BOSTON

NEW HAMPSHIRE
POPULATION: 1,185,000 * CAPITAL: CONCORD

NEW JERSEY
POPULATION: 8,115,000 * CAPITAL: TRENTON

NEW YORK
POPULATION: 18,175,000 * CAPITAL: ALBANY

PENNSYLVANIA
POPULATION: 12,002,000 * CAPITAL: HARRISBURG

RHODE ISLAND
POPULATION: 988,500 * CAPITAL: PROVIDENCE

VERMONT
POPULATION: 590,900 * CAPITAL: MONTPELIER

VIRGINIA
POPULATION: 6,791,000 * CAPITAL: RICHMOND

WEST VIRGINIA
POPULATION: 1,811,000 * CAPITAL: CHARLESTON

◆ PROJECT: *Iroquois Beads* ◆

According to the custom of the native Iroquois people, a person saying something important must give the listener a gift to confirm the truth of the statement. This gift is often a string of white and purple shell beads known as wampum. Try making your own Iroquois friendship beads. Thread some colored beads onto pieces of string and attach the strings to a length of yarn. Remember to explain the meaning of your gift to the receiver.

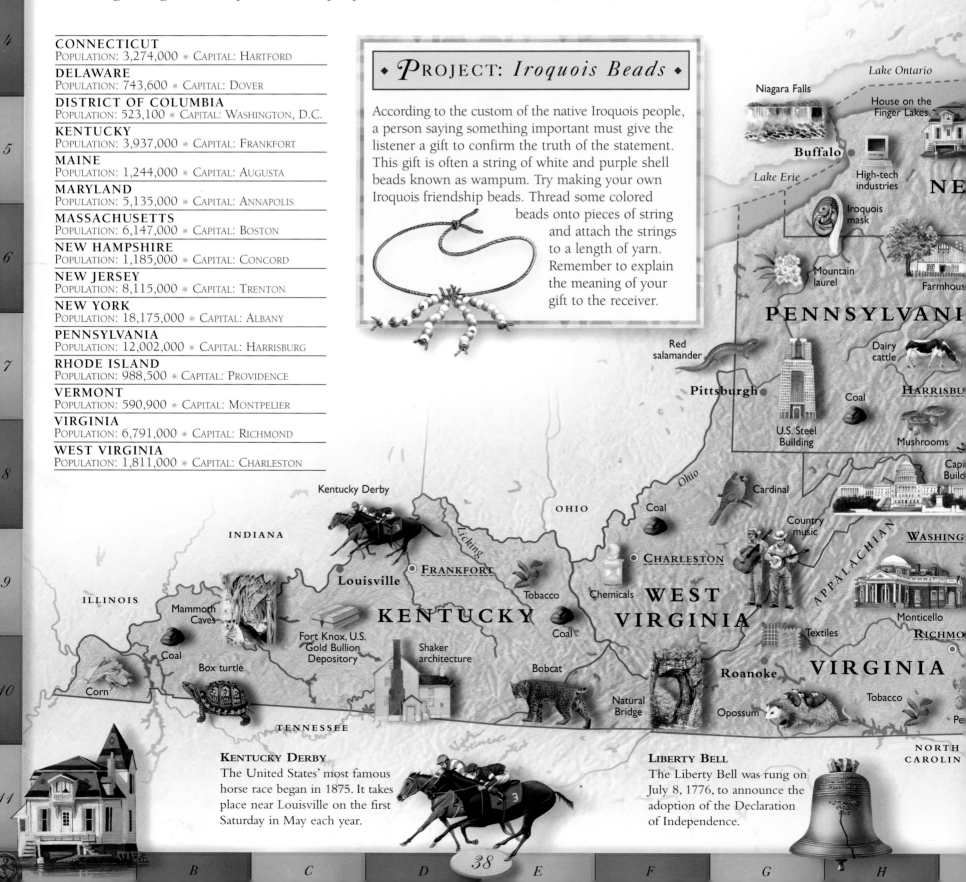

KENTUCKY DERBY
The United States' most famous horse race began in 1875. It takes place near Louisville on the first Saturday in May each year.

LIBERTY BELL
The Liberty Bell was rung on July 8, 1776, to announce the adoption of the Declaration of Independence.

Fort Kent

Potatoes

Chickadee

Chipmunk

Timber

Blueberries

MAINE

Mt. Washington Cog Railway

CANADA

VERMONT

Zinc

Apples

MONTPELIER

Dairy cattle

Skiing

Paper

AUGUSTA

Poultry

Portland

Lighthouse

Bluebird

Fort Ticonderoga

Maple syrup

NEW HAMPSHIRE

CONCORD

Timber

Manchester

Salmon

ALBANY

ORK

Baseball Hall of Fame

Basketball Hall of Fame

High-tech industries

MASSACHUSETTS

BOSTON

Cranberries

Amish people

Chrysler Building

CONNECTICUT

HARTFORD

PROVIDENCE

RHODE ISLAND

Mayflower

Chocolate

Rhode Island Red

Tourism

Minke whale

New York

NEW JERSEY

Liberty Bell

Statue of Liberty

iladelphia

TRENTON

Poultry

timore

Tourism

Atlantic City

NAPOLIS

DOVER

DELAWARE

Blue marlin

ARYLAND

Crab

Norfolk

ATLANTIC OCEAN

AMAZING FACT

The Statue of Liberty was a gift from the people of France to the people of the United States. It was designed by Frédéric-Auguste Bartholdi and engineered by Alexandre Gustave Eiffel, who built the Eiffel Tower in Paris, France. The statue took nine years to build and was unveiled in 1886. It is made up of 300 copper sheets and stands 151 feet (46 m) tall on a base 154 feet (47 m) high.

LOCATION

N
W E
S

SCALE

MILES

0 25 50 75 100 125

0 50 100 150 200

KILOMETERS

Aircraft carrier

CHRYSLER BUILDING

This skyscraper was built by Walter Chrysler, founder of the Chrysler car empire. The steel arches at the top are modeled on car hubcaps.

MAYFLOWER

In 1620 the Mayflower carried the Pilgrims from England to America to establish one of the first permanent colonies.

Southern United States

THE SOUTHERN UNITED STATES is a warm, humid region of plains, rivers, swamps and coastal lagoons. From southern Texas, a broad belt of lowland stretches around the Gulf of Mexico, across Florida and along the shores of the Atlantic Ocean. In the north and west, the coastal plains rise to plateaus and mountain ranges, including the Appalachian Mountains, which formed about 400 million years ago and are North America's oldest mountains. Mixed crop and livestock farms cover the fertile eastern and southern plains. In the west, on the dry Texas grasslands, ranch hands tend huge herds of cattle. Texas is the second-biggest American state after Alaska, and its beef industry and large oil reserves have made it one of the richest parts of the country. Numerous rivers cross the southern United States, including the Mississippi, one of North America's longest rivers and busiest inland waterways. Along the Gulf Coast and in northern Florida, these rivers have formed shallow lakes, muddy deltas and steamy swamps that are home to snakes, turtles and alligators. Florida's sunny climate and sandy beaches make it a popular vacation spot. The Walt Disney World theme park near Orlando is the world's number one tourist attraction, with more than 25 million visitors each year.

Many of the first Europeans to settle in this region came from France and Spain in the 17th century, and their descendants are called Creoles. Other French-speakers known as Cajuns arrived soon afterward from Canada. Florida's large Spanish-speaking population includes immigrants from the island of Cuba, which lies just 135 miles (217 km) south of Key West, the southernmost tip of Florida and the United States.

ALABAMA
POPULATION: 4,352,000 * CAPITAL: MONTGOMERY

ARKANSAS
POPULATION: 2,539,000 * CAPITAL: LITTLE ROCK

FLORIDA
POPULATION: 14,916,000 * CAPITAL: TALLAHASSEE

GEORGIA
POPULATION: 7,642,000 * CAPITAL: ATLANTA

LOUISIANA
POPULATION: 4,369,000 * CAPITAL: BATON ROUGE

MISSISSIPPI
POPULATION: 2,753,000 * CAPITAL: JACKSON

NORTH CAROLINA
POPULATION: 7,547,000 * CAPITAL: RALEIGH

OKLAHOMA
POPULATION: 3,347,000 * CAPITAL: OKLAHOMA CITY

SOUTH CAROLINA
POPULATION: 3,836,000 * CAPITAL: COLUMBIA

TENNESSEE
POPULATION: 5,431,000 * CAPITAL: NASHVILLE

TEXAS
POPULATION: 19,760,000 * CAPITAL: AUSTIN

KANSAS

Wheat — Camping

Beef cattle — Capitol Building — Tulsa — Natural gas

Amarillo — **OKLAHOMA CITY**

American kestrel — **OKLAHOMA** — Cherokee powwow

Red

Lubbock — Natural gas

Cotton — Oil pump — Fort Worth — Dallas

Brazos — Dallas skyline

El Paso — Pecos — Oil — **TEXAS**

Longhorn cattle — Rodeo — Armadillo

Peanuts

Lassoing cattle — Sheep — The Alamo — **AUSTIN** — Houston

Rio Grande — San Antonio

MEXICO — Concepción Mission — Oil — GULF COASTAL P — Galves

Roseate spoonbill

Laredo — Corpus Christi

Oil tanker

Brownsville

RODEO
Rodeo events test the riding and roping skills of both men and women. In the bull-riding event, riders have to stay on the bucking bull for eight seconds.

PADDLE STEAMER
In the 19th century, more than 400 of these elegant steamers provided transportation for people and goods along the Mississippi River.

• AMAZING FACT •

The Everglades, the vast wetland that covers southern Florida, is actually an enormous, slow-moving river 50 miles (80 km) wide, 100 miles (160 km) long and, on average, only six inches (15 cm) deep. The water comes from Lake Okeechobee, which overflows during the summer wet season.

• LOOK AGAIN •

- What kind of grain is grown in Arkansas?
- In which state is the space shuttle launch site found?
- Which river forms part of the border between the United States and Mexico?

LOCATION

VIRGINIA

KENTUCKY

Tennessee walking horse

Country music

Zinc

NASHVILLE

APPALACHIAN MTS.

Black bear

Tobacco

Gray squirrel

RALEIGH

NORTH CAROLINA

Mt. Mitchell 6,684 ft (2,037 m)

Charlotte

TENNESSEE

Mockingbird

Memphis

Poultry

SOUTH CAROLINA

Venus flytrap

Wilmington

ARK PLATEAU

SSOURI

ARKANSAS

Wild turkey

Soybeans

Tennessee

Stone Mountain Memorial Carving

Birmingham

Sewing a quilt

Pecans

Carolina wren

COLUMBIA

ATLANTIC COASTAL PLAIN

Blue marlin

ATLANTIC OCEAN

LITTLE ROCK

Rice

Harvesting cotton

ATLANTA

Peanuts

Macon

Charleston

Savannah

Savannah

MISSISSIPPI

ALABAMA

Columbus

Cotton

JACKSON

MONTGOMERY

GEORGIA

LOUISIANA

Raccoon

Alabama

Shorter Mansion

Albany

Tobacco

Flying squirrel

Shrimp

Cotton

Chattahoochee

Jambalaya

Mobile

Purple gallinule

TALLAHASSEE

Avocadoes

Jacksonville

BATON ROUGE

Jackson Square

Lake Charles

Jazz

New Orleans

Lobster

FLORIDA

Kennedy Space Center, Cape Canaveral

Epcot Center and Walt Disney World

Orlando

Oil rig

Tampa

Oranges

Alligator

Lake Okeechobee

THE BAHAMAS

Great blue heron

Airboat in the Everglades

Miami

Gulf   o f   M e x i c o

Tourism

Straits of Florida

N

W   E

S

Scuba diving

FLORIDA KEYS

Key West

Straits of Florida

SCALE

MILES
0   50   100   150   200

0   100   200   300
KILOMETERS

41

J   K   L   M   N   O   P

COUNTRY MUSIC

Nashville, Tennessee, is known as the home of country music. The city has about 180 record companies, 25 recording studios and 450 music publishers.

Central United States

THE CENTRAL UNITED STATES consists of a vast area of lowland known as the Midwest or prairies. In the northeastern part of this region lie the Great Lakes, the largest group of freshwater lakes in the world. Rivers and canals connect the lakes to the Atlantic Ocean and the Gulf of Mexico, forming a major transportation network. This network and the area's many natural resources (including coal and iron ore) have helped turn the Great Lakes region into the industrial heart of the United States. Factories now line the southern shores of Lake Michigan and Lake Erie, and supply most of the country's iron, steel and cars. Unfortunately, these industries create a great deal of waste, and the Great Lakes are now badly polluted. The area south and west of the lakes was once an enormous natural grassland, roamed by millions of bison and deer, and home to Native American tribes such as the Sioux and the Comanche. Now it is one of the world's most important farming regions. Iowa lies at the center of an area known as the Corn Belt because it produces half of the world's corn. Almost all of this corn is used to fatten the region's pigs and cattle, which provide most of the United States' meat. Farther west, on the Great Plains, is a "wheat belt." Here, immense fields of wheat stretch as far as the eye can see.

ILLINOIS
POPULATION: 12,045,000 ✳ CAPITAL: SPRINGFIELD

INDIANA
POPULATION: 5,899,000 ✳ CAPITAL: INDIANAPOLIS

IOWA
POPULATION: 2,862,000 ✳ CAPITAL: DES MOINES

KANSAS
POPULATION: 2,629,000 ✳ CAPITAL: TOPEKA

MICHIGAN
POPULATION: 9,817,000 ✳ CAPITAL: LANSING

MINNESOTA
POPULATION: 4,725,000 ✳ CAPITAL: ST. PAUL

MISSOURI
POPULATION: 5,439,000 ✳ CAPITAL: JEFFERSON CITY

NEBRASKA
POPULATION: 1,663,000 ✳ CAPITAL: LINCOLN

NORTH DAKOTA
POPULATION: 638,300 ✳ CAPITAL: BISMARCK

OHIO
POPULATION: 11,210,000 ✳ CAPITAL: COLUMBUS

SOUTH DAKOTA
POPULATION: 738,200 ✳ CAPITAL: PIERRE

WISCONSIN
POPULATION: 5,224,000 ✳ CAPITAL: MADISON

BISON
Before European settlers arrived, 25 million bison lived on the Plains. Hunters wiped out most of them, and now only 30,000 remain.

SIOUX HEADDRESS
The northern Great Plains is the traditional homeland of the Sioux people. Headdresses like this are still worn by their chiefs.

♦ AMAZING FACT ♦

At Mount Rushmore in South Dakota, sculptor Gutzon Borglum carved the faces of four great U.S. presidents— Washington, Jefferson, Theodore Roosevelt and Lincoln. Each face is more than 60 feet (18 m) high!

CANADA

Timber

Kayaking

Moose

Iron ore

Duluth

Superior

Container ship

Lake Superior

Sailing

Marquette

Iron ore

Black bear

Escanaba

Lake Michigan

Sault Ste. Marie

Mackinac Bridge

ESOTA

Paper

St. Croix

ST. PAUL

Maple trees

WISCONSIN

Green Bay

MICHIGAN

Lake Huron

CANADA

nneapolis

Robin

High-tech industries

Cranberries

Appleton

Apples

Bay City
Saginaw

Skunks

Lake Erie

Rochester

La Crosse

Grand Rapids

PENNSYLVANIA

itional building

Gopher

Dairy cattle

Beer

MADISON

Mississippi

Milwaukee

Fishing

LANSING

Cherries

Car manufacturing

Detroit

Lake Erie

Cleveland

oodchuck

Dubuque

Sears Tower

National Professional Football Hall of Fame

IOWA

Soybeans

Hamburger

Chicago

Fort Wayne

Toledo

Corn

OHIO

Coal

COLUMBUS

LOCATION

DES MOINES

Davenport

Gary

INDIANA

Serpent Mound (ancient native burial ground)

Ohio

Iowa Capitol Building

Rock Island

Iron and steel

Natural gas

WEST VIRGINIA

Corn

Hogs

Peoria

Car racing

Wabash

Hogs

Mark Twain's house

SPRINGFIELD

Abraham Lincoln's house

INDIANAPOLIS

St. Joseph

Hannibal

Cincinnati

Kansas City

ILLINOIS

Covered bridge

Aircraft manufacturing

St. Louis

East St. Louis

Corn silos

OPEKA

JEFFERSON CITY

Gateway Arch

Mississippi

Ohio

KENTUCKY

MISSOURI

Evansville

N

Springfield

Cottontail rabbit

Coal

Cairo

W E

Tornado

Zinc

OZARK PLATEAU

Soybeans

S

ARKANSAS

SCALE
MILES

0   50   100   150

0   50   100   150   200   250
KILOMETERS

MARK TWAIN'S HOUSE
In 1835, author Mark Twain was born in this tiny cabin, which is now part of the Mark Twain Museum in Hannibal, Missouri.

AMERICAN FOOTBALL
Following the growth of this sport in the 19th century, the first American professional football association was founded in Canton, Ohio, in 1920.

Western United States

THE COLOSSAL ROCKY MOUNTAINS separate the western United States from the plains of the Midwest. Among the valleys and peaks of this spectacular range, mountain goats bound up steep rock faces and elk feed beside fast-flowing streams. There is little agriculture here, but herds of cattle graze the mountain meadows. West of the Rockies lies a series of dry plateaus, valleys and ranges. The Colorado Plateau has some of the continent's most spectacular scenery, including the world's largest gorge, the Grand Canyon. The states of Washington, Oregon and Idaho are known as the Pacific Northwest. The wet, densely forested western part of this area provides 40 percent of the United States' timber. The largest state in the region, California, is home to more people than any other American state. Most of the population lives in or near the coastal cities of Los Angeles and San Francisco. Inland, between the mountains of the Coast Ranges and the Sierra Nevada, farms form a patchwork of fields across the fertile, irrigated Central Valley. The most westerly state, Hawaii, lies 2,500 miles (4,000 km) off the coast, in the middle of the Pacific Ocean. Hawaii consists of 132 islands, which were formed by undersea volcanoes. Several Hawaiian volcanoes still erupt, including Mauna Loa, the largest active volcano in the world.

HAWAII (U.S.A.)

Pineapple
Kauai
Niihau
Lihue
Hula dancer
Oahu
HONOLULU
Surfing
Molokai
Lahaina
Lanai
Maui
Kahoolawe
Hawaii
Mauna Kea 13,796 ft (4,205 m)
Hilo
Ancient Hawaiian totem pole
Mauna Loa 13,680 ft (4,170 m)

MILES
0   50   100
0   100   200
KILOMETERS

PACIFIC OCEAN

CANADA

Aircraft manufacturing

Seattle skyline
Tacoma
Seattle
Spokane
Coeur d'Alene Mission
OLYMPIA
WASHINGTON
Missou
Mt. Rainier 14,410 ft (4,392 m)
Apples
Rock climbing
Timber
Columbia
Beef cattle
Mint Portland
SALEM
Timber
Beef cattle
Hell's Canyon
Roses
OREGON
IDAH
BOISE
Silver City ghost town
Eugene
Snake
Pacific giant salamander
Pronghorn
California quail
Crater Lake
Twin Falls
Eureka
Redwood tree
Sacramento
Skiing
Winnemucca
Gold
Humboldt
Jackrabbit
Wine
Reno
NEVADA
CARSON CITY
Lake Tahoe
TransAmerica Building
SACRAMENTO
Oakland
SIERRA NEVADA
Bristlecone pine
Mountain lion
San Francisco
High-tech industries
GREAT BASIN
Golden Gate Bridge
Oranges
Fresno
Casino
General Sherman tree
Mt. Whitney 14,495 ft (4,418 m)
DEATH VALLEY
Las Vegas
Lake Mead
COAST RANGES
Rattlesnake
In-line skating
CALIFORNIA
Disneyland
Desert tortoise
Santa Barbara
Los Angeles
HOLLYWOOD
Hollywood sign
Colorado
San Diego
MEXICO

PACIFIC OCEAN

ARIZONA POPULATION: 4,669,000 ∗ CAPITAL: PHOENIX	**NEVADA** POPULATION: 1,747,000 ∗ CAPITAL: CARSON CITY
CALIFORNIA POPULATION: 32,667,000 ∗ CAPITAL: SACRAMENTO	**NEW MEXICO** POPULATION: 1,737,000 ∗ CAPITAL: SANTA FE
COLORADO POPULATION: 3,971,000 ∗ CAPITAL: DENVER	**OREGON** POPULATION: 3,282,000 ∗ CAPITAL: SALEM
HAWAII POPULATION: 1,193,000 ∗ CAPITAL: HONOLULU	**UTAH** POPULATION: 2,100,000 ∗ CAPITAL: SALT LAKE CITY
IDAHO POPULATION: 1,229,000 ∗ CAPITAL: BOISE	**WASHINGTON** POPULATION: 5,689,000 ∗ CAPITAL: OLYMPIA
MONTANA POPULATION: 880,500 ∗ CAPITAL: HELENA	**WYOMING** POPULATION: 480,900 ∗ CAPITAL: CHEYENNE

GENERAL SHERMAN TREE
This giant sequoia is the world's largest living thing. It is as tall as a 23-story building and is at least 2,300 years old.

◆ PROJECT: *Sand-Art Jars* ◆

The Navajo and Pueblo people of the southwestern United States make ceremonial paintings with colored sand. After the ceremony, the paintings are erased. You can make your own colored-sand painting in a jar.

❶ First sift the sand to make sure it is clean and fine. Divide the sand into small piles, adding a few drops of food coloring to each to make different-colored sands. Stir the sand every few hours to dry it.

❷ When the sand is dry, slowly pour some into a clean glass jar. Then pour a layer of another color. Keep pouring layers of different colors until the jar is full.

❸ Now make patterns by pushing a length of wire, or the end of a thin paintbrush, down the inside of the glass, between the sand and the jar. Be careful not to stir the sand! As the wire goes up and down, different colors will slide into the spaces and create designs.

❹ Finally, top off the jar with more of the colored sand and put on the lid.

🅐 AMAZING FACT ◆

Carved out by the Colorado River, the Grand Canyon is 220 miles (350 km) long and about one mile (1.6 km) deep. The rocks at the bottom of the canyon are more than two billion years old!

LOCATION

Map labels

Wheat
Whitewater rafting
Oil
Natural gas
NORTH DAKOTA
Great Falls
Missouri
HELENA
MONTANA
Yellowstone
Billings
Bighorn sheep
Grizzly bear
Bighorn Canyon
Coal
Devil's Tower
SOUTH DAKOTA
Old Faithful geyser
WYOMING
Uranium
Beef cattle
Idaho Falls
Potatoes
American kestrel
Casper
Great Salt Lake
Rock Springs
Coyote
CHEYENNE
NEBRASKA
Ogden
Salt Lake City
Provo
Skiing
Boulder
DENVER
Stegosaur skeleton
KANSAS
non Temple
UTAH
Arches National Park
COLORADO
Grand Junction
Colorado Springs
Pueblo
COLORADO PLATEAU
Cedar City
Monument Valley
Lake Powell
Mountain goat
Arkansas
Cumbres and Toltec Scenic Railroad
Plains Indian dancer
Natural gas
Taos Pueblo (native village)
Appaloosa horses
Grand Canyon
Flagstaff
Navajo woman weaving
Uranium
SANTA FE
Albuquerque
Pueblo pottery
TEXAS
Zuni jewelry
NEW MEXICO
ARIZONA
uaro ctus
PHOENIX
Gila
High-tech industries
Copper
Rio Grande
Roswell
National Astronomy Observatory
Oil
Tucson
San Xavier de Bac Mission
Roadrunner
TEXAS

N
W   E
S

SCALE
MILES
0   50   100   150   200
0   100   200   300
KILOMETERS

ROADRUNNER
Roadrunners seldom fly, preferring to race along on their powerful legs. They can reach speeds of 20 miles per hour (32 kph).

PLAINS INDIAN DANCER
By dressing as buffalo (bison), dancers appeal to the sacred spirits of these animals to bring them health and good fortune.

Mexico, Central America and the Caribbean

MEXICO AND CENTRAL AMERICA form a land bridge between the United States and South America. At its narrowest point, this strip of land is only 50 miles (80 km) wide and is split by the Panama Canal, an artificial waterway that links the Atlantic and Pacific oceans. Mexico is more than twice the size of the seven Central American countries combined. It is dominated by a large dry plateau, and only 18 percent of the land can be farmed. The narrow plains on the east coast are warm and humid, and contain large oil reserves. Three-quarters of Mexicans live in cities and towns, and Mexico City is one of the largest and fastest-growing cities in the world. Most of Central America is mountainous, and much of the land is covered in rain forests where colorful parrots shriek from the treetops and chattering monkeys swing among branches. Although only a small proportion of Central America can be farmed, about half of the people live in rural areas and many grow their own food on small plots of land. To the east lie the Caribbean Islands, most of which are covered by tropical forests and surrounded by sandy beaches. Spain ruled much of Mexico, Central America and the Caribbean for centuries, and today most of the people speak Spanish. Their ancestors may be settlers from Europe, Native American peoples or Africans who were first brought to the region as slaves.

ANTIGUA AND BARBUDA
POPULATION: 64,300 ✳ CAPITAL: ST. JOHN'S

THE BAHAMAS
POPULATION: 284,800 ✳ CAPITAL: NASSAU

BARBADOS
POPULATION: 259,200 ✳ CAPITAL: BRIDGETOWN

BELIZE
POPULATION: 235,800 ✳ CAPITAL: BELMOPAN

COSTA RICA
POPULATION: 3,675,000 ✳ CAPITAL: SAN JOSÉ

CUBA
POPULATION: 11,097,000 ✳ CAPITAL: HAVANA

DOMINICA
POPULATION: 64,900 ✳ CAPITAL: ROSEAU

DOMINICAN REPUBLIC
POPULATION: 8,130,000 ✳ CAPITAL: SANTO DOMINGO

EL SALVADOR
POPULATION: 5,840,000 ✳ CAPITAL: SAN SALVADOR

GRENADA
POPULATION: 97,100 ✳ CAPITAL: ST. GEORGE'S

GUATEMALA
POPULATION: 12,336,000 ✳ CAPITAL: GUATEMALA

HAITI
POPULATION: 6,885,000 ✳ CAPITAL: PORT-AU-PRINCE

HONDURAS
POPULATION: 5,998,000 ✳ CAPITAL: TEGUCIGALPA

JAMAICA
POPULATION: 2,653,000 ✳ CAPITAL: KINGSTON

MEXICO
POPULATION: 100,295,000 ✳ CAPITAL: MEXICO CITY

NICARAGUA
POPULATION: 4,718,000 ✳ CAPITAL: MANAGUA

PANAMA
POPULATION: 2,779,000 ✳ CAPITAL: PANAMA

ST. KITTS–NEVIS
POPULATION: 42,900 ✳ CAPITAL: BASSETERRE

ST. LUCIA
POPULATION: 154,100 ✳ CAPITAL: CASTRIES

ST. VINCENT AND THE GRENADINES
POPULATION: 120,600 ✳ CAPITAL: KINGSTOWN

TRINIDAD AND TOBAGO
POPULATION: 1,103,000 ✳ CAPITAL: PORT-OF-SPAIN

SINGING GRASSHOPPER MOUSE
This mouse is named for its habit of squeaking or "singing" to warn off rivals. Grasshoppers are its favorite food.

◆ Amazing Fact ◆

The saguaro cactus is found only in the deserts of northwestern Mexico and the southwestern United States. It grows incredibly slowly, taking 25 years to reach a height of one foot (30 cm). But it can live for 200 years and grow as high as a four-story house. Like other cacti, the saguaro survives on water stored in its stem. A fully grown saguaro may contain enough water to fill 100 bathtubs!

◆ Project: *Make a Mexican Piñata* ◆

A piñata is a pot made from papier-mâché and filled with toys and candy, often shaped like a star or animal. It is a popular part of many celebrations and festivals in Mexico and Central America. Children hang the piñata from the ceiling or a tree branch and take turns trying to break it open. You can make a Mexican piñata for your next party.

❶ Cover a large balloon with strips of newspaper dipped in flour-and-water paste or white glue. Wait for this papier-mâché to dry and then repeat with at least two more layers of newspaper.

❷ When the papier-mâché is completely dry, cut a small hole in the top and fill the piñata with all sorts of goodies. Re-cover the hole with more papier-mâché.

❸ Make star points out of cardboard as shown. Tape them onto the ball using the tabs. Decorate the star with paint and colored tissue paper.

Step 3A   Step 3B

❹ Make two small holes next to each other at the top of the piñata. Thread curved wire through one hole and out the other. Hang up the piñata and have guests take turns hitting it with a stick to open it.

ATLANTIC OCEAN

Queen angelfish

Tourism

THE BAHAMAS

★ NASSAU

TURKS AND CAICOS ISLANDS (U.K.)

Scuba diving

VIRGIN ISLANDS (U.S.A./U.K.)

ANGUILLA (U.K.)

ANTIGUA AND BARBUDA

Traditional dancers

HAVANA ★

Cigars

CUBA

Ⓔ Cuban crocodile

Palm tree

SAN JUAN ★

PUERTO RICO (U.S.A.)

ST. KITTS–NEVIS

MONTSERRAT (U.K.)

GUADELOUPE (FRANCE)

DOMINICA

Tourism

MARTINIQUE (FRANCE)

LOCATION

Bananas

SANTO DOMINGO ★

PORT-AU-PRINCE ★

DOMINICAN REPUBLIC

HAITI

Fort-de-France

ST. LUCIA

BARBADOS

Cricket

CAYMAN ISLANDS (U.K.)

★ KINGSTON

JAMAICA

ST. VINCENT AND THE GRENADINES

Sugarcane

Caribbean Sea

Sailing

Fishing boat

GRENADA

Steel band

NETHERLANDS ANTILLES (NETHERLANDS)

PORT-OF-SPAIN ★

TRINIDAD AND TOBAGO

ARUBA (NETHERLANDS)

HONDURAS

Fishing boat

VENEZUELA

N

UCIGALPA

Coffee

COLOMBIA

W   E

NICARAGUA

Beef cattle

Panama Canal

Cuna Indian

NAGUA

Bananas

SAN JOSÉ ★

PANAMA

PANAMA

COSTA RICA

Coffee

Sugarcane

Howler monkey

S

GREAT PLAZA, TIKAL
Tikal is an ancient city in Guatemala. It was built by the Maya between AD 75 and 900, and then mysteriously abandoned. It is now completely surrounded by jungle.

SCALE
MILES
0   100   200   300

0   100   200   300   400   500
KILOMETERS

South America

FROM ITS TROPICAL NORTHERN SHORE, South America stretches 4,500 miles (7,240 km) southward to the chilly, storm-battered peninsula of Cape Horn, just 600 miles (1,000 km) from Antarctica. The Andes run the entire length of the continent's west coast, forming the longest mountain chain in the world. In the north, the Amazon River (the world's second-longest river) snakes eastward from the Andes to the Atlantic Ocean, through vast rain forests that once covered more than one-third of the continent. To the south, the forests give way to the grasslands of the Gran Chaco and the Pampas. The southern tip of South America is a dry, windswept plateau known as Patagonia. South America's inhabitants include people of European, native Indian and African origin. Most people speak Spanish, but Portuguese is the official language in Brazil.

Major Mountains and Rivers

Aconcagua, Argentina
22,834 ft (6,960 m)

Cerro Ojos del Salado,
Argentina-Chile
22,664 ft (6,908 m)

Bonete, Argentina
22,546 ft (6,872 m)

Huascarán, Peru
22,205 ft (6,768 m)

Mount Illimani, Bolivia
21,201 ft (6,462 m)

Chimborazo, Ecuador
20,702 ft (6,310 m)

Amazon 4,010 miles (6,450 km)
Paraná-Río de la Plata 2,800 miles (4,500 km)
Purus 2,080 miles (3,350 km)
São Francisco 1,800 miles (2,900 km)
Paraná 1,740 miles (2,800 km)
Orinoco 1,550 miles (2,500 km)

Political Map

VENEZUELA
GUYANA
COLOMBIA
SURINAME
FRENCH GUIANA
(FRANCE)
GALÁPAGOS
ISLANDS
(ECUADOR)
ECUADOR
BRAZIL
PERU
BOLIVIA
MARTIN VAZ
ISLANDS (BRAZIL)
PARAGUAY
EASTER ISLAND
(CHILE)
CHILE
JUAN FERNANDEZ
ISLANDS (CHILE)
URUGUAY
ARGENTINA
FALKLAND
ISLANDS (U.K.)
SOUTH
GEORGIA (U.K.)

Continent Facts

Regional land area: 6,877,943 sq. miles (17,818,505 sq. km)
Regional population: 343,131,400
Independent countries: Argentina, Bolivia, Brazil, Chile, Colombia, Ecuador, Guyana, Paraguay, Peru, Suriname, Uruguay, Venezuela

World Records

WORLD'S LONGEST MOUNTAIN CHAIN
ANDES, WESTERN SOUTH AMERICA 4,700 MILES (7,600 KM)

WORLD'S DRIEST PLACE
ATACAMA DESERT, CHILE, AVERAGE ANNUAL RAINFALL LESS THAN 1/250 IN (0.1 MM)

WORLD'S HIGHEST WATERFALL
ANGEL FALLS, VENEZUELA, 3,212 FT (979 M)

WORLD'S HIGHEST CAPITAL CITY
LA PAZ, BOLIVIA, 11,913 FT (3,631 M)

WORLD'S HIGHEST NAVIGABLE LAKE
LAKE TITICACA, PERU-BOLIVIA, 12,500 FT (3,810 M)

WORLD'S LARGEST RIVER BY VOLUME
AMAZON, PERU-BRAZIL, DISCHARGES 7,100,000 CUBIC FEET (200,000 CUBIC M) PER SECOND INTO ATLANTIC OCEAN

WORLD'S LARGEST RIVER BASIN
AMAZON BASIN, NORTHERN SOUTH AMERICA, 2,720,000 SQ. MILES (7,045,000 SQ. KM)

WORLD'S LARGEST LAGOON
LAGOA DOS PATOS, BRAZIL, 3,803 SQ. MILES (9,850 SQ. KM)

Continent Records

HIGHEST MOUNTAIN
ACONCAGUA, ARGENTINA, 22,834 FT (6,960 M)

LOWEST POINT
VALDÉS PENINSULA, ARGENTINA, 131 FT (40 M) BELOW SEA LEVEL

LARGEST LAKE
LAKE TITICACA, PERU-BOLIVIA, 3,200 SQ. MILES (8,288 SQ. KM)

LONGEST RIVER
AMAZON RIVER, PERU-BRAZIL, 4,010 MILES (6,450 KM)

LARGEST COUNTRY BY AREA
BRAZIL, 3,284,426 SQ. MILES (8,506,663 SQ. KM)

LARGEST COUNTRY BY POPULATION
BRAZIL, POPULATION 171,854,000

LARGEST CITY BY POPULATION
SÃO PAULO, BRAZIL, POPULATION 16,800,000

◆ Amazing Fact ◆

The Atacama Desert in northern Chile is the driest place in the world. Rain showers occur only once or twice a century, and in some parts of the desert rain has never been recorded!

PHYSICAL MAP

NORTH AMERICA

AFRICA

Tropic of Cancer

Caribbean Sea

Lake
Maracaibo

Orinoco

GUIANA HIGHLANDS

Gulf of
Panama

LLANOS

Rio Negro

Rio Branco

Amazon
Delta

GALÁPAGOS
ISLANDS

Chimborazo

Marañon

AMAZON
BASIN

Amazon

PACIFIC

Equator

Gulf of
Guayaquil

A N D E S

SELVAS

Purus

Madeira

Tapajos

Xingu

Tocantins

São Francisco

ATLANTIC OCEAN

Huascarán

Lake
Titicaca

Mt. Illimani

MATO GROSSO
PLATEAU

BRAZILIAN
HIGHLANDS

Lake
Poopó

GRAN CHACO

Paraguay

Paraná

SERRA DO MAR

Tropic of Capricorn

ATACAMA DESERT

Cerro Ojos
del Salado

Bonete

A N D E S

Uruguay

Lagoa dos
Patos

OCEAN

Easter
Island

Aconcagua

Colorado

PAMPAS

Rio de la
Plata

PATAGONIA

Blanca Bay

San Matias Gulf

VALDÉS
PENINSULA

San Jorge Gulf

FALKLAND
ISLANDS

Tierra del Fuego

South
Georgia

CAPE HORN

Drake Passage

Antarctic Circle

ANTARCTICA

J K L M N O P Q

Northern South America

MOST OF NORTHERN SOUTH AMERICA is drained by the world's second-longest river, the Amazon, and its more than 200 tributaries. These waterways flow through lush tropical rain forests that are home to a tenth of all the plants and animals on Earth. Sadly, the rain forests are rapidly disappearing as a growing population clears the land for farming. Every minute, an area of forest the size of five football fields is cut down. More than a quarter of the world's rain forests lie within Brazil, the largest country in South America. Brazil has many resources, including iron ore, oil and gold. It is the continent's most industrialized country and the world's leading producer of coffee, bananas and sugarcane. Northwest of Brazil lies Venezuela, a sparsely populated country that is South America's top oil producer. From Venezuela, the Andes curve southward through Colombia, Ecuador and Peru. At the northern end of this mountain range, the climate is wet, and large coffee and banana plantations cover the hillsides. Farther south, little rain falls and crops can only be grown by using water from mountain streams. On the upper slopes of the Peruvian Andes, farmers grow potatoes and wheat and raise animals, including llamas and alpacas. Six hundred miles (1,000 km) off the coast of Ecuador lie the Galápagos Islands. These volcanic islands are famous for their unusual wildlife, which includes marine iguanas and giant tortoises.

BRAZIL
POPULATION: 171,854,000 ✳ CAPITAL: BRASÍLIA

COLOMBIA
POPULATION: 39,310,000 ✳ CAPITAL: BOGOTÁ

ECUADOR
POPULATION: 12,563,000 ✳ CAPITAL: QUITO

GUYANA
POPULATION: 705,200 ✳ CAPITAL: GEORGETOWN

PERU
POPULATION: 26,625,000 ✳ CAPITAL: LIMA

SURINAME
POPULATION: 431,200 ✳ CAPITAL: PARAMARIBO

VENEZUELA
POPULATION: 23,204,000 ✳ CAPITAL: CARACAS

GALÁPAGOS ISLANDS
(ECUADOR)

Pinta
Marchena
Genovesa
PACIFIC OCEAN
Giant tortoise
Isabela
San Salvador
Blue-footed booby
Fernandina
Santa Cruz
Puerto Ayora
San Cristóbal
Marine iguana
Puerto Baquerizo Moreno
Santa María
Española

MILES
0   20   40
0   25   50   75
KILOMETERS

STRAWBERRY POISON DART FROG
The skin of this colorful frog contains one of the strongest poisons on Earth. Native hunters use the poison on their arrow tips.

MACHU PICCHU
This ancient, mountaintop city in Peru was built by the Incas, a native people who ruled western South America between 1400 and 1532.

TRINIDAD AND
TOBAGO

ATLANTIC OCEAN

Oil

Cacao

inoco

Ciudad Bolívar

Angel Falls

GEORGETOWN

Cock-of-
the-rock

ef
le

PARAMARIBO

European Space
Agency Ariane rocket

Making
cassava
cakes

Cayenne

SURINAME

FRENCH GUIANA
(FRANCE)

GUYANA

Black
caiman

Tapirs

Hummingbird

Amazon
Delta

Manaus Opera
House

Piranha

mami
ter

Negro

Amazon

Manaus

Passenger boat

Belém

São Luís

ⓔ Green
turtle

Shrimp

Thresher shark

Fortaleza

Bananas

Brazil
nuts

Cotton

Fishing boat

SIN

Clearing
trees

Amazon
River dolphin

Madeira

Tapajós

Amazon river and
rain forest

Xingu

Iron ore

Sloth

Kayapó
man

Toucan

Conga
drum

Harvesting
sugarcane

Recife

Tarantula

Txukahamai
hunters with anaconda

BRAZIL

Gold

Tocantins

Topaz

Beef cattle

Oil

Lobster

Tin

Guaporé

ⓔ Giant armadillo

**MATO GROSSO
PLATEAU**

**BRAZILIAN
HIGHLANDS**

São Francisco

Tourism

Salvador

BOLIVIA

Purple
gallinule

Diamonds

BRASÍLIA

Church of Nosso
Senhor de Bomfim

Soccer

Brasília Cathedral

Cacao

Rio de Janeiro
carnival dancer

Oranges

Beef cattle

Statue of
Christ

Belo Horizonte

Paraná

Coffee

Rio de Janeiro

Car
manufacturing

São Paulo

Sugarloaf Mountain

PARAGUAY

ARGENTINA

Uruguay

Soybeans

**Pôrto
Alegre**

Shrimp

Iguazú Falls

Sheep

*Lagoa
dos Patos*

URUGUAY

◆ AMAZING FACT ◆

The Amazon Basin is home to more wildlife than any other part of our planet. At least 1,000 species of birds live in the forests, and more than 3,000 species of fish swim in the rivers. A single tree may be home to as many as 400 animals!

LOCATION

SCALE

MILES

0   100   200   300   400

0 100 200 300 400 500 600

KILOMETERS

N

W   E

S

KAYAPÓ MAN

The Kayapó people of northeastern Brazil are known for their elaborate headdresses made from the tail feathers of macaws.

Southern South America

SOUTHERN SOUTH AMERICA IS SHAPED like a long, narrow triangle that tapers to a point on the southern island of Tierra del Fuego. The Andes run down the western side of the region, separating the country of Chile from its neighbors. Twenty times as long as it is wide, Chile has a variety of climates and landscapes. In the cold, wet, sparsely populated south, mountains rise steeply from the ocean, and glaciers snake through valleys. Central Chile has milder weather and many farms, vineyards and orchards. The north is very arid and includes the driest place in the world, the Atacama Desert. East of the Atacama, the Andes spread into Bolivia, one of the poorest countries in South America. From eastern Bolivia, wide plains stretch southward through Paraguay, Uruguay and northern Argentina. Enormous herds of cattle and sheep roam the eastern and southern parts of these plains, tended by ranch hands called gauchos. Argentina has more than 50 million cattle, and beef production is one of its most important industries. The country's most fertile grasslands, the Pampas, surround the capital, Buenos Aires. This city is home to one-third of the Argentinian population. Few people live in southern Argentina, a cold, barren plateau known as Patagonia, but the area is rich in minerals. The seas around Tierra del Fuego in the far south are often stormy. Hundreds of ships have been wrecked attempting to round Cape Horn or navigate the Strait of Magellan.

PROJECT: Easter Island Moai

Easter Island is covered with huge statues called "moai." Some are more than 30 ft (9 m) high! The early inhabitants of Easter Island may have built the statues to honor their ancestors. You can make an Easter Island statue, too.

1. Mix equal parts of plaster and vermiculite (both available at hardware stores). Stir as you add enough water to make a thick plaster. Pour the mixture into an old shoe box.

2. When the mixture hardens, tear away the cardboard. Carve the stone using tools such as a plastic knife or an ice pop stick.

3. Alternatively, make your carving out of a block of modeling clay; plaster of Paris or any other modeling material.

LLAMA
A common domestic animal in South America, the llama is a relative of the camel. It is kept for its wool and is also used for carrying goods through mountainous terrain.

ARGENTINA
POPULATION: 36,738,000 * CAPITAL: BUENOS AIRES

BOLIVIA
POPULATION: 7,983,000 * CAPITALS: LA PAZ, SUCRE

CHILE
POPULATION: 14,974,000 * CAPITAL: SANTIAGO

PARAGUAY
POPULATION: 5,435,000 * CAPITAL: ASUNCION

URUGUAY
POPULATION: 3,309,000 * CAPITAL: MONTEVIDEO

Map labels: PERU, BRAZIL, BOLIVIA, PARAGUAY, GRAN CHACO, ATACAMA DESERT, ANDES

Gold, Giant anteater, Spectacled bear, Zinc, Timber, Motmot, Trinidad, Guaporé, Mamoré, LA PAZ, Mt. Illimani 21,201 ft (6,462 m), Lake Titicaca, Arica, Iquique, Antofagasta, Copiapó, Tin, Cochabamba, SUCRE, Santa Cruz, Bolivian folk costume, Oil, Natural gas, Corn, Beef cattle, Cotton, Greater rhea, Chacoan peccary, Pilcomayo, Presidential palace, ASUNCIÓN, Streetcar, Paraguay, Maté (tea), Corrientes, Sugarcane, Polo, Maned wolf, Río Salado, San Miguel de Tucumán, Llamas, Andean condor, Village musicians, Silver, Giant bromelia, Lake Poopó, Cerro Ojos del Salado 22,664 ft (6,908 m), Bonete 22,546 ft (6,877 m), Copper, Hydroelectricity

The United Kingdom and the Republic of Ireland

THE UNITED KINGDOM AND THE REPUBLIC OF IRELAND occupy islands known as the British Isles. The United Kingdom is made up of the countries of England, Wales, Scotland and Northern Ireland, which are ruled by one government based in London but have their own cultures. Scotland and Wales also have their own parliaments, and Scotland has its own legal and educational systems, churches and bank notes. England is a crowded country with many large cities. Almost eight million people live in London, the capital city. London is one of the world's most important centers of trade and finance and is famous for its many historic buildings. Southeastern England is flat and fertile and is famous for its many historic buildings. Southeastern England is flat and fertile and its farms provide most of the United Kingdom's crops. The country's most important industries are located in central England, an area known as the Midlands, and around the coalfields of the Pennine hills. To the west and north, the countryside is wet and mountainous and is used mainly for grazing animals. In the rugged, sparsely populated Scottish Highlands, red deer and sheep roam the hills and eagles soar overhead. The Republic of Ireland occupies about 85 percent of the island of Ireland. It is a land of green plains surrounded by coastal mountains. Most of the country's industries are located in the capital, Dublin, and the southern city of Cork.

IRELAND
POPULATION: 3,633,000 ★ CAPITAL: DUBLIN

UNITED KINGDOM
POPULATION: 59,114,000 ★ CAPITAL: LONDON

ENGLAND
POPULATION: 49,089,000 ★ CAPITAL: LONDON

NORTHERN IRELAND
POPULATION: 1,663,000 ★ CAPITAL: BELFAST

SCOTLAND
POPULATION: 5,128,000 ★ CAPITAL: EDINBURGH

WALES
POPULATION: 2,921,000 ★ CAPITAL: CARDIFF

◆ AMAZING FACT ◆

In the 19th century, as a hoax, the name of the village Llanfairpwllgwyngyll was lengthened to the tongue-twisting Llanfairpwllgwyngyllgogerychwyn-drobwllllantysiliogogogoch. The name means "St. Mary's church by the pool of white hazel trees, near the rapid whirlpool, by the red cave of the Church of St. Tysilio." In 1988 the village officially returned to using the shorter name. However, the railway station is still called by the 58-letter version.

LLANFAIRPWLLGWYNGYLLGOGERYCHWYRNDROBWLLLLANTYSILIOGOGOGOCH

◆ LOOK AGAIN ◆

- Which famous railway bridge is located near the capital of Scotland?
- Name a sport that is played in Ireland.
- What is the name of the group of islands near Land's End?

**Map labels:**

Fishing trawler

Giant's Causeway rock formation

Iona Abbey

Islay

North Uist

South Uist

OUTER HEBRIDES

Lewis with Harris

Stornoway

Textiles

Sheep

Skye

Mull

Arran

Otter

Oban

Salmon

Ben Nevis 4,406 ft (1,343 m)

Capercaillie

Urquhart Castle and Loch Ness

Red deer

SCOTLAND

Inverness

Thurso

John o'Groats

Kirkwall

ORKNEY ISLANDS

Cod

SHETLAND ISLANDS

Shetland pony

Lerwick

Highland piper

Glasgow

Clyde

GRAMPIAN MTS.

Coal

Forth

EDINBURGH

Beef cattle

Tweed

Tay

Dee

Glamis Castle

Hammer throwing, Highland Games

Highland cattle

Golf

Dundee

Aberdeen

Hadrian's Wall

Forth railway bridge

Coal

Oil rig

North

Haddock

Cod

EUROPE

PHYSICAL MAP

ATLANTIC OCEAN

NORTH AMERICA

ARCTIC OCEAN

NORTH POLE
×

Greenland

Iceland

FAEROE ISLANDS

Arctic Circle

Barents Sea

Norwegian Sea

Ireland

Great Britain

North Sea

English Channel

Baltic Sea

Lake Vänern

Gulf of Bothnia

Lake Ladoga

Lake Onega

SCANDINAVIA

EUROPEAN PLAIN

URAL MOUNTAINS

ASIA

Volga

Don

Dnieper

Dniester

Danube

Elbe

Rhine

Seine

Loire

CARPATHIAN MTS

ALPS

Mont Blanc

Monte Rosa

Matterhorn

Jungfrau

Bay of Biscay

PYRENEES

IBERIAN PENINSULA

Strait of Gibraltar

BALEARIC IS.

Corsica

Sardinia

APENNINES

Sicily

Mt Etna

Adriatic Sea

Ionian Sea

Aegean Sea

BALKAN PENINSULA

Crete

Mediterranean Sea

Black Sea

CAUCASUS MTS

Mt Elbrus

Caspian Sea

AFRICA

Tropic of Cancer

Equator

Sea

LOCATION

Thatched cottage

Norwich

Sugar beets

Ipswich

Poultry

Big Ben and the Houses of Parliament

Canal barge

Tennis

Brighton Pavilion

FRANCE

Castle Howard

Hull

York

Middlesbrough

Iron and steel

Iron and steel

Tyne

Carlisle

Black pudding

PENNINES

Trent

Sheffield

Nottingham

ENGLAND

Leicester

Coventry

LONDON

Thames

Coldstream Guard

Brighton

Hovercraft

Hedgehog

Red squirrel

Tourism

Leeds

Manchester

Cricket

Textiles

Chatsworth House garden maze

Tudor architecture

Birmingham

Cambridge

Oxford

Southampton

Isle of Wight

English Channel

Blackpool

Blackpool rock candy

Liverpool

High-tech industries

Car manufacturing

Reading

Bath

Stonehenge

Isle of Man

Motorcycle racing

Tourism

Mt. Snowdon ▲ 3,561 ft (1,085 m)

WALES

Wye

Coal mining

Wheat

Bristol

Dairy cattle

CHANNEL ISLANDS (U.K.)

Guernsey Jersey

Stranraer

Irish Sea

Anglesey

Severn

Caernarfon Castle

Aberystwyth

CARDIFF

Rugby

Swansea

Exeter

Tourism

Morris dancing

Plymouth

Pollock

Bangor

Stormont Castle

Llanfairpwllgwyngyll

NORTHERN IRELAND

BELFAST

Dundalk

Beer

Irish harp

DUBLIN

Liffey

St. George's Channel

Milford Haven

Puffins

Royal Navy rescue helicopter

Historic tin mine

LAND'S END

ISLES OF SCILLY

STONEHENGE

This prehistoric stone monument, or megalith, was a religious and ceremonial site for thousands of years.

Sligo

Beef cattle

Newgrange prehistoric burial mound

IRELAND

Shannon

Kingfisher

Carlow

Waterford crystal

Waterford

Sailing

Mackerel

Cross of Muireadach

Limerick

Tipperary

Blarney Castle

Cork

BLARNEY CASTLE

It is said that if you kiss the Blarney Stone in the tower of this castle you will become a clever and persuasive talker.

Galway

Donkey

Crofter's cottage

Sugar beets

▲ Carrauntuohill 3,414 ft (1,041 m)

Sheep

Bantry

N

E

S

W

SCALE

MILES

0 50 100 150

KILOMETERS

0 50 100 150 200 250

Peat

Potatoes

Hurling

Dairy cattle

Gallarus Oratory

Lobster

Celtic Sea

10 11 12 13 14 15 16

A B C D E F G H J K

Spain and Portugal

SPAIN AND PORTUGAL OCCUPY the Iberian Peninsula, a wide, square-shaped piece of land in southwestern Europe. This peninsula is separated from the rest of the continent by the Pyrenees, a mountain range that contains the tiny country of Andorra. Most of the Iberian Peninsula consists of a huge plateau known as the Meseta, which is covered with dry grasslands, olive groves and forested hills. At the center of the Meseta, 2,120 feet (646 m) above sea level, lies Madrid—the largest city in Spain and the highest capital city in Europe. Spain's second-largest city, Barcelona, lies on the narrow plains of the east coast. This coastline and the nearby Balearic Islands are warm and sunny for much of the year, and in summer, crowds of vacationers from all over Europe sunbathe on the sandy beaches. The southern tip of Spain lies only nine miles (15 km) from Africa. Between AD 711 and the 12th century, most of Spain was ruled by the Moors, an Arabic people from North Africa, and towns such as Granada and Seville have many ornate Moorish buildings. West of Spain lies Portugal. Once the heart of a vast, worldwide empire, Portugal is now one of the poorest countries in western Europe. Olive groves and cork oak forests cover the dry, southern plains. In the many river valleys that cross the country, farmers grow grapes for winemaking. Among the best-known Portuguese wines is port, which is named after the country's second-largest city, Porto.

ANDORRA
POPULATION: 66,000 * CAPITAL: ANDORRA
PORTUGAL
POPULATION: 9,919,000 * CAPITAL: LISBON
SPAIN
POPULATION: 39,168,000 * CAPITAL: MADRID

ATLANTIC OCEAN

PORTUGAL

La Coruña · Mussels · Apples · Potatoes
Santiago · Farmer and hay cart · Corn
Vigo · Sheep
Anchovies
Woman in folk costume
Porto · Port wine · Transporting wine
Douro
Farmer plowing
Mondego · Coimbra · Textiles
Cistercian monastery
Tagus
Torre de Belem
LISBON
Setúbal · Évora · Cork oak · Badajoz · Olives · Cork oak
Wine
Bluefin tuna
Fisherman mending a net
Guadiana
ALGARVE
CAPE ST. VINCENT · Tourism · Faro · Spanish lynx
Gulf of Cádiz

AZORES (PORTUGAL)

Corvo
Flores
Wine · Graciosa · Terceira · Windmill
Faial
Pico · São Jorge
São Miguel
Santa Maria

MILES
0   50   100
0   50   100   150
KILOMETERS

MADEIRA (PORTUGAL)

Wine
Tourism
Funchal

MILES
0   25   50
0   25   50   75
KILOMETERS

AZORES
MADEIRA
CANARY ISLANDS

CANARY ISLANDS (SPAIN)

La Palma
Cigars
Tenerife
Santa Cruz de Tenerife
Camel
Lanzarote
Gomera · Tourism
Bananas
Las Palmas
Goat
Fuerteventura
Hierro
Pineapples
Grand Canary

MILES
0   25   50   75
0   50   100   150
KILOMETERS

FLAMENCO DANCER
Flamenco is a style of music and dance created by the gypsies of southern Spain. Dancers in colorful costumes are accompanied by guitarists and singers.

Bay of Biscay
Gijón
Santander
Oviedo

Basque folk dancer

FRANCE

P Y R E N E E S

Bearded vulture

ANDORRA
ANDORRA

UNTAINS

Brown bear

Altamira cave paintings

Bilbao

Donostia-San Sebastián

Pamplona

Running of the bulls

Iron and steel

Beef cattle

Pico de Aneto 11,168 ft (3,404 m)

Barley

Vacationer

Costa Brava

Wheat

Potatoes

Valladolid

Douro

Wild boars

Saragossa

Torre de Aragón

Textiles

Barcelona

Holy Week procession

Alcazar

Segovia

Wine

Sagrada Familia church

Salamanca

eat

High-tech industries

El Escorial

★ MADRID

Statue of Don Quixote and Sancho Panza

Spanish guitarist

Olives

Oil

BALEARIC ISLANDS

Minorca

Mahón

Toledo

M E S E T A

SPAIN

Tagus

Bullfighting

Paella

Oranges

Jara Gate

Palma

Olives

Majorca

Car manufacturing

Valencia

Sardines

Tourism

Ibiza

Ibiza

Farmhouse

Guadiana

Windmills of La Mancha

Tourism

Alicante

Fishing boat

Mezquita Mosque

Wine

Sunflowers

Collecting saffron

ERRA MORENA

Guadalquivir

Córdoba

Olives

Flamenco dancer

Citrus fruit

Murcia

Cartagena

Mediterranean Sea

Alhambra Palace

Mulhacén 11,407 ft (3,477 m)

Granada

Almería

ville

Andalucian ranch hand

Tajo Bridge

Málaga

Tourism

COSTA DEL SOL

Sailing

GIBRALTAR (U.K.)

Sardines

Algeciras

Ceuta (SPAIN)

MOROCCO

Melilla (SPAIN)

ALGERIA

N
W   E
S

◆ AMAZING FACT ◆

Two-thirds of the world's cork is produced in Spain and Portugal. Cork is obtained from the thick bark of the cork oak tree and is used to make bottle stoppers, shoes, floor coverings and bulletin boards.

SAGRADA FAMILIA CHURCH

The spires of this Barcelona church are covered with shells and ceramics, and stand 350 foot (110 m) high. The building was begun in 1884. More than 100 years later, it is still being built.

SCALE

MILES

0   25   50   75   100

0   50   100   150

KILOMETERS

J K L M N O P Q

ENGLAND

France

FRANCE, THE LARGEST COUNTRY in western Europe, has a varied climate and landscape. In the north, the weather is mild and wet, and much of the land is flat. As you travel south, the climate becomes warmer and the land more mountainous. Three-quarters of the population live in towns and cities, but most of the country is farmland, and France is Europe's leading farming country. The northern plains are covered in fields of wheat and sugar beets, and in central and southern France vineyards dot the hillsides—more wine is produced in France than in any other country except Italy. The area around Paris, the capital, is the most densely populated region. It is home to one-fifth of the country's population and most of its industries. Several great rivers, including the Seine and the Loire, cross France's northern and western plains. These waterways were once the country's main transportation routes, and their banks are lined with historic villages and magnificent castles known as châteaus. In the south, the mountains of the Pyrenees and the Alps separate France from Spain and Italy. Among their snow-capped peaks lie popular ski resorts and national parks that are home to eagles, marmots and goatlike antelopes called chamois. Along the Mediterranean coast there are many busy beach resorts. Near the Italian border lies Monaco, the second-smallest country in the world. Monaco is famous for its casinos and its annual Grand Prix motor race.

FRANCE
POPULATION: 58,979,000 ∗ CAPITAL: PARIS
MONACO
POPULATION: 32,200 ∗ CAPITAL: MONACO

◆ AMAZING FACT ◆

France is now connected to Great Britain by an undersea rail link known as the Channel Tunnel. The tunnel took seven years to build and includes two rail tracks. Trains take 35 minutes to pass through the tunnel. Travelers can journey from London to Paris in about three hours.

Cross-channel ferry

English Channel

Channel Tunnel

Tourism

Cherbourg

Le Havre

Mont-St-Michel

Bayeux Tapestry

Ver

Brest

Medieval houses

Camembert cheese

Apples

Rennes

Car racing, Le Mans

Quimper

Tourism

Standing stones

Dairy cattle

St-Nazaire

Tou

Nantes

Fishing boat

Tourism

Château Chenonceau

Beef cattle

La Rochelle

S

ATLANTIC OCEAN

Tourism

Lim chi

Mackerel

Château de la Brède

Oysters

Bordeaux

Lascaux paint

Bay of Biscay

Wine

French breads

Ga

Windsurfing

Boule

Biarritz

Natural gas

Ⓔ Pyrenean ibex

P Y R E N

SPA I

SPAI

BOULES
Boules is a bowling game that is popular in France. It is played with metal balls on a hard dirt surface.

EIFFEL TOWER
Once the tallest structure in the world, the Eiffel Tower was erected for the Paris Exposition of 1889 by engineer Alexandre-Gustave Eiffel.

Dunkerque
Calais
oulogne
Nuclear energy
Lille
ssels
Potatoes
Sugar beets
BELGIUM
Dieppe
Wheat
Amiens
Rouen
LUXEMBOURG
Car manufacturing
Cafe
GERMANY
PARIS
Reims
Fashion
Metz
Nuclear energy
Nancy
Coal
Strasbourg
Chartres Cathedral
Eiffel Tower
Champagne
Iron ore
Iron and steel
Wine
Seine
Troyes
Folk costume
Tour de France
Gaul fort
Loire
Château de Chambord
Dijon
Chapel of Notre Dame du Haut
Bourges
Mustard
Besançon
Mountain climbing
T.G.V. high-speed train
Saône
FRANCE
Doubs
Dairy cattle
SWITZERLAND
Snail
Marmot
Textiles
Tungsten
Farmer with goats
Coal
Lyon
Rhône
ALPS
Mont Blanc 15,771 ft (4,807 m)
Playing the cabrette
St-Étienne
Chamois
Chapel of St-Michel D'Aiguilhe
French breads
Wine
Grenoble
Skiing
Hunting for truffles
Geese
ITALY
Durance
Nuclear energy
Casino, Monte Carlo
Avignon
Harvesting lavender
Perfume
Mackerel
Aircraft manufacturing
MONACO
Toulouse
Montpellier
Pont du Gard
Cannes Film Festival
Nice
Cannes
Walled town of Carcassonne
Marseille
Tourism
RRA
Sailing
Flamingo
Waterskiing
Perpignan
Mediterranean Sea
Osprey
Corsica
Tourism
Solar furnace
Ajaccio
Statue of Napoleon

TOUR DE FRANCE
France's most famous sporting event, this cycle race around the entire country covers about 2,500 miles (4,000 km).

Rhône
Moselle
Meuse

• PROJECT: *Cave Painting* •

The cave paintings at Lascaux were created about 15,000 years ago. Here's how you can create your own painting that will look thousands of years old.

❶ Stuff a strong paper bag with crumpled newspaper and then staple the bag closed.

❷ Mix some glue and sand and use this to paint the whole bag. When it dries it will look like a rock.

❸ Collect three or four different-colored soils. Sift out the lumps and then mix each color with glue to make earth paints (add water if the paints are too thick). Now you are ready to paint. Like the artists who created the Lascaux cave paintings, you can paint animals living in your area.

• LOOK AGAIN •

● Which cathedral lies southwest of Paris?

● Name a horned animal found in the Pyrenees.

● What kind of food is produced in Dijon?

● Which small country is located east of Nice?

LOCATION

N
W   E
S

SCALE
MILES
0   25   50   75   100

0   50   100   150
KILOMETERS

The Low Countries

THE DENSELY POPULATED COUNTRIES of the Netherlands (also called Holland), Belgium and Luxembourg are known as the Low Countries because they have no high mountains and few hills. Much of the land, including one-third of the Netherlands, actually lies below sea level. Over the centuries, local people have built large barriers known as dikes to keep the sea out, pumped water out of the marshes behind the dikes to create areas of new land called polders, and constructed thousands of miles of canals. Throughout the region, barges chug along these waterways, past windmills, dairy farms and colorful fields of tulips—both Belgium and the Netherlands export flowers and bulbs all over the world. The capital of the Netherlands, Amsterdam, has more than 150 canals, many of which are lined with tall, narrow, 17th-century buildings. In Belgium, canals link the country's ports to the historic cities of Bruges and Ghent, and to Brussels, the capital. Brussels is often referred to as the capital of Europe because it is the headquarters of the European Union (EU). Southeast of Brussels lies the only high part of the Low Countries, the Ardennes. This range of forest-covered hills spreads across the northern half of Luxembourg, one of Europe's smallest countries but also one of its most important financial centers.

BELGIUM
POPULATION: 10,183,000 * CAPITAL: BRUSSELS
LUXEMBOURG
POPULATION: 429,100 * CAPITAL: LUXEMBOURG
THE NETHERLANDS
POPULATION: 15,808,000 * CAPITALS: AMSTERDAM, THE HAGUE

THE ATOMIUM
The Atomium represents an iron molecule and is one of the rare remains of the World Exhibition held in Brussels in 1958.

♦ AMAZING FACT ♦

The Low Countries have more than 5,000 miles (8,000 km) of canals, which are used for transportation and for draining the land. Because much of the region lies below sea level, water has to be pumped into canals built high above ground level. You could be standing in a field in the Low Countries and see a ship pass by above your head!

THE NETHERLANDS

Groningen — Wheat — Natural gas — Prehistoric hunebed (burial tomb) — Sheep — Dairy cattle — Pigs — Folk dancers — Beef cattle — Cycling — Clogs — Apeldoorn — Poultry — Arnhem — Rhine — Beef cattle — Leeuwarden — Zuider Zee folk costume — Dairy cattle — Windmill — Eurasian spoonbill — Soccer — Lek — Dom Cathedral tower — Utrecht — Amsterdam — AMSTERDAM — Tulips — Flowers — Alkmaar — Diamond cutting — Haarlem — Iron and steel — Alkmaar cheese market — Herring — Mackerel — Peace Palace — THE HAGUE — Rotterdam — Container ship — Ijsselmeer — Waddenzee — WEST FRISIAN ISLANDS — Ameland — Terschelling — Vlieland — Texel — Harbor seals — Potatoes — Tourism

LOCATION

CLOGS
Worn by Dutch farmers, these traditional wooden shoes help keep feet warm and dry in damp fields. They are known locally as *klompen*.

LUXEMBOURG

Wine

Iron and steel

National Savings Bank

LUXEMBOURG

Esch-sur-Alzette

Red squirrel

ALKMAAR CHEESE MARKET
Every Friday during summer in the Dutch town of Alkmaar, round balls of cheese are carried to the market on traditional wooden "sledges."

GERMANY

Rye

Vegetables

Dairy cattle

Wheat

Eindhoven
High-tech industries

's Hertogenbosch Cathedral

Tilburg

Breda

Sugar beets

BAARLE-HERTOG (BELGIUM)

Vegetables

Bicycle racing

Crystal

Liège

Iron and steel

Meuse

Red deer

Ardennes

Wild boars

A R D E N N E S

Louvain Town Hall

Sugar beets

Chemicals

Antwerp

Diamond cutting

Atomium building

Beer

★ **BRUSSELS**

Chocolate

B E L G I U M

Sambre

Fortress and town of Dinant

Beef cattle

Dockside cranes, Antwerp port

Iron and steel

Ghent

Brugge
High-tech industries

F L A N D E R S

Ghent

Textiles

Vegetables

Dairy cattle

Wheat

Barley

FRANCE

Mussels

Wheat

Oysters

Ostende

Damme Canal

Pigs

Sugar beets

Tourism

North Sea

Maas

SCALE
MILES
0 10 20 30
KILOMETERS
0 10 20 30 40 50

W N E S

63

◆ PROJECT: *Make a Paper Windmill* ◆

At one time, much of the land in the western part of the Netherlands lay under water. Windmills were used to pump and drain water from land as well as to grind grain. Windmills harness the force of the wind to produce energy. The wind turns the sails of the windmill, which are connected to a pillar. This pillar transmits the energy through a system of gears to a vertical shaft that carries the power to a water pump or mill. You can make a paper windmill and power it by blowing on it.

① Cut a 7½- x 7½-inch (19- x 19-cm) piece of paper. Draw an **X** across the paper. Using a large coin or a compass, trace a circle in the center of the square.

② Cut along the four diagonal lines up to the edge of the circle. Without folding the paper, bend every other point in to the center of the circle.

③ Stick a pushpin through the center of the circle and through all the bent-in points. Now stick the pushpin into the side of the eraser at the end of a pencil. Hold the windmill by the pencil tip and blow on it.

Western Central Europe

AFTER WORLD WAR II, GERMANY was divided into two countries: East Germany and West Germany. They were reunited in 1990 and Germany is now home to more than 80 million people, the largest population of any European country except Russia. Many of Germany's cities lie on rivers. The Rhine River connects the country's most important industrial region, the Ruhr Valley, to the ports of the Netherlands and the Swiss city of Basel. On its journey northward, the Rhine meanders past forests of spruce and fir, steep hillsides covered with vineyards, and cliffs crowned by medieval castles. From southern Germany, the spectacular Alps mountain range stretches across the countries of Switzerland and Austria, where it covers about two-thirds of the land. Throughout these mountains, roads and railways wind through narrow river valleys and cross steep passes. In summer, cows graze in the alpine meadows; in winter, skiers hurtle down the slopes. Switzerland is a peaceful country which hasn't been involved in a war since 1814. This has encouraged people from all over the world to deposit money in Swiss banks, and the country is now a leading financial center. In Austria, many farms and industries lie on the northeastern lowlands. This area is crossed by the Danube, Europe's second-longest river. The Danube passes through Austria's capital, Vienna—home to one-fifth of Austria's population and one of Europe's grandest cities.

AUSTRIA
POPULATION: 8,140,000 ✦ CAPITAL: VIENNA

GERMANY
POPULATION: 82,088,000 ✦ CAPITAL: BERLIN

LIECHTENSTEIN
POPULATION: 32,100 ✦ CAPITAL: VADUZ

SWITZERLAND
POPULATION: 7,276,000 ✦ CAPITAL: BERN

SCALE
MILES
0   25   50   75
KILOMETERS
0   25   50   75   100   125

✦ PROJECT: Swiss Chocolate Fondue ✦

The Swiss eat a dish called fondue, which is often made from cheese. Pieces of bread are dipped in a mixture of hot melted cheese and white wine. This fondue is different—it's made with chocolate!

❶ Place 8 oz (250 g) semisweet chocolate pieces into a saucepan with 1 cup (8 oz/250 ml) whipping cream.

❷ Ask an adult to help you warm the ingredients gently until the chocolate has melted. Beat the mixture until it becomes glossy.

❸ Let the mixture cool a little. Then spear a piece of fruit (strawberries or grapes are good) on a fork, dip it in the fondue and have a taste. Yum!

✦ AMAZING FACT ✦

The country of Liechtenstein is home to only 32,100 people and is just four miles (6 km) wide. That means you could walk across it in less than two hours! The prince of Liechtenstein lives in this castle at Vaduz, the capital.

Baltic Sea

North Sea

POLAND

DENMARK

THE NETHERLANDS

Oder

Shipbuilding

Wheat

Horses

BERLIN

Hurdy-gurdy player

Brandenburg

White stork

Potatoes

Herring

Rostock

Sheep

Magdeburg

Shipbuilding

Lübeck

Rye

Beaver

Kiel

Vegetables

Hamburg

Elbe

Brunswick

High-tech industries

Sausages

Lüneburg heath

Car manufacturing

Nord-Ostsee Canal

Musicians of Bremen statue

Bremen

Hannover

Textiles

Oats

Weser

Cod

Natural gas

Pigs

Oldenburg

Münster

Iron

Blackbird

Dairy cattle

Ems

Tourism

Oil

ALPENHORN

For hundreds of years, the farmers of the Swiss Alps used these gigantic wooden horns to call in their cattle from high mountain pastures.

NEUSCHWANSTEIN CASTLE

This spectacular building was the model for the fairy-tale castles in Walt Disney theme parks. It was built in the late 19th century by King Ludwig II.

LIPIZZANER HORSE

Lipizzaners are trained to perform graceful steps and leaps at the Winter Riding School in Vienna. They are named after the town of Lipizza in Slovenia where they were first bred.

ITALY *See World Fact File page 108*

Italy

ITALY CONSISTS OF A LONG, boot-shaped peninsula, the large islands of Sicily and Sardinia, and about 70 smaller islands. Within Italy lie two other countries: San Marino and the Vatican City (the world's smallest country) in the city of Rome. The Vatican City is the home of the Pope, the head of the Roman Catholic Church. Most of mainland Italy is mountainous. The Alps form a great arc around the northern border, and the Apennines stretch almost the entire length of the peninsula. Between these two mountain ranges lies the Northern Plain, a flat, fertile region drained by the Po River. This plain has Italy's richest farmland and is home to the country's most important industries, including the car factories of Turin, and Milan's fashion and design houses.

Each year, more than 50 million tourists travel to Italy to visit its ancient ruins, historic cities and museums, and to enjoy the sunny summer weather. The country's mild climate allows farmers to grow large quantities of wheat, citrus fruit, olives and grapes—Italy is the world's leading producer of olive oil and wine. Parts of Italy are regularly rocked by earthquakes, and the country has the only active volcanoes on mainland Europe. On the island of Sicily, Mount Etna has erupted at least 260 times since the first recorded eruption in 70 BC. About 60 miles (95 km) south of Sicily lie the islands of Malta. At various times in its history, Malta was ruled by the Romans, Arabs, Turks, French and British. It is now an independent republic.

ITALY
POPULATION: 56,736,000 * CAPITAL: ROME
MALTA
POPULATION: 381,700 * CAPITAL: VALLETTA
SAN MARINO
POPULATION: 25,100 * CAPITAL: SAN MARINO
VATICAN CITY
POPULATION: 870 * CAPITAL: VATICAN CITY

◆ AMAZING FACT ◆

The Leaning Tower of Pisa was constructed as a bell tower between AD 1173 and 1370. Unfortunately, it was built on unstable ground, and it began to sink and tilt to one side after completion of the first three stories. Although the tower leans about 15 feet (4.5 m) out of line, it has recently been stabilized so that it will not fall over.

MOUNT VESUVIUS AND POMPEII
In AD 79, Mount Vesuvius erupted, burying the town of Pompeii under stone and ash. The ruins were not discovered until the 18th century.

COLOSSEUM
This Roman stadium was built in the first century AD and used for events such as gladiator contests. It was even flooded for mock sea battles.

**Map labels:**

FRANCE
SWITZERLAND
AUSTRIA
SLOVENIA
CROATIA

Mont Blanc 15,771 ft (4,807 m)
Matterhorn 14,691 ft (4,478 m)
Monte Rosa 15,203 ft (4,634 m)
ALPS
DOLOMITES
APENNINES

Skiing
Hydroelectricity
Turin
Car manufacturing
Wine
Rice
Olives
Milan
Fashion
Car manufacturing
Lake Maggiore
Lake Como
Lake Garda
Parma Baptistry
Parmesan cheese
Parma
Modena
Bologna
Brescia
Violin making
Skiing
Marmot
Chamois
Rock climbing
Bolzano
Pinnacles of the Dolomites
Rialto Bridge
Venice
Padua
Verona
Dairy cattle
Sugar beets
Corn
Trieste
Gulf of Venice
Sole
Po
Wheat
Rice
Ferrara
Florence Cathedral
Ravenna
Church of San Vitale
RIMINI
SAN MARINO
Rocca Tower, San Marino
Ancona
Pasta
Arezzo
Siena
Chianti wine
Florence
Arno
Livorno
Pisa
Leaning Tower of Pisa
La Spezia
Marble
Genoa
Milan Cathedral
Walnuts
Tourism
Fishing boat
Squid
Liguarian Sea
Elba

N W E S

LOCATION

Adriatic Sea

Strait of Otranto

Trulli houses

Crabs

Octopus

Winemaking

Brindisi

Bari

Oysters

Taranto

Gulf of Taranto

Ionian Sea

Sea horse

Red mullet

Potatoes

Oil

Foggia

Appian Way (Roman road)

Great barracuda

Vesuvius and the ruins of Pompeii Forum

Goats

Olives

Wall lizard

Cosenza

Reggio di Calabria

Sheep

ITALY

Wolf

Abbey of Monte Cassino

Soccer

Pescara

Pizza maker

Naples

Salerno

Wine

Anchovies

Oranges

Vatican City

Ischia

Mt. Vesuvius 4,190 ft (1,277m)

Capri

Tourism

Garfish

LIPARI ISLANDS

Stromboli

Messina

Tourism

Syracuse

Tibur

Sunflowers

Vatican guard

VATICAN CITY ★ ROME

Colosseum

Container ship

Tyrrhenian Sea

Swordfish

Ustica

Palermo

Temple of Concordia

Sicily

Mt. Etna 10,902 ft (3,323 m)

Citrus fruit

Wheat

Oil

Mediterranean Sea

Wine

Sardines

MALTA ★ VALLETTA

Tourism

SAN MARINO

The smallest republic in Europe and the oldest republic in the world, San Marino was founded around AD 300 by Christians fleeing religious persecution.

Giglio

CORSICA (FRANCE)

Scuba diving

Bluefin tuna

Sardines

Iron ore

Sassari

Sardinia

Goats

Sheep

Olives

Woman in folk costume

Cagliari

Tourism

Sardines

MILES
0   25   50   75   150
KILOMETERS
0   50   100   150

◆ PROJECT: *Making a Mosaic* ◆

A mosaic is a design made by pressing small pieces of cut stone or colored glass into a soft plaster surface. In ancient Rome, the walls and floors of public places and private homes were decorated with mosaics. There are many colorful mosaics in the Church of San Vitale in Ravenna, which were made around AD 526–47. You can make your own mosaic using tiny pieces of colored paper instead of stone or glass.

❶ Cut ¼-inch (0.5-cm) squares out of several sheets of different-colored paper.

❷ On a surface of white or colored paper, draw the outline of a simple design for your mosaic. It could be a landscape, a flower, an animal or even a portrait of a friend.

❸ To create your mosaic, carefully glue the tiny pieces of paper close together within the outlines of your design.

Southeastern Europe

THIS REGION IS OFTEN REFERRED TO as the Balkans. It lies at the edge of Europe, close to Asia, and is home to many peoples from both continents. Throughout history, disputes between countries and ethnic groups have occurred here regularly. In 1991, the republics of Slovenia, Croatia, Bosnia and Herzegovina, and Macedonia declared their independence from Yugoslavia. This led to a war that destroyed cities, farms and industries, and left thousands of people homeless. Most of southeastern Europe is rugged and mountainous. Along the coast of Croatia, rocky slopes rise steeply from the water. Inland, forests and farms surround the peaks that spread eastward through Yugoslavia and into Romania and Bulgaria. In Bulgaria's Balkan

Mountains, an area known as the Valley of the Roses, produces more than two-thirds of the world's rose oil, an essential ingredient in most perfumes. Southeastern Europe's best farmland lies along the Danube River, which connects many of the region's towns to the ports of the Black Sea. In Greece, overgrazing by sheep and goats has stripped some of the land of trees and shrubs, but the warm climate allows farmers to grow olives, grapes, citrus fruit and wheat. Greece's sunny weather and scenic attractions bring tourists from all over the world. In Athens, home to one-third of Greece's population, rush-hour traffic roars past 2,000-year-old temples. On the Greek islands, clusters of white buildings cling to cliffs, and fishing boats drift across clear turquoise bays.

ALBANIA
POPULATION: 3,365,000 • CAPITAL: TIRANË

BOSNIA AND HERZEGOVINA
POPULATION: 3,483,000 • CAPITAL: SARAJEVO

BULGARIA
POPULATION: 8,195,000 • CAPITAL: SOFIA

CROATIA
POPULATION: 4,677,000 • CAPITAL: ZAGREB

GREECE
POPULATION: 10,708,000 • CAPITAL: ATHENS

MACEDONIA
POPULATION: 2,023,000 • CAPITAL: SKOPJE

ROMANIA
POPULATION: 22,335,000 • CAPITAL: BUCHAREST

SLOVENIA
POPULATION: 1,971,000 • CAPITAL: LJUBLJANA

YUGOSLAVIA
POPULATION: 11,207,000 • CAPITAL: BELGRADE

Black Sea

LOCATION

TURKEY

Shipka Memorial Church

Food processing

Plovdiv

Tobacco

Mt. Musala
9,596 ft
(2,925 m)

Skiing

RHODOPE MTS.

Struma

Wheat

Greek Orthodox monk

Alexandroúpolis

Thásos

Samothráce

TURKEY

Olives

Lemnos

Lesbos

Sailing

Aegean Sea

Chíos

Sámos

Iron and steel

Thessaloníki

Goats

Vardar

Skiing

SKOPJE

MACEDONIA

Eastern Orthodox Church

Cotton

Bitola

Korçë

Monastery, Meteora

Mt. Olympus
9,570 ft
(2,917 m)

Volos

GREECE

Ruins of Delphi

Wine

Sardines

NORTHERN SPORADES

Skyros

Euboea

Khalkis

Lignite

Mackerel

ATHENS

Piraeus

Parthenon

Andros

Tínos

Mykonos

CYCLADES

Páros

Naxos

Tourism

DODECANESE

Windmill

Traditional church

Rhodes

Kárpathos

Sea of Crete

Bull's head sculpture, Knossos

Iráklion

Crete

Canea

Wine

Mediterranean Sea

Copper

Shkodër

Corn

Black kite

ALBANIA

TIRANË

Durrës

Vlorë

Inspecting carpets

Tourism

Corfu

IONIAN ISLANDS

Levkás

Olives

Zákinthos

Cephalonia

Kíthira

PELOPONNESE

Patras

Tripolis

Ruins of Olympia

King Agamemnon's gold death mask

Evzones guards

Bouzouki

Ionian Sea

Adriatic Sea

ITALY

KOSOVO

Black Sea

◆ PROJECT: *Make a Cave* ◆

The Postojna Caves in Slovenia are famous for their stalactites and stalagmites. These formations took thousands of years to develop, but you can make your own cave with stalactites and stalagmites in just a few days.

❶ Draw a cave scene on the inside bottom of a shoe box. Line the outside and inside walls of the box with aluminum foil. Turn the box on its side so that the scene becomes the cave's back wall. Ask an adult to help you punch two holes close together at each end of the top of the box. Place a glass outside each end of the box.

❷ Thread a length of string in through one hole at one end and out through one hole at the other end. Repeat with the other two holes. Make sure the strings reach the bottom of each glass and hang down a little inside the cave.

❸ Fill the glasses with hot water and stir in washing soda until no more will dissolve. Make sure you wash your hands well after using the washing soda. Over the next few days, as the water soaks into the strings and then starts to evaporate, small salt formations will appear where the strings sag. At the same time, small mounds of salt will form where the water drips onto the cave floor. Gradually, these formations will grow into stalactites and stalagmites.

BLACK KITE

These birds of prey are found throughout southeastern Europe. At night, they roost in trees in huge flocks of as many as 100 birds.

CASTLE OF VLAD TEPES

Vlad Tepes, a 15th-century Romanian prince known as Vlad the Impaler, is said to have inspired the legend of Dracula the vampire.

EVZONES GUARDS

Wearing their traditional skirts and tasseled hats and shoes, the evzones stand guard outside the parliament in Athens.

Eastern Europe

IN RECENT YEARS, MANY POLITICAL CHANGES have occurred within this vast region. During 1990 and 1991, the republics of Latvia, Estonia, Lithuania, Belarus, Moldova and the Ukraine, all formerly part of the Soviet Union, became independent countries. In 1993, Czechoslovakia divided into two countries, the Czech Republic and Slovakia. Mountains line the borders of the Czech Republic and cover most of Slovakia, but elsewhere eastern Europe is generally flat. Wide grasslands cover central Hungary and most of the Ukraine. In Poland, rivers that rise in the southern mountains meander northward across a wide plain of rich farmland toward coastal swamps and sand dunes. The Baltic States of Lithuania, Latvia and Estonia are covered with meadows, marshes and more than 9,000 lakes. Around the Baltic Sea, winters can be bitterly cold, and icebreaker ships often have to clear a path between the region's ports. About two-thirds of eastern Europe's people live in cities, and many work in heavy industries such as mining, steelmaking and shipbuilding. These industries have created serious pollution problems. Acid rain has destroyed forests in Poland and the Czech Republic, and people are no longer allowed to swim in some polluted lakes in Hungary. In the Ukraine and Belarus, large areas of land can no longer be farmed because they were contaminated by radioactivity after an accident at the Chernobyl nuclear power plant near Kiev in 1986. Despite this, the Ukraine remains one of the largest producers of wheat in the world.

◆ LOOK AGAIN ◆

- What kind of glassware is produced in the Czech Republic?
- Name a mineral that is mined in eastern Hungary.
- Ukrainians eat a soup called borscht. What is it made of?

BELARUS
POPULATION: 10,402,000 ◆ CAPITAL: MINSK

CZECH REPUBLIC
POPULATION: 10,281,000 ◆ CAPITAL: PRAGUE

ESTONIA
POPULATION: 1,409,000 ◆ CAPITAL: TALLINN

HUNGARY
POPULATION: 10,187,000 ◆ CAPITAL: BUDAPEST

LATVIA
POPULATION: 2,354,000 ◆ CAPITAL: RIGA

LITHUANIA
POPULATION: 3,585,000 ◆ CAPITAL: VILNIUS

MOLDOVA
POPULATION: 4,461,000 ◆ CAPITAL: CHIŞINĂU

POLAND
POPULATION: 38,609,000 ◆ CAPITAL: WARSAW

SLOVAKIA
POPULATION: 5,397,000 ◆ CAPITAL: BRATISLAVA

UKRAINE
POPULATION: 49,812,000 ◆ CAPITAL: KIEV

Black stork

Gulf

Baltic Sea

Shipbuilding

Folk costumes

Gdańsk

Timber

Camping

KALININGRA OBLAST (RUSS

Herring

Amber

Pigs

European b

Szczecin

Chemicals

POLAND

Horse-drawn sled

Bydgoszcz

Royal Castle

Poznań

Food processing

Łódź

Textiles

★ WARSAW

GERMANY

Oder

Oleśnica Castle

Wheat

Pig

Potatoes

Church of Our Lady Before Tyn

Karkonosze Mountains

SUDETEN MTS.

Wrocław

Baroque houses

Iron and steel

Brow bear

Coal

Plzeň

Bohemian crystal

PRAGUE

Car manufacturing

CZECH REPUBLIC

Soccer

Katowice

Coal

Kraków

Vistula

Brown bear

Stalagmites Krásnohor Cave

Brno

SLOVAKIA

Košice

BOHEMIAN FOREST

Coal

Bratislava Castle

Hortobágy horseman

AUSTRIA

★ **BRATISLAVA**

Bauxite (aluminum

BUDAPEST

★

Debre

HUNGARY

Parliament Building

SLOVENIA

Poultry

Danube

Corn

Curing ham

CROATIA

Pécs

YUGOSLAVIA

CHURCH OF OUR LADY BEFORE TYN
The towers of this 14th-century church are known as Adam and Eve towers because one (the right-hand tower) is larger than the other.

HORTOBÁGY HORSEMAN
The Hortobágy region of Hungary is a famous horse-breeding center. Locals pride themselves on their riding skills.

Gulf of Finland

Old Town, Tallinn

Lake Peipus

...ALLINN

...rism

ESTONIA

...ga

Fallow deer

Beef cattle

LATVIA

RIGA

Food processing

Folk dancers

...IUANIA

Daugava

Timber

Island Castle, Trakai

Red foxes

Vitsyebsk

Rye

VILNIUS

Chemicals

Neman

Station Square

MINSK

High-tech industries

Mahilyow

Clocks and watches

Dnieper

Flax

RUSSIA

Dairy cattle

BELARUS

Barley

Potatoes

Homyel'

Pripyat'

Folk costume

Brest Fortress

Cossack dancer

Osprey

Dairy cattle

Chernobyl nuclear reactor

Tobacco

Kharkiv

Borscht (beet soup)

Natural gas

Wolf

Sugar beets

KIEV

St. Sophia's Cathedral

Porcelain manufacturing

High-tech industries

Textiles

Hydroelectricity

Collecting corn

Sugar beets

Wild boars

Painted eggs

Manganese

L'viv

Natural gas

Car manufacturing

UKRAINE

Wheat

Dnieper

Dnipropetrovs'k

Coal

Lynx

Geese

Wheat

Iron and steel

Donets'k

Wine

Bug

Folk dancers

CARPATHIAN MTS.

...ildcat

Dniester

Prut

Corn

Hydroelectricity

Kakhovka Reservoir

ROMANIA

MOLDOVA

Sunflowers

Caviar

RUSSIA

CHIŞINĂU

Odessa

Tourism

Swallow's Nest Castle

Ⓔ Sturgeon

Sea of Azov

Harvesting hay

Wheat

Fishing boat

Wine

CRIMEAN MTS.

EUROPEAN BISON
Bison once roamed through the forests of Europe. They still live in their natural environment in parts of Poland.

Food processing

Sevastapol'

Black Sea

LOCATION

◆ PROJECT: *Painted Eggs* ◆

Symbols of rebirth and a new beginning, decorated eggs are an Easter tradition in eastern Europe. It's easy to paint an egg—the tricky part is preparing the shell. Take the raw eggs out of the refrigerator a few hours before you start. If they are too cold, they will be hard to blow.

❶ Take an egg and gently prick the larger end of the shell with a pin. Chip the shell away until the hole is about ¹/₄-inch (0.5 cm) across.

❷ Make a tiny hole in the smaller end. Put your fingers over both holes and gently shake the egg to break up the yolk. Hold the egg over a dish and blow through the small hole. The insides of the egg will slowly empty into the dish. Rinse the eggshell with water and let it dry.

❸ Now you are ready to paint. Carefully thread a piece of stiff wire through the holes in the shell. Hold the egg by the wire and paint your design on it.

❹ Lay the wire across a bowl so the painted egg can dry without being touched.

SCALE

MILES

0   50   100   150

0   50 100 150 200 250

KILOMETERS

Northern Europe

THE COUNTRIES OF NORTHERN EUROPE are known as the Nordic countries. They are sometimes called Scandinavia, but strictly speaking this name refers only to the wide peninsula occupied by Norway and Sweden. On the western side of this peninsula, fjords—spectacular, steep-sided bays formed by glaciers—and more than 150,000 islands create a maze of waterways. Inland, mountain peaks and high plateaus cover most of Norway. To the east, the marshy plains of Sweden and Finland are studded with thousands of lakes and cloaked in coniferous forests that are home to moose, brown bears and wolves. The northern half of this region has a cold climate, with long, dark, snowy winters. In the far south, the climate is more temperate and the land more fertile.

Only one-twentieth of Norway can be farmed, but more than three-quarters of Denmark is used for agriculture. There is little farmland on Iceland, a volcanic island which lies 600 miles (1,000 km) west of Norway. The island's barren interior consists mainly of volcanoes, hot springs and lava fields. Parts of Iceland are so like the surface of the moon that astronauts trained there for moon landings. Some upland areas are covered by huge sheets of ice. Vatnajökull, an ice sheet in the southeast, is larger than all the glaciers in Europe combined.

DENMARK
POPULATION: 5,357,000 ∗ CAPITAL: COPENHAGEN
FINLAND
POPULATION: 5,159,000 ∗ CAPITAL: HELSINKI
ICELAND
POPULATION: 272,600 ∗ CAPITAL: REYKJAVIK
NORWAY
POPULATION: 4,439,000 ∗ CAPITAL: OSLO
SWEDEN
POPULATION: 8,912,000 ∗ CAPITAL: STOCKHOLM

Barents Sea

North Cape monument

NORTH CAPE

Hammerfest

Orca (killer whale)

Cod

Tromsø

Puffins

Fishing boat

LOFOTEN ISLANDS

Narvik

Salmon

Bodø

Herring

Arctic Circle pyramid

Reindeer

Sami man

Sami man and woman

Lake Inari

Wolverine

Brown bear

Gällivare

Iron ore

Torne

Kebnekaise 6,965 ft (2,123 m)

Rune stone

Kemi

Elk (moose)

Timber

Hydroelectricity

FINLAND

Sauna

Oulu

Zinc

Cross-country skiing

RUSSIA

Luleå

Giant chess board

Skellefte

Umeå

St. Lucia

Sailing

Timber

Ice hockey

Hydroelectricity

LAPLAND

Norwegian Sea

SCALE
MILES
KILOMETERS

N E S W

ICELAND

White-tailed eagle

Akureyri

Svartifoss waterfall

VATNAJÖKULL

Sheep

REYKJAVIK

Strokkur geyser

ATLANTIC OCEAN

MILES
KILOMETERS

LOCATION

◆ PROJECT: *Sami Tent* ◆

Some of the nomadic Sami people of Northern Europe still live in tents made from reindeer skins stretched over poles. These tents are easily set up and taken down as the Sami follow their grazing herds of reindeer. Here's an easy way to make a model of a Sami home.

1 Use several straws for the poles. Loosely tie one end of the straws together with string. Spread out the other ends of the straws to form the base of the tent.

2 Now use parchment paper for the reindeer-skin covering. Roll the paper into a cone shape and tape it together. Leave a hole at the top of the cone (real Sami tents have a large smoke hole at the top). Slip the cone over the straws and cut an opening for the door.

3 You can also create a full-size Sami tent for backyard camping. Use bamboo poles about 4 to 5 feet (1.2 to 1.5 m) long, canvas and strong twine.

LITTLE MERMAID STATUE

At the edge of Copenhagen harbor sits this statue of the main character in Danish author Hans Christian Andersen's much-loved fairy tale, *The Little Mermaid*.

ST. ANDREW'S CHURCH

Built about AD 1150 in Norway, this wooden church stands more than four stories tall. Its gables are carved in the shape of dragons, important symbols in Viking mythology.

Kuopio
Hydroelectricity
Joensuu
Paper
Jyväskylä
Trout
Lake Sainaa
Lahti
Helsinki Cathedral
Hydrofoil
ESTONIA
Timber
Kick-sledding
Tampere
Ice pool
Dairy cattle
Vaasa
Pori
Turku
HELSINKI ★
Gulf of Finland
LATVIA
ÅLAND ISLANDS
Parliament building
Gulf of Bothnia
Icebreaker ship
Capercaillie
Hydroelectricity
Indal
Sundsvall
Traditional church and bell tower
Fiddle player in national dress
Drottningholm Palace
Uppsala
STOCKHOLM ★
Norrköping
Linköping
Orrefors glass
Gotland
Folk dancing
Osterdal
Cross-country skiing
Iron and steel
Örebro
Karlstad
Lake Vättern
Jönköping
Baltic Sea
Öland
Kalmar Castle
POLAND
Trondheim
Traditional storehouse
Skiing
Galdhøpiggen 8,100 ft (2,469 m)
NORWAY
JOTUNHEIM MOUNTAINS
Ski jumping
Chemicals
OSLO ★
Fredrikstad
Drammen
Shipbuilding
Fredrikstad
Lake Vänern
Borås
Goteborg
Car manufacturing
Hälsingborg
Pigs
Bornholm
Malmö
Oil rig
Natural gas
Nordfjord
Sognefjord
Bergen wharf
Bergen
St. Andrew's Church
Hydroelectricity
Jarlsberg cheese
Stavanger
Fishing boat
Kristiansand
Ice fishing
Folk costume
Skagerrak
North Sea
Ålborg
Århus
DENMARK
Little Mermaid statue
Fyn
Odense
COPENHAGEN ★
Sjælland
Lolland
Legoland
Esbjerg
Pigs
Egeskov Castle
Cod
GERMANY

Asia

THE WORLD'S BIGGEST CONTINENT, Asia stretches almost halfway around the globe and covers one-third of Earth's landmass. It has the world's tallest mountains, the world's largest lake and the world's lowest point on land. It was the birthplace of many great religions and important civilizations, and is now home to 60 percent of the people on Earth. Most Asians live in the east and south, where the climate is warm and wet and there are large areas of forest, fertile plains and hundreds of tropical islands. Deserts and barren mountain ranges dominate the southwest and center of the continent. To the north, the grasslands, or steppes, of central Asia give way to the immense coniferous forests of Russia. A belt of freezing tundra extends along the continent's north coast. Russia is the world's largest country by area, but China has the world's largest population.

Major Mountains and Rivers

Mount Everest, China-Nepal
29,028 ft (8,848 m)

Kanchenjunga,
India-Nepal
28,169 ft (8,586 m)

Communism Peak,
Tajikistan
24,590 ft (7,495 m)

K2,
China-Pakistan
28,250 ft (8,611 m)

Annapurna, Nepal
26,504 ft (8,078 m)

Mount Ararat, Turkey
16,945 ft (5,165 m)

Chang (Yangtze) 3,960 miles (6,380 km)
Yenisey-Angara 3,445 miles (5,550 km)
Huang (Yellow) 3,395 miles (5,464 km)
Ob'-Irtysh 3,360 miles (5,410 km)
Mekong 2,795 miles (4,500 km)
Lena 2,730 miles (4,400 km)

Political Map

RUSSIA

KAZAKSTAN

MONGOLIA

GEORGIA
1 2
UZBEKISTAN KYRGYZSTAN
TURKMENISTAN
TURKEY
TAJIKISTAN
NORTH
KOREA
CYPRUS
SYRIA
AFGHANISTAN
CHINA
SOUTH
KOREA
JAPAN
4 3
IRAQ
JORDAN 5
IRAN
PAKISTAN
NEPAL 9
6
7 8
INDIA 10
TAIWAN
SAUDI
ARABIA OMAN
MYANMAR
(BURMA)
LAOS
YEMEN
THAILAND
PHILIPPINES
CAMBODIA
SRI
LANKA
VIETNAM
12
MALDIVES
MALAYSIA
11
INDONESIA
EAST TIMOR

Continent Facts

Regional land area: 17,139,445 sq. miles (44,391,162 sq. km) (excluding European Russia)
Regional population: 3,660,642,000 (excluding European Russia)
Independent countries: Afghanistan, Armenia, Azerbaijan, Bahrain, Bangladesh, Bhutan, Brunei, Cambodia, China, Cyprus, East Timor, Georgia, India, Indonesia, Iran, Iraq, Israel, Japan, Jordan, Kazakstan, Kuwait, Kyrgyzstan, Laos, Lebanon, Malaysia, Maldives, Mongolia, Myanmar (Burma), Nepal, North Korea, Oman, Pakistan, Philippines, Qatar, Russia, Saudi Arabia, Singapore, South Korea, Sri Lanka, Syria, Taiwan, Tajikistan, Thailand, Turkey, Turkmenistan, United Arab Emirates, Uzbekistan, Vietnam, Yemen

World Records

WORLD'S HIGHEST MOUNTAIN
MOUNT EVEREST, CHINA-NEPAL, 29,028 FT (8,848 M)

WORLD'S LOWEST POINT ON LAND
DEAD SEA, ISRAEL-JORDAN, 1,300 FT (400 M) BELOW SEA LEVEL

WORLD'S LARGEST LAKE BY AREA
CASPIAN SEA, WESTERN ASIA, 143,550 SQ. MILES (371,800 SQ. KM)

WORLD'S OLDEST, DEEPEST AND LARGEST (BY VOLUME) LAKE
LAKE BAIKAL, RUSSIA, 25 MILLION YEARS OLD; 5,371 FT (1,637 M) DEEP; 5,500 CUBIC MILES (23,000 CUBIC KM) OF WATER

WORLD'S LARGEST COUNTRY BY AREA
RUSSIA, 6,592,812 SQ. MILES (17,075,383 SQ. KM)

WORLD'S LARGEST COUNTRY BY POPULATION
CHINA, POPULATION 1,246,872,000

WORLD'S LARGEST CITY BY POPULATION
TOKYO, JAPAN, POPULATION 27,200,000

WORLD'S LONGEST WALL
GREAT WALL OF CHINA, 2,150 MILES (3,460 KM)

WORLD'S LONGEST RAILWAY LINE
TRANS-SIBERIAN, RUSSIA, 5,777 MILES (9,297 KM)

Continent Records

LONGEST RIVER
CHANG (YANGTZE), 3,960 MILES (6,380 KM)

Key to Numbered Countries

1 ARMENIA	7 QATAR
2 AZERBAIJAN	8 UNITED ARAB EMIRATES
3 LEBANON	9 BHUTAN
4 ISRAEL	10 BANGLADESH
5 KUWAIT	■ 11 SINGAPORE
■ 6 BAHRAIN	12 BRUNEI

*P*HYSICAL **MAP**

ARCTIC OCEAN
× NORTH POLE

Barents Sea

Kara Sea

Laptev Sea

East Siberian Sea

Bering Sea

EUROPE

URAL MOUNTAINS

Ob

Arctic Circle

Lena

VERKHOYANSKI MTS.

KAMCHATKA PENINSULA

CENTRAL SIBERIAN PLATEAU

WEST SIBERIAN PLAIN

Yenisey

Angara

Sea of Okhotsk

Sakhalin

KURIL ISLANDS

Black Sea

Mt. Elbrus ▲

CAUCASUS MTS.

Mt. Ararat ▲

Irtysh

SIBERIA

Lake Baikal

Amur

Hokkaidō

Caspian Sea

Lake Balkhash

Aral Sea

ALTAY MTS.

MANCHURIAN PLAIN

Honshū

Sea of Japan

SYRIAN DESERT

ZAGROS MTS.

TIEN MTS.

GOBI DESERT

Persian Gulf

PLATEAU OF IRAN

Communism Peak ▲

TAKLIMAKAN DESERT

▲ K2

KUNLUN MTS.

Huang (Yellow)

Yellow Sea

Shikoku

Kyūshū

Red Sea

HINDU KUSH

Indus

HIMALAYAS

PLATEAU OF TIBET

East China Sea

RYUKYU ISLANDS

Tropic of Cancer

ARABIAN PENINSULA

GREAT INDIAN DESERT

▲ Annapurna
▲ Mt. Everest
▲ Kanchenjunga

Chang (Yangtze)

Gulf of Oman

INDO-GANGETIC PLAIN

Ganges

NAN MTS.

Gulf of Aden

DECCAN

Bay of Bengal

Irrawaddy

Taiwan

Arabian Sea

Hainan

Luzon

South China Sea

PHILIPPINE ISLANDS

ANDAMAN ISLANDS

Andaman Sea

Mekong

MALDIVES

Sri Lanka

NICOBAR ISLANDS

Gulf of Thailand

Mindanao

MALAY PENINSULA

Equator

New Guinea

Borneo

MOLUCCAS

Sumatra

Sulawesi

Java Sea

INDIAN OCEAN

GREATER SUNDA ISLANDS

Java

LESSER SUNDA ISLANDS

AUSTRALIA AND OCEANIA

PACIFIC OCEAN

Tropic of Capricorn

Russia

RUSSIA IS THE LARGEST country in the world. It covers two-thirds of Asia and one-third of Europe, and is so wide that it has eleven time zones. When the citizens of St. Petersburg are getting ready for bed, the miners and reindeer herders who live in the remote far east are already starting their next day's work. Most of Russia has a cold climate, with mild to cool summers and cold to freezing winters. In the far north, where most of the land is tundra, winter temperatures can drop to –94°F (–70°C). South of the tundra, a wide band of coniferous woodland stretches almost all the way across the country. The Ural Mountains divide Russia into two regions. West of the Urals is European Russia, which has only one-quarter of the land, but four-fifths of the population, the largest industries and the most fertile farmland. East of the Urals, in Asia, is Siberia, a vast wilderness region that is bigger than the United States and western Europe combined. In the southern part of this region near Mongolia lies Lake Baikal, the world's deepest lake, which holds one-fifth of the world's fresh water. Siberia is also rich in minerals, such as coal and oil. The Chukchi Peninsula in eastern Siberia is the most easterly point in Asia. It lies only 50 miles (82 km) from North America. Before 1991, Russia was part of an even larger country—the Soviet Union—which also included 14 present-day countries in eastern Europe and central Eurasia.

RUSSIA
POPULATION: 146,394,000 ∗ CAPITAL: MOSCOW

Map labels

ARCTIC
FRANZ JOSEF LAND
SEVERNAYA ZEMLY
NOVAYA ZEMLYA
NORWAY
Icebreaker ship
Murmansk
Barents Sea
Kara Sea
Harp seals
Iron ore and copper
Puffins
Haddock
Fishing through ice
Ptarmig
Nickel and platinum
FINLAND
Coal
Natural gas
KALININGRAD OBLAST (RUSSIA)
ESTONIA
Lake Ladoga
Lake Onega
Arkhangel'sk
Nenet woman
LATVIA
St. Petersburg
Chess
Timber
LITHUANIA
Fabergé egg
Troika
Yenisey
Dairy cattle
Demetrius Cathedral
Woolly mammoth fossils
BELARUS
Russian Orthodox priest
URAL MOUNTAINS
Khanty tribesmen
Oil
St. Basil's Cathedral
Ballet
Yaroslavl'
Ob'
WEST SIBERIAN PLAIN
MOSCOW
Vyatka
Steppe herder
Nizhniy Novgorod
Matreshka dolls
Rye
Iron ore
The Kremlin
Church of the Nativity
Perm'
Geese
Ob'
Kazan'
Bauxite (aluminum)
Hay cart
Yenisey
Ti
Gymnastics
Balalaika
Ufa
RU
UKRAINE
Dom
Samara
Corn
Yekaterinburg
Capercaillie
Saratov
Chelyabinsk
Oats
Rostov-na-Donu
Volgograd
Wheat
Samovar
Omsk
Novosibirsk
Wild boars
Black Sea
Volga
Krasnoya
Krasnodar
Farm workers
KAZAKSTAN
Trans-Siberian Railroad
Volga-Don Canal
Astrakhan
Wheat
CAUCASUS MTS.
Mt. Elbrus 18,510 ft (5,642 m) ▲
Caviar
Fisherman with sturgeon
Hydroele
Grozny
GEORGIA
Caspian Sea
Sheep
AZERBAIJAN

ST. BASIL'S CATHEDRAL
This colorful Moscow cathedral was built in the 16th century to celebrate Czar Ivan the Terrible's victory over his Tartar enemies.

ALASKA
(U.S.A.)

◆ AMAZING FACT ◆

Stretching almost one-quarter of the way around the globe, the Trans-Siberian Railroad is the longest railway in the world. The journey from Moscow to Vladivostok takes eight days and covers a distance of 5,777 miles (9,297 km).

◆ LOOK AGAIN ◆

- What kind of fossils have been discovered on the West Siberian Plain?
- On which peninsula is the Klyuchevskaya volcano located?
- Name a form of dance that is popular in Moscow.

Chukchi Sea
Bering Strait

CHUKCHI PENINSULA

Harbor seals

Chukchi hunter

East Siberian Sea

NEW SIBERIAN ISLANDS

OCEAN

Polar bears

Reindeer

Wolf

Furs

Bering Sea

Laptev Sea

Kittiwake

Arctic fox

Nordvik

Snowy owl

Walrus

Lynx

Gold

Timber

KAMCHATKA PENINSULA

Yakut woman and children

Verkhoyansk

Natural gas

VERKHOYANSKI MTS.

Reindeer sled

Lena

Klyuchevskaya volcano 15,580 ft (4,749 m)

Petropavlovsk-Kamchatskiy

Evenki woman and baby

CENTRAL SIBERIAN PLATEAU

Brown bear

Magadan

Okhotsk

Elk (moose)

Timber

Yakutsk

Osprey

Salmon

Diamonds

Herring

Sea of Okhotsk

Furs

Lena

Wolf

Gold

Oil

Natural gas

Sakhalin

KURIL ISLANDS

STANOVOY MTS.

Coal

Coal

Hydroelectricity

YABLANOVYY MTS.

Hydroelectricity

Siberian tiger Ⓔ

Amur

Khabarovsk

Udegei dancers

JAPAN

Bratsk

Baroque architecture

Buryat archer

CHINA

Wheat

Coal

Irkutsk

Siberian house

Lake Baikal

Ulan-Ude

Udegei building

Sea of Japan

MONGOLIA

Vladivostok

LOCATION

MATRESHKA DOLLS

...ese traditional wooden dolls ...e shaped so that they fit inside ...e another. Some matreshka ...s include more than 12 dolls.

SIBERIAN TIGER

Siberian tigers are the world's biggest tigers. They live in southeastern Siberia and hunt bears, deer and, occasionally, people!

SCALE

MILES

0   100   200   300   400   500

0   200   400   600   800

KILOMETERS

Central Eurasia

EURASIA IS THE LANDMASS that contains Europe and Asia. Central Eurasia extends from the southeastern corner of Europe into the dry heart of Asia. Turkey forms a bridge between the two continents, which are separated by the narrow Bosporus strait. Turkey's interior is hilly and barren, but its fertile coastal regions produce tea, tobacco, and the world's largest crops of hazelnuts and raisins. South of Turkey lies the island of Cyprus, which is home to people of Turkish and Greek descent. Beyond Turkey's eastern border, the countries of Georgia, Armenia and

Azerbaijan are flanked by the massive Caucasus mountains. These countries are rich in minerals: at one time, Baku, the capital of Azerbaijan, supplied half of the world's oil. Across the Caspian Sea, deserts cover most of Turkmenistan, Uzbekistan and Kazakstan. Ancient trade routes between China and Europe passed through these lands, linking cities such as Samarquand and Tashkent. In the north, the desert merges with the Kirgiz Steppe, a vast grassland; in the southeast, the Tian Mountains cover most of Kyrgyzstan and Tajikistan. Many of central Eurasia's rivers are diverted to irrigate crops. This has lowered the levels of some lakes. The Aral Sea, once the world's fourth-largest lake, has shrunk to half its former size, stranding fishing villages and boats more than 20 miles (30 km) from the shore.

ARMENIA
POPULATION: 3,410,000 * CAPITAL: YEREVAN

AZERBAIJAN
POPULATION: 7,909,000 * CAPITAL: BAKU

CYPRUS
POPULATION: 754,100 * CAPITAL: NICOSIA

GEORGIA
POPULATION: 5,067,000 * CAPITAL: TBILISI

KAZAKSTAN
POPULATION: 16,825,000 * CAPITAL: ASTANA

KYRGYZSTAN
POPULATION: 4,547,000 * CAPITAL: BISHKEK

TAJIKISTAN
POPULATION: 6,103,000 * CAPITAL: DUSHANBE

TURKEY
POPULATION: 65,600,000 * CAPITAL: ANKARA

TURKMENISTAN
POPULATION: 4,367,000 * CAPITAL: ASHKHABAD

UZBEKISTAN
POPULATION: 24,103,000 * CAPITAL: TASHKENT

BLUE MOSQUE
Built for Sultan Ahmet I in the 17th century, this mosque in Istanbul, Turkey, is named for the more than 21,000 blue tiles that cover its interior.

♦ AMAZING FACT ♦

In Cappadocia in central Turkey, an eerie landscape of strange rock formations has been created by wind and water erosion. Early Christians made homes and churches inside caves cut into the rock. Some of these caves are still in use today.

♦ PROJECT: *Kilim Weaving* ♦

A kilim is a flat, woven rug traditionally made in Turkey. To make a simple kilim, you will first need to make a loom.

❶ Cut notches into the corners of a rectangular piece of cardboard. Tie a length of string to the left-hand notch and then wrap it around the cardboard, moving from left to right and leaving about ½ inch (1 cm) between strings. Tie the string off on the right-hand notch.

❷ Now weave by threading wool under and then over the strings. If you begin the first row weaving under, begin the second row weaving

over, and so on. When you add a new piece of wool, tie it to the old piece. As you weave, push the rows tightly together.

❸ When the loom is full, turn it over so that it is face down and cut the two middle strings. Tie them together at the top and bottom edges of the weaving. Repeat with the rest of the strings.

❹ When all the strings have been cut and tied, remove the weaving from the loom. Trim the ends of the tied-off strings to make a fringe for your weaving.

Step 1   Step 2   Step 3

SNOW LEOPARD
Living high in the mountains, the snow leopard needs strong paws for rock climbing and long, thick fur to keep warm.

LOCATION

Qostanay
Petropavl
Iron ore
Marmot
Wheat
Ishim
Sarsembek herder
ASTANA
Pavlodar
Barley
Irtysh
RUSSIA
Gold
Textiles
Aktyubinsk
KIRGIZ STEPPE
Bearded vulture
Yurts (nomad tents)
stranded fishing boats, Aral Sea
Manganese
Copper
Qaraghandy
Semey
Oskemen
Hydroelectricity
Lake Zaysan
Aral Sea
KAZAKSTAN
Baykonur Cosmodrome
Coal
Baking bread in traditional oven
White-throated kingfisher
Cotton
Folk costume
Syr Dar'ya
Cotton
Saiga antelope
Lake Balkhash
Spoonbill
ukus
UZBEKISTAN
Kirgiz farmer
Chemicals
Street vendor selling apples
CHINA
N
W   E
S
Registan Square
Shymkent
Almaty
Ⓔ Snow leopard
Bukhara
Samarkand
TASHKENT
BISHKEK
KYRGYZSTAN
Namangan
Rice
Sheep
rdzhou
Cotton
Osh
Cotton
Yak
Sheep
DUSHANBE
Communism Peak 24,590 ft (7,495 m)
Musician playing longhorn
TAJIKISTAN
Hissar fortress
AFGHANISTAN
Amu Dar'ya
akumskiy Canal
TIAN MTS.

SCALE
MILES
0   100   200   300
0   100   200   300   400   500
KILOMETERS

BAYKONUR COSMODROME
Formerly a Soviet Union space center, Baykonur is now leased from Kazakstan by Russia for use as its main space shuttle and rocket launching site.

The Middle East

THE MIDDLE EAST IS A LAND of ancient cities and vast deserts. It is home to some of the world's oldest civilizations and was the birthplace of three of the most widespread religions—Islam, Christianity and Judaism. Though there are narrow strips of fertile land on the densely populated Mediterranean coast, along the Tigris and Euphrates rivers in Iraq, and in the highlands of northern Iran and Yemen, most of this region is hot, dry and barren. Deserts extend southward from Syria, Jordan and Israel, covering most of the Arabian Peninsula. Parts of this peninsula receive no rain for up to 10 years! Deserts also cover two-thirds of Iran. The enormous Dasht-e Kavīr salt desert in eastern Iran has almost no vegetation. Among its few inhabitants are gazelles that survive on tiny amounts of salty water. Over the centuries, the people of the Middle East have made skillful use of their limited water supplies. For thousands of years, the Tigris and Euphrates rivers have been used to water crops. Today, desalination plants on the shores of the Persian Gulf turn sea water into fresh water. The Gulf region holds half the world's reserves of oil and gas, and this has made some countries very wealthy. On average, people in the United Arab Emirates earn twice as much as people in the United States. In contrast, Yemen, which has little oil, is one of the poorest countries in the world.

BAHRAIN
POPULATION: 629,100 ∗ CAPITAL: MANAMA

IRAN
POPULATION: 65,180,000 ∗ CAPITAL: TEHRAN

IRAQ
POPULATION: 22,428,000 ∗ CAPITAL: BAGHDAD

ISRAEL
POPULATION: 5,750,000 ∗ CAPITAL: JERUSALEM

JORDAN
POPULATION: 4,562,000 ∗ CAPITAL: AMMAN

KUWAIT
POPULATION: 1,992,000 ∗ CAPITAL: KUWAIT

LEBANON
POPULATION: 3,563,000 ∗ CAPITAL: BEIRUT

OMAN
POPULATION: 2,447,000 ∗ CAPITAL: MUSCAT

QATAR
POPULATION: 723,600 ∗ CAPITAL: DOHA

SAUDI ARABIA
POPULATION: 21,505,000 ∗ CAPITAL: RIYADH

SYRIA
POPULATION: 17,214,000 ∗ CAPITAL: DAMASCUS

UNITED ARAB EMIRATES
POPULATION: 2,345,000 ∗ CAPITAL: ABU DHABI

YEMEN
POPULATION: 16,943,000 ∗ CAPITAL: SANAA

◆ AMAZING FACT ◆

The Rub' al-Khali Desert, or Empty Quarter, in southern Saudi Arabia is the biggest sand desert in the world. It is as large as France and has no towns or villages. Its only inhabitants are nomadic Bedouin people.

Map labels

TURKEY

Aleppo
Krak des Chevaliers
Euphrates

Latakia
CYPRUS
Mediterranean Sea
LEBANON
SYRIA
SYRIAN DESERT

Beirut
Damascus

Dome of the Rock, Jerusalem
WEST BANK
Amman

Tel Aviv-Jaffa
Gaza
JERUSALEM
Dead Sea
GAZA STRIP

Date palm

Scorpion

ISRAEL
JORDAN

Royal Tombs, Petra
Lappet-faced vulture

Western Wall, Jerusalem

AN NAFŪD DESERT

EGYPT

HEJAZ

Rock tombs, Madain Salah

Lyre-tailed goldfish

Date palm

Leopard gecko

Pearls

Medina

Red Sea

Veiled woman

Jiddah
Mecca

SUDAN

Barracuda

Dhow

ERITREA

Huda

DOME OF THE ROCK
This Muslim temple in Jerusalem backs onto the Western Wall, a site sacred to Jews. Inside the temple is a rock that some say marks the center of the world.

VEILED WOMAN
Traditionally, Muslim women must keep their face and hair hidden from strangers. Many wear a long black cloak and a veil or eye-mask.

◆ LOOK AGAIN ◆

- In which country could you shop at a floating market?
- Name a weapon used by hunters in Malaysia.
- What kind of "dragon" lives on an island in Indonesia?

SCALE

MILES

0   100   200   300   400

0   150   300   450   600

KILOMETERS

N
W · E
S

◆ PROJECT: *Erupting Volcano* ◆

Southeast Asia has more active volcanoes than any other part of the world. The island of Java alone has 50 volcanoes that could erupt at any time. Here's a volcano that will erupt whenever you want it to.

❶ On a tray, use moist soil to model a mountain.

❷ Scoop out a hole from the top of the mountain and put in a container, such as the lid from a spray can.

❸ Pour about ¼ cup warm water into the container. Now stir in 1 tablespoon baking soda, a few drops of red food coloring and a few drops of dishwashing liquid. Pour in ¼ cup vinegar and watch your volcano erupt.

Adding vinegar to the baking soda produces carbon dioxide gas. This causes pressure to build up until the volcano erupts, forcing lava suds out the top. This is similar to the pressure inside Earth's crust that causes a real volcano to erupt.

Dugongs

Jeepney bus

Luzon Baguio

Basket boat

Copper

Ⓔ Philippine eagle

Swordfish

MANILA

Parrot fish

Mindoro Legazpi

PHILIPPINES

Pineapples *Samar*

Panay Bacolod

Tiger shark

Palawan Fishing with a frame-net

Cebu

Negros

Rice

South China Sea

Dayak woman

Sulu Sea

Mindanao

Muslim dancer Davao

Kota Kinabalu

Sandakan

BANDAR SERI BEGAWAN

Mt. Kinabalu 13,455 ft (4,101 m)

SABAH

Sea gypsy collecting sea urchins

Celebes Sea

il

BRUNEI

SARAWAK

Mulu Caves

Hunter with blowpipe

Coconuts Manado

Diver and giant clam

Halmahera

PACIFIC OCEAN

LOCATION

Orangutan

Oil

Sail-tailed water lizard

Cloves

Oil

Banded pitta

KALIMANTAN

Borneo

Balikpapan

Peppercorns

Greater bird of paradise

Jayapura

Rafflesia flower

Proboscis monkey

Sulawesi

Nutmeg

Ceram

Asmat tribesman

IRIAN JAYA

Banjarmasin

Rice

Tarsier

Buru Ambon

Puncak Jaya 16,535 ft (5,040 m)

New Guinea

Ⓔ Leatherback turtle

Ujung Pandang

Banda Sea

Kai

Aru

PAPUA NEW GUINEA

INDONESIA

Bumblebee goby

Bananas

robudur Temple

Surabaya

Flores Sea

Komodo dragon

Tanimbar

Manta ray

Arafura Sea

Bali *Sumbawa*

Tourism

Flores

Ⓢ DILI
EAST TIMOR

Balinese mask

Lombok Shadow puppet

Coconuts

Sumba

Corn

Hammerhead shark

Timor Sea

Kupang

AUSTRALIA

Eastern Asia

EASTERN ASIA INCLUDES ONE-QUARTER of the Asian mainland as well as several small islands. It is dominated by China, the third-largest (and most populous) country in the world. China is only slightly larger than the United States, but it has more than four times as many people. Eighty percent live in the eastern third of the country, where the climate is mild and wet, and most of the land is fertile. There are many large cities in eastern China, but most people live in villages where they raise pigs and chickens, and grow rice, wheat and vegetables. Western China is dry, rugged and sparsely populated. The southwestern region—Tibet—is sometimes called the "roof of the world" because it lies on the highest plateau on Earth and contains part of the tallest mountain range, the Himalayas. In the north, the barren Gobi Desert stretches into Mongolia, where many people are nomadic herders. On and around China's coast lie a number of rapidly developing countries and territories. South Korea and Taiwan have many thriving industries, including textile, car and electrical goods manufacturers. Macao, a tiny Portuguese colony on the south coast of China, is the world's most crowded place, with 57,100 people for every square mile (22,150 per sq. km). Macao will revert to Chinese rule in 1999. Neighboring Hong Kong, a former British territory which was given back to China in 1997, is the world's third-largest financial center. Its modern, high-rise office buildings tower over one of Asia's busiest harbors.

CHINA
POPULATION: 1,246,872,000 * CAPITAL: BEIJING

MONGOLIA
POPULATION: 2,618,000 * CAPITAL: ULAANBAATAR

NORTH KOREA
POPULATION: 21,386,000 * CAPITAL: P'YŎNGYANG

SOUTH KOREA
POPULATION: 46,885,000 * CAPITAL: SEOUL

TAIWAN
POPULATION: 22,113,000 * CAPITAL: TAIPEI

•AMAZING FACT•

The Great Wall of China stretches for 2,150 miles (3,460 km) across northern China and is so large that astronauts can see it from space. It was built in the third century BC to keep out invaders from the north, and then rebuilt and expanded in the 14th century AD.

Map labels

KAZAKSTAN

Oil

Rice

Donkey cart

KYRGYZSTAN

TIEN MTS.

Ürümqi

Playing the dotar

Coal

Camel train

Kashgar

Cotton

TAJIKISTAN

TAKLIMAKAN DESERT

PAKISTAN

Cotton

Apak Hoja Tomb

Jade

ALTUN MTS.

KUNLUN MTS.

INDIA

K2 28,250 ft (8,611 m)

PLATEAU OF TIBET

Milking a yak

Snow leopard

Tibetan monks

TIBET

HIMALAYAS

Potala Palace

NEPAL

Lhasa

Xiagazê

Gyangze

Mt. Everest 29,028 ft (8,848 m)

BHUTAN

N
W   E
S

SCALE

MILES
0   100   200   300

KILOMETERS
0   100   200   300   400   500

TERRA-COTTA WARRIORS
Chinese emperor Qin Shi Huang had more than 6,000 life-sized clay warriors built to guard his body after his death.

GIANT PANDA
There are only 1,000 giant pandas left in the wild, and they all live in bamboo forests in central China, near Chengdu.

J K L M N O P Q

Lake Uvs
Lake Hövsgöl
Elk (moose)
RUSSIA
Amur
(E) Tiger
Coal mining

Darhan
Qiqihar
Ice sledding
Timber

ULAANBAATAR
Traditional costume
Choybalsan
Harbin

Mongolian family and ger (tent)
Car manufacturing
Soybeans

MONGOLIA
Wild boars
Wheat
Changchun
Coal
Farmer carrying grain

(E) Bactrian camel
Corn
Ch'ŏngjin

GOBI DESERT
Great Wall of China
Iron and steel
Fushun
NORTH KOREA

Goats
Shenyang

Oil
Temple of Heaven
P'YŎNGYANG
Iron and steel

Yumen
Baotou
BEIJING
Tangshan

CHINA
Iron and steel
Forbidden City
Tianjin
Dalian
SEOUL
SOUTH KOREA

Pallas's cat
Cycling
Zibo
Fortune cookies
Textiles

Lake Qinghai
Chemicals
Taiyuan
Jinan
Wheat
Pusan

Lanzhou
Cotton
Silk worm and cocoon
Traditional costume

Reeves's pheasant
Xi'an
Zhengzhou
Grand Canal
Yellow Sea
Cheju

Terra-cotta warriors
Chemicals
Taking cabbages to market
Nanjing Pagoda

(E) Giant panda
Golden snub-nosed monkey
Ping-pong
Nanjing
Shanghai
Container ship

Chengdu
Tai chi
Hangzhou

(E) Red panda
Iron and steel
Wuhan
Lake Poyang
Ming vase
Textiles
East China Sea

Chongqing
Lake Dongting
Lychees
Nanchang
Shrimp

Asiatic golden cat
Grand Buddha
Farmhouse
Changsha
Sweet potatoes

Guiyang
Tea
Fuzhou
TAIPEI

Kunming
Fishing with cormorants
Limestone hills of Guilin
Pigs
High-tech industries

Herding ducks
Rice
Bank of China
TAIWAN

Stone forest (rock formations)
Guangzhou
Chiang Kai Shek monument

Nanning
Paper
Hong Kong

Hydroelectricity
Macao

MYANMAR (BURMA)
VIETNAM

LAOS

TRADITIONAL COSTUME
Most Korean men used to wear a white jacket and baggy pants, and a black horsehair hat. Now they wear these only on special occasions.

Coffee
Haikou
South China Sea

Hainan
Junk

Mandarin fish

JAPAN

LOCATION

PACIFIC OCEAN

Sea of Japan
Korea Strait
Taiwan Strait

Japan

JAPAN CONSISTS OF A long chain of 4 main islands and more than 4,000 smaller islands that lies off the east coast of the Asian mainland. The northern half of Japan has a cold temperate climate with snowy winters and mild summers. In the south the weather is more tropical, with mild winters and a summer wet season. Most of the land is mountainous, and almost two-thirds is covered in forests. Earthquakes are common, and there are many active volcanoes. Japan occupies an area smaller than the U.S. state of Montana but has 150 times as many people. Three-quarters live in cities, the largest of which are located on the large island of Honshū. Japan's capital, Tokyo, sprawls across more than 80 neighboring towns, forming the biggest urban area in the world, and is home to almost 27 million people. So many workers commute to the city center each day that railroad stations employ guards known as "pushers" to cram passengers into trains. Despite having little farmland, Japan manages to produce most of its food, including large quantities of rice. Fish is the country's most important resource, and the Japanese fishing fleet is the largest in the world. Although it has few other natural resources, Japan has become a major industrial power by importing raw materials and manufacturing high-quality goods. It is the world's top car manufacturer, has the world's foremost shipbuilding industry, and is a leading exporter of electronic goods.

JAPAN
POPULATION: 126,182,000 ▪ CAPITAL: TOKYO

◆ LOOK AGAIN ◆

- What kind of festival takes place in Sapporo?
- Name two kinds of shark found off the west coast of Honshū.
- Which famous mountain lies southwest of Japan's capital?

Map labels

RUSSIA

Sea of Okhotsk

RUSSIA

Hokkaidō

Salmon
Dairy cattle
Ainu man
Kushiro
Coal
Great white shark
Pollock
Brown bear
Timber
Skiing
Wakkanai
Rebun
Rishiri
Halibut
Rice
Asahikawa
Sapporo snow festival
Sapporo
Otaru
Serows
Hakodate
Japanese crane
Mackerel

Tsugaru Strait

Macaques
Aomori
Apples
Japanese spider crab
Akita
Sushi
Morioka
Kokechi doll
Carp streamers
Making chopsticks
Rice
Sendai
Shiogama festival
Sardines
Dancer in traditional costume
Mako shark
Fukushima
Niigata
Shinano

JAPAN

Sado

Ninja

Sea of Japan

RYUKYU ISLANDS

East China Sea

OKINAWA ISLANDS

AMAMI ISLANDS

Rice
Long-tailed carpet shark
Karate
Tourism
Naha
Pineapples

MILES
0   25   50   75

KILOMETERS
0   50   100   150

LOCATION

◆ PROJECT: *Origami Penguin* ◆

Origami is the ancient Japanese art of folding paper to create decorative models. Origami models usually represent animals or people and sometimes have movable parts. In ancient Japan, origami was a highly prized art form and models often consisted of hundreds of folds. You can make your own origami model of a penguin if you follow these steps.

1. Fold a square of paper in half to make a crease. Unfold.

2. Fold the bottom corner up as shown.

3. Fold the paper in half again.

4. Fold the sides in as shown, to form the wing flaps.

5. Fold the top down to make a crease. Unfold.

6. Open the paper out and pull the tip forward.

7. Close the paper again and press the "head" flat.

Your origami penguin is finished!

**Map labels:**

SOUTH KOREA

Korea Strait

Tsushima Strait

Tsushima

Kitakyūshū

Nagasaki

GOTŌ ISLANDS

Koto player

Fukuoka

Rice

Shipbuilding

Traditional fishing boat

Kumamoto

Kendo

Miyazaki

Sweet potatoes

Kagoshima

Ōsumi ISLANDS

TOKARA ISLANDS

Kyūshū

Octopus

White-sided dolphin

Bluefin tuna

Shikoku

Kōchi

Matsuyama

Tokushima

Mandarin oranges

Autumn harvest festival

INLAND SEA

Sumo wrestlers

Torii Gate

Hiroshima

World War II monument

Shinto priest

Matsue

OKI ISLANDS

Squid

Swordfish

Tiger shark

Himeji Castle

Okayama

Geisha preparing tea

Iron and steel

Kōbe

Wakayama

Ōsaka

Ōsaka Castle

Kyōto

Temple of the Golden Pavilion

Rice

Kabuki theater

Honshū

Kanazawa

Nagoya

Chemicals

Horyuji Temple

Hamamatsu

Tea

Shizuoka

Mt. Fuji 12,388 ft (3,776 m)

Bullet train

Kawasaki

Great Buddha

Pearl divers

Yokohama

Car manufacturing

Solar-powered ship

TOKYO

skyline

High-tech industries

PACIFIC OCEAN

N E S W

SCALE

MILES

0   25   50   75   100

KILOMETERS

0   50   100   150

ŌSAKA CASTLE

Completed in AD 1584, Ōsaka Castle was the fortress of Toyotomi Hideyoshi, the general who unified feudal Japan. At the time, it was the biggest castle in Asia.

KABUKI THEATER

A blend of music, drama, acrobatics and colorful costumes, kabuki first appeared in the 17th century. All the parts—even female roles—are played by men.

Africa

THE WORLD'S SECOND-LARGEST CONTINENT, Africa is an enormous plateau surrounded by narrow coastal plains. A thick band of tropical rain forest covers much of the center of the continent. To the north and south of this forest lie grasslands, known as savannas, and deserts. The Sahara Desert, the biggest desert in the world, spans the entire width of northern Africa, from the Atlantic Ocean to the Red Sea, and covers an area almost as large as the United States. The Kalahari and Namib deserts extend across much of the southwest. In the east, the Great Rift Valley, a series of valleys formed by cracks in Earth's crust, stretches from Syria, in Asia, to Mozambique. Africa includes 53 countries ranging from vast, mainly arid Sudan to the tiny tropical islands of the Seychelles. Arab peoples form the majority of the population in the north. The south's mainly black population is made up of hundreds of native tribes.

Continent Facts

Regional land area: 11,716,972 sq. miles (30,354,852 sq. km)
Regional population: 777,338,000
Independent countries: Algeria, Angola, Benin, Botswana, Burkina Faso, Burundi, Cameroon, Cape Verde Islands, Central African Republic, Chad, Comoros, Congo, Côte d'Ivoire (Ivory Coast), Democratic Republic of the Congo (Zaire), Djibouti, Egypt, Equatorial Guinea, Eritrea, Ethiopia, Gabon, Gambia, Ghana, Guinea, Guinea-Bissau, Kenya, Lesotho, Liberia, Libya, Madagascar, Malawi, Mali, Mauritania, Mauritius, Morocco, Mozambique, Namibia, Niger, Nigeria, Rwanda, São Tomé and Príncipe, Senegal, Seychelles, Sierra Leone, Somalia, South Africa, Sudan, Swaziland, Tanzania, Togo, Tunisia, Uganda, Zambia, Zimbabwe

Major Mountains and Rivers

Mount Kilimanjaro, Tanzania 19,341 ft (5,895 m)
Mount Kenya, Kenya 17,058 ft (5,199 m)
Margherita Peak, Uganda-Democratic Republic of the Congo (Zaire) 16,763 ft (5,109 m)
Ras Dashen, Ethiopia 15,158 ft (4,620 m)
Mount Meru, Tanzania 14,954 ft (4,558 m)
Mount Toubkal, Morocco 13,665 ft (4,165 m)

Nile 4,140 miles (6,670 km)
Congo (Zaire) 2,900 miles (4,670 km)
Niger 2,595 miles (4,180 km)
Zambezi 2,200 miles (3,540 km)
Ubangi-Uele 1,400 miles (2,250 km)
Kasai 1,210 miles (1,950 km)

World Records

WORLD'S LARGEST DESERT
SAHARA DESERT, NORTHERN AFRICA, 3,579,000 SQ. MILES (9,269,000 SQ. KM)

WORLD'S LONGEST RIVER
NILE RIVER, NORTHERN AFRICA, 4,140 MILES (6,670 KM)

WORLD'S LARGEST ARTIFICIAL LAKE
LAKE VOLTA, GHANA, 3,275 SQ. MILES (8,482 SQ. KM)

WORLD'S HIGHEST TEMPERATURE
AL-'AZĪZĪYA, LIBYA, SHADE TEMPERATURE OF 136°F (58°C) RECORDED ON SEPTEMBER 13, 1922

Continent Records

HIGHEST MOUNTAIN
KILIMANJARO, TANZANIA, 19,341 FT (5,895 M)

LOWEST POINT
LAKE ASSAL, DJIBOUTI, 500 FT (152 M) BELOW SEA LEVEL

LARGEST LAKE
LAKE VICTORIA, EAST AFRICA, 26,828 SQ. MILES (69,485 SQ. KM)

LARGEST COUNTRY BY AREA
SUDAN, 967,500 SQ. MILES (2,505,825 SQ. KM)

LARGEST COUNTRY BY POPULATION
NIGERIA, POPULATION 113,829,000

LARGEST CITY BY POPULATION
CAIRO, EGYPT, POPULATION 9,700,000

Political Map

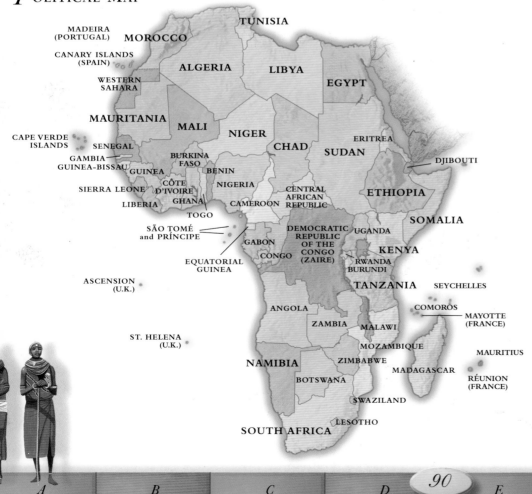

MADEIRA (PORTUGAL)
MOROCCO
TUNISIA
CANARY ISLANDS (SPAIN)
ALGERIA
LIBYA
EGYPT
WESTERN SAHARA
MAURITANIA
MALI
NIGER
CHAD
SUDAN
ERITREA
CAPE VERDE ISLANDS
SENEGAL
GAMBIA
GUINEA-BISSAU
GUINEA
BURKINA FASO
BENIN
DJIBOUTI
SIERRA LEONE
CÔTE D'IVOIRE
NIGERIA
CENTRAL AFRICAN REPUBLIC
ETHIOPIA
LIBERIA
GHANA
TOGO
CAMEROON
SOMALIA
SÃO TOMÉ and PRÍNCIPE
DEMOCRATIC REPUBLIC OF THE CONGO (ZAIRE)
UGANDA
KENYA
GABON
CONGO
RWANDA
BURUNDI
EQUATORIAL GUINEA
ASCENSION (U.K.)
TANZANIA
SEYCHELLES
ANGOLA
COMOROS
MAYOTTE (FRANCE)
ST. HELENA (U.K.)
ZAMBIA
MALAWI
MOZAMBIQUE
MAURITIUS
NAMIBIA
ZIMBABWE
MADAGASCAR
RÉUNION (FRANCE)
BOTSWANA
SWAZILAND
LESOTHO
SOUTH AFRICA

• Amazing Fact •

The huge volume of water that pours over Victoria Falls, on the border between Zambia and Zimbabwe, creates a deafening roar and a cloud of spray that can be seen from more than 20 miles (32 km) away. Because of this, locals refer to the falls as "the smoke that thunders."

AFRICA

PHYSICAL MAP

Arctic Circle

EUROPE

ASIA

Mediterranean Sea

Madeira

Strait of Gibraltar

ATLAS MOUNTAINS

CANARY
ISLANDS

▲ Mt. Toubkal

AHAGGAR
MOUNTAINS

LIBYAN DESERT

Nile

Tropic of Cancer

SAHARA DESERT

TIBESTI
MOUNTAINS

Lake
Nasser

NUBIAN
DESERT

Red Sea

Gulf of Aden

CAPE
VERDE
ISLANDS

Senegal

Niger

Lake
Chad

S A H E L

▲ Ras Dashen
Lake
Assal

Socotra

Lake Volta

Benue

ADAMAWA
HIGHLANDS

Uele

Blue Nile

White Nile

ETHIOPIAN
PLATEAU

Bioko

Ubangi

Margherita
Peak ▲

Lake

Equator

Príncipe

São Tomé

Congo (Zaire)

CONGO
BASIN

Kasai

Victoria

▲ Mt. Kenya

GREAT RIFT VALLEY

Gulf of
Guinea

Mt. Meru ▲ ▲ Mt. Kilimanjaro

A
T
L
A
N
T
I
C

Ascension

Lake
Tanganyika

Zanzibar

SEYCHELLES

Lake
Nyasa

COMOROS
ISLANDS

St. Helena

O
C
E
A
N

NAMIB DESERT

Okavango

Okavango
Delta

Lake
Kariba

Zambezi

Limpopo

KALAHARI
DESERT

Mozambique Channel

Madagascar

Mauritius

Réunion

Tropic of Capricorn

I
N
D
I
A
N

Orange

DRAKENSBERG MTS.

O
C
E
A
N

CAPE OF
GOOD HOPE

Antarctic Circle

Northern Africa

THE SAHARA DESERT, the largest desert in the world, covers more than half of northern Africa. On its barren, rocky plains and rolling sand dunes, the heat is fierce, water is scarce and there is little land that can be farmed. Most of the people of the Sahara are nomads, who move their camels, sheep and goats around the desert in search of water and pasture. The only usable fertile land north or east of the Sahara lies in the valleys of the Atlas Mountains and along the banks of the Nile River in Egypt. People have farmed the Nile valley for thousands of years, and it is now one of the most densely populated places on Earth. There is little farmland in Algeria and Libya, but both countries possess large oil and gas reserves which have helped them overcome serious poverty. South of the Sahara lies a wide belt of dry grasslands known as the Sahel. These grasslands suffer frequent droughts, and overfarming is turning some areas

into desert. Farther south, the Sahel gives way to the tropical rain forests of central Africa. Around the Gulf of Guinea, much of the forest has been cleared to make way for farms and large plantations where cocoa beans, coffee and cotton are grown. Oil and other minerals have been discovered in a number of Gulf countries, and this has created some wealth and industries. However, only a minority of the region's huge population benefit and most people are still very poor.

ALGERIA
POPULATION: 31,134,000 • CAPITAL: ALGIERS

BENIN
POPULATION: 6,306,000 • CAPITALS: COTONOU, PORTO-NOVO

BURKINA FASO
POPULATION: 11,576,000 • CAPITAL: OUAGADOUGOU

CAMEROON
POPULATION: 15,456,000 • CAPITAL: YAOUNDÉ

CAPE VERDE ISLANDS
POPULATION: 405,800 • CAPITAL: PRAIA

CENTRAL AFRICAN REPUBLIC
POPULATION: 3,445,000 • CAPITAL: BANGUI

CHAD
POPULATION: 7,558,000 • CAPITAL: N'DJAMENA

CÔTE D'IVOIRE (IVORY COAST)
POPULATION: 15,818,000 • CAPITALS: ABIDJAN, YAMOUSSOUKRO

DJIBOUTI
POPULATION: 447,500 • CAPITAL: DJIBOUTI

EGYPT
POPULATION: 67,274,000 • CAPITAL: CAIRO

EQUATORIAL GUINEA
POPULATION: 465,800 • CAPITAL: MALABO

ERITREA
POPULATION: 3,985,000 • CAPITAL: ASMARA

ETHIOPIA
POPULATION: 59,681,000 • CAPITAL: ADDIS ABABA

GAMBIA
POPULATION: 1,337,000 • CAPITAL: BANJUL

GHANA
POPULATION: 18,888,000 • CAPITAL: ACCRA

GUINEA
POPULATION: 7,539,000 • CAPITAL: CONAKRY

GUINEA-BISSAU
POPULATION: 1,235,000 • CAPITAL: BISSAU

LIBERIA
POPULATION: 2,924,000 • CAPITAL: MONROVIA

LIBYA
POPULATION: 4,993,000 • CAPITAL: TRIPOLI

MALI
POPULATION: 10,429,000 • CAPITAL: BAMAKO

MAURITANIA
POPULATION: 2,582,000 • CAPITAL: NOUAKCHOTT

MOROCCO
POPULATION: 29,662,000 • CAPITAL: RABAT

NIGER
POPULATION: 9,963,000 • CAPITAL: NIAMEY

NIGERIA
POPULATION: 113,829,000 • CAPITAL: ABUJA

SENEGAL
POPULATION: 10,052,000 • CAPITAL: DAKAR

SIERRA LEONE
POPULATION: 5,297,000 • CAPITAL: FREETOWN

SOMALIA
POPULATION: 7,141,000 • CAPITAL: MOGADISHU

SUDAN
POPULATION: 34,476,000 • CAPITAL: KHARTOUM

TOGO
POPULATION: 5,082,000 • CAPITAL: LOMÉ

TUNISIA
POPULATION: 9,514,000 • CAPITAL: TUNIS

OSTRICH
The largest bird in the world, the ostrich, is unable to fly but can run at up to 40 miles per hour (65 kph).

N W E S

CAPE VERDE ISLANDS

Santo Antão
Mindelo
São Vicente
São Nicolau
Sal
Bananas
Boa Vista
São Tiago
Maio
African fish eagle
Brava   Fogo   Praia

MILES
0   50   100   150

KILOMETERS
0   100   200

SCALE

MILES
0   100   200   300   400   500

KILOMETERS
0   200   400   600   800

◆ PROJECT: *Khamsa Hand* ◆

A *khamsa* is a Moroccan good luck charm in the form of a hand. A *khamsa* with spread fingers is said to keep away bad luck. A *khamsa* with closed fingers is supposed to bring good luck. Some *khamsas* are worn as pendants, but you can hang this *khamsa* on the door of your house or bedroom.

❶ Trace around your hand onto a piece of cardboard and cut out the shape.

❷ Glue sequins, buttons and shapes cut from colored paper or foil onto the hand shape.

❸ When you are happy with your design, leave it to dry and then hang it on your door. If you want to carry your good luck with you, make a tiny *khamsa* and thread it on a string to make a necklace.

TUNIS   ITALY
Constantine   MALTA   GREECE   TURKEY
TUNISIA
Mediterranean Sea   CYPRUS   SYRIA
Tripoli   LEBANON
Misrātah   Benghazi   ISRAEL
Musicians   Oil   Port Said
Ghadāmis   Oil   Alexandria   Suez
Leptis Magna   CAIRO
LIBYA   Giza pyramids   *Suez Canal*
Oil   Collecting water   *Nile*
Dama gazelle   LIBYAN DESERT   **EGYPT**   Luxor   Feluccas (traditional boats)
Gerboa   Cotton   Aswān
Oil   Lake Nasser   *Red Sea*   SAUDI ARABIA
Sphinxes at Temple of Karnak   Hydroelectricity
A   D   E   S   E   R   T   TIBESTI MTS.   Lappet-faced vulture   NUBIAN DESERT   LOCATION
Tuaregs   **CHAD**   Port Sudan   Lyre-tailed goldfish   YEMEN
SUDAN
NIGER   Two Niles Mosque   **ERITREA**   Asmara
Porcupine   Zinder   Lake Chad   Goatherd   KHARTOUM   Kassala   Castle at Gondar   *Gulf of Aden*
El Obeid   Blue Nile falls   Ras Dashen 15,158 ft (4,620 m)
N'DJAMENA   Storage bales   Ras Dashen
Cotton   Traditional house   *White Nile*   *Blue Nile*   **DJIBOUTI**   Berbera
IA   Giraffes   DJIBOUTI   Hoopoe
Kano Mosque   Sarh   Cotton   ETHIOPIAN PLATEAU   Donkeys
Tapping a rubber tree   **CENTRAL AFRICAN REPUBLIC**   Crocodile   ADDIS ABABA   Dire Dawa
CAMEROON   Cocoa   Cotton   Coffee   Statue of the Lion   **SOMALIA**
AOUNDÉ   Ⓔ Elephants   Rhinoceroses   Juba   Dinka herdsman   **ETHIOPIA**   Grinding grain
BANGUI   Ⓔ Rhinoceroses   Lions   MOGADISHU
LABO   DEMOCRATIC REPUBLIC OF THE CONGO (ZAIRE)   UGANDA   Ⓔ Zebra
UATORIAL   INDIAN OCEAN
INEA   Clay house   CONGO   KENYA   Bananas
GABON   Kismaayo

BORORRO MAN
The Bororro people in Niger hold beauty contests—for men! They wear makeup and fine clothes, and the winner is selected by female judges.

GIZA PYRAMIDS
The Giza pyramids were built about 4,500 years ago as tombs for Egyptian kings. The largest pyramid is made of two million blocks of stone.

Southern Africa

IN THE NORTHWESTERN PART of this region, the Congo River and its many tributaries flow through immense tropical rain forests. Crocodiles swim the waterways, and the jungles are home to chimpanzees, gorillas and tropical birds. Most of the local people live in villages near the rivers and grow their own food on small plots of cleared land. The rain forests stretch eastward across the continent toward the Great Rift Valley, a chain of dramatic, steep-sided valleys that runs down the eastern side of Africa. Within these valleys lie many deep lakes as well as a number of volcanoes, including Mount Kilimanjaro, Africa's highest mountain. On the valley floors and across the surrounding grassland plateaus, enormous herds of zebras, wildebeests and antelopes are hunted by lions, cheetahs and other predators. To protect the region's wildlife, many countries have created nature preserves, which attract tourists from all over the world. From the southern end of the Rift Valley, in Mozambique, high grasslands known as the veld spread westward toward the Kalahari and Namib deserts. In South Africa the veld is an important farming region rich in mineral resources including copper, gold and diamonds. Off the coast of Mozambique lies Madagascar, the world's fourth-largest island. Madagascar is famous for its unique wildlife, which includes many species of lemurs, unusual relatives of monkeys.

ANGOLA
POPULATION: 11,178,000 * CAPITAL: LUANDA

BOTSWANA
POPULATION: 1,465,000 * CAPITAL: GABORONE

BURUNDI
POPULATION: 5,736,000 * CAPITAL: BUJUMBURA

COMOROS
POPULATION: 562,800 * CAPITAL: MORONI

CONGO
POPULATION: 2,717,000 * CAPITAL: BRAZZAVILLE

DEMOCRATIC REPUBLIC OF THE CONGO (ZAIRE)
POPULATION: 50,482,000 * CAPITAL: KINSHASA

GABON
POPULATION: 1,226,000 * CAPITAL: LIBREVILLE

KENYA
POPULATION: 28,809,000 * CAPITAL: NAIROBI

LESOTHO
POPULATION: 2,129,000 * CAPITAL: MASERU

MADAGASCAR
POPULATION: 14,874,000 * CAPITAL: ANTANANARIVO

MALAWI
POPULATION: 10,001,000 * CAPITAL: LILONGWE

MAURITIUS
POPULATION: 1,183,000 * CAPITAL: PORT LOUIS

MOZAMBIQUE
POPULATION: 19,125,000 * CAPITAL: MAPUTO

NAMIBIA
POPULATION: 1,649,000 * CAPITAL: WINDHOEK

RWANDA
POPULATION: 8,155,000 * CAPITAL: KIGALI

SÃO TOMÉ AND PRÍNCIPE
POPULATION: 154,900 * CAPITAL: SÃO TOMÉ

SEYCHELLES
POPULATION: 79,200 * CAPITAL: VICTORIA

SOUTH AFRICA
POPULATION: 43,427,000 * CAPITALS: BLOEMFONTEIN, CAPE TOWN, PRETORIA

SWAZILAND
POPULATION: 986,000 * CAPITAL: MBABANE

TANZANIA
POPULATION: 31,271,000 * CAPITALS: DAR ES SALAAM, DODOMA

UGANDA
POPULATION: 22,805,000 * CAPITAL: KAMPALA

ZAMBIA
POPULATION: 9,664,000 * CAPITAL: LUSAKA

ZIMBABWE
POPULATION: 11,164,000 * CAPITAL: HARARE

SCALE

MILES
0   100   200   300   400

0 100 200 300 400 500 600
KILOMETERS

CAMEROON

SÃO TOMÉ AND PRÍNCIPE
Príncipe
São Tomé
SÃO TOMÉ

EQUATORIAL GUINEA

Chimpanzees
Gray parrot
Baboon

CONGO

Timber
LIBREVILLE
GABON
Pygmies
Okapi

Port-Gentil
Manganese

Mandrill
Oil
BRAZZAVILLE
Rhinoceros viper

Pointe-Noire
Kasai

CABINDA (ANGOLA) Matadi KINSHASA
Traditional dancers
Diam

Cubatas (huts)

LUANDA
Cuanza
Colobus monkey

ANGOLA

Flying fish
Coffee
Cassava

Benguela
Huambo
Hornbill

Oil
Iron ore

Cunene
Okavango
Springbok

Uranium

Khoisan woman with fishing net

Meerkats

NAMIBIA
Herero woman

Anchovies
WINDHOEK

Walvis Bay
KA...

NAMIB DESERT
Topnaar family

Kokerboom tree
Khoi...

Hake

Orange
Diamonds
SOUT... AFRIC...

Table Mountain

CAPE TOWN
Cape of Good Hope
Wine

CENT...

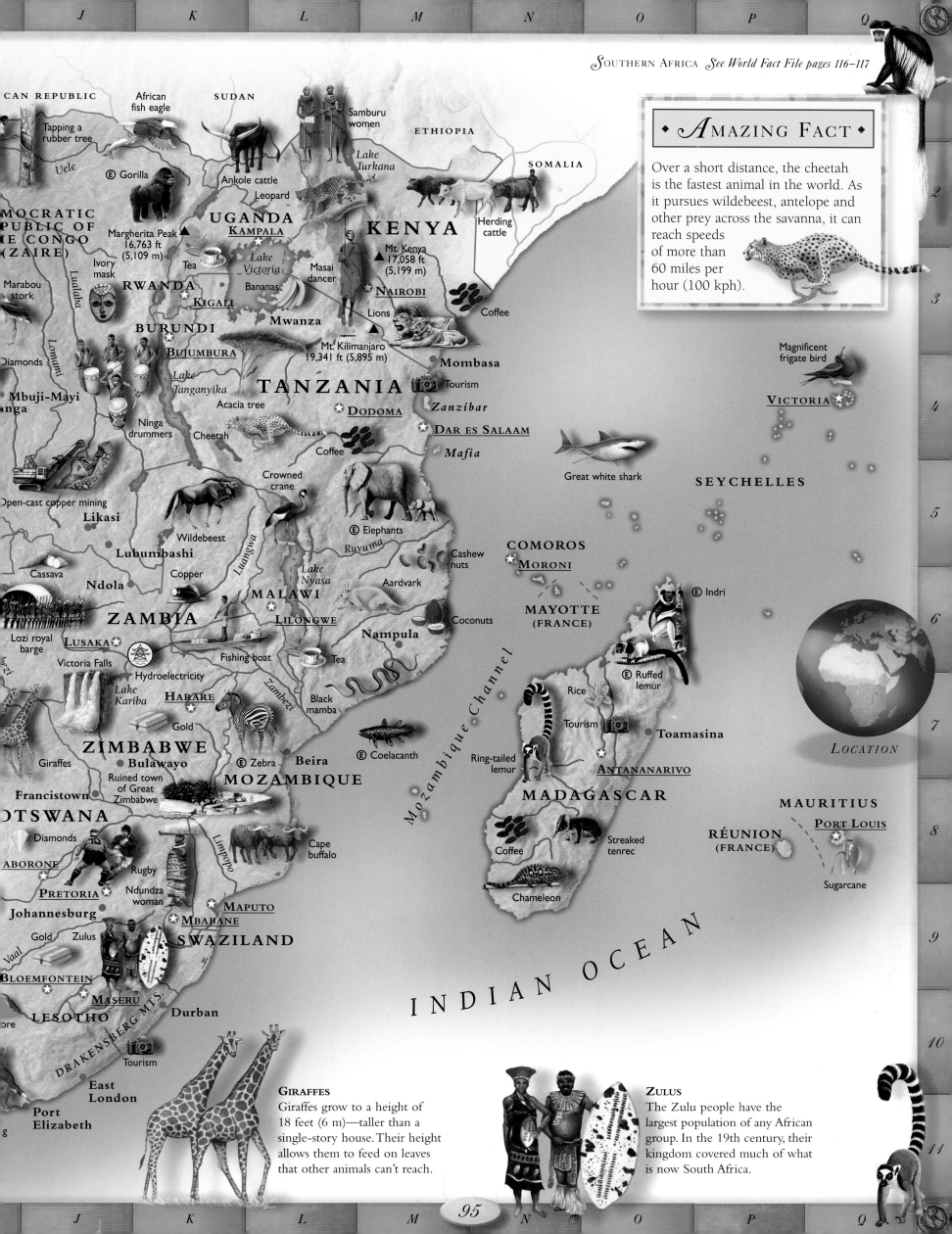

CAN REPUBLIC

African fish eagle

Tapping a rubber tree

Uele

Ⓔ Gorilla

MOCRATIC
PUBLIC OF
HE CONGO
(ZAIRE)

Margherita Peak ▲
16,763 ft
(5,109 m)

Ivory mask

Lualaba

RWANDA

★ KIGALI

BURUNDI

★ BUJUMBURA

Marabou stork

Diamonds

Lomami

Mbuji-Mayi

anga

Ninga drummers

Lake Tanganyika

Open-cast copper mining

Likasi

Lubumbashi

Cassava

Ndola

ZAMBIA

Lozi royal barge

★ LUSAKA

Victoria Falls

Hydroelectricity

Lake Kariba

★ HARARE

ZIMBABWE

● Bulawayo

Giraffes

Francistown

Ruined town of Great Zimbabwe

OTSWANA

Diamonds

ABORONE

★ PRETORIA

Johannesburg

Gold

Zulus

BLOEMFONTEIN

★ MASERU

LESOTHO

ore

Port Elizabeth

East London

DRAKENSBERG MTS.

Ⓒ Tourism

Durban

SUDAN

Ankole cattle

Leopard

UGANDA

★ KAMPALA

Tea

Lake Victoria

Bananas

Lake Turkana

Samburu women

ETHIOPIA

SOMALIA

Herding cattle

KENYA

Mt. Kenya
17,058 ft
(5,199 m) ▲

★ NAIROBI

Lions

Masai dancer

Mwanza

Mt. Kilimanjaro
19,341 ft (5,895 m) ▲

Mombasa

Zanzibar

Ⓒ Tourism

★ DODOMA

★ DAR ES SALAAM

Mafia

TANZANIA

Acacia tree

Cheetah

Coffee

Crowned crane

Ⓔ Elephants

Ruvuma

Cashew nuts

Coconuts

COMOROS

★ MORONI

MAYOTTE
(FRANCE)

Wildebeest

Copper

MALAWI

★ LILONGWE

Lake Nyasa

Aardvark

Nampula

Fishing boat

Tea

Black mamba

Luangwa

Zambezi

Beira

Ⓔ Coelacanth

Mozambique Channel

Gold

Zebra

Ⓔ Zebra

MOZAMBIQUE

Limpopo

Cape buffalo

Rugby

Ndundza woman

★ MAPUTO

★ MBABANE

SWAZILAND

Vaal

Coffee

UGANDA

TANZANIA

Ⓔ Indri

VICTORIA ★

SEYCHELLES

Magnificent frigate bird

Great white shark

Rice

Ⓔ Ruffed lemur

Tourism

Ⓒ Tourism

Toamasina

Ring-tailed lemur

★ ANTANANARIVO

MADAGASCAR

Coffee

Streaked tenrec

Chameleon

MAURITIUS

★ PORT LOUIS

RÉUNION
(FRANCE)

Sugarcane

INDIAN OCEAN

LOCATION

AMAZING FACT

Over a short distance, the cheetah is the fastest animal in the world. As it pursues wildebeest, antelope and other prey across the savanna, it can reach speeds of more than 60 miles per hour (100 kph).

GIRAFFES

Giraffes grow to a height of 18 feet (6 m)—taller than a single-story house. Their height allows them to feed on leaves that other animals can't reach.

ZULUS

The Zulu people have the largest population of any African group. In the 19th century, their kingdom covered much of what is now South Africa.

Australia and Oceania

STRETCHING FROM THE INDIAN OCEAN to the center of the Pacific Ocean, Australia and Oceania cover a vast area of the globe. But because most of this region is ocean, it has a relatively small population. Australia is by far the largest landmass. This island is so big that it is considered a continent. Oceania consists of thousands of much smaller islands that are scattered across the Pacific Ocean to the east of Australia. They are divided into three groups: Micronesia, Melanesia, and Polynesia, which includes the large islands of New Zealand. There are two main types of Pacific island: high, rugged islands that are the peaks of undersea volcanoes and submerged mountain ranges; and coral atolls—low, sandy islands formed by coral reefs growing on the tops of undersea mountains. Many of the Pacific islands are so small that they do not appear on regular maps.

Continent Facts

Regional land area: 3,283,993 sq. miles (8,507,753 sq. km)
Regional population: 29,300,000
Independent countries: Australia, Federated States of Micronesia, Fiji, Kiribati, Marshall Islands, Nauru, New Zealand, Palau, Papua New Guinea, Solomon Islands, Tonga, Tuvalu, Vanuatu, Western Samoa

World Records

WORLD'S LONGEST CORAL REEF
THE GREAT BARRIER REEF, AUSTRALIA, 1,260 MILES (2,025 KM)

WORLD'S LARGEST ROCK
ULURU (AYERS ROCK), AUSTRALIA, 1,143 FT (348 M) HIGH; 1.5 MILES (2.5 KM) LONG; 1 MILE (1.6 KM) WIDE

WORLD'S LARGEST SAND ISLAND
FRASER ISLAND, AUSTRALIA, 75 MILES (120 KM) LONG

Continent Records

HIGHEST MOUNTAIN
MOUNT WILHELM, PAPUA NEW GUINEA, 14,762 FEET (4,500 M)

LOWEST POINT
LAKE EYRE, AUSTRALIA, 52 FT (16 M) BELOW SEA LEVEL

LARGEST LAKE
LAKE EYRE, AUSTRALIA, 3,600 SQ. MILES (9,324 SQ. KM)

LONGEST RIVER
MURRAY-DARLING, AUSTRALIA, 2,330 MILES (3,750 KM)

LARGEST COUNTRY BY AREA
AUSTRALIA, 2,967,909 SQ. MILES (7,686,884 SQ. KM)

LARGEST COUNTRY BY POPULATION
AUSTRALIA, population 18,784,000

LARGEST CITY BY POPULATION
SYDNEY, AUSTRALIA, population 3,934,000

Major Mountains and Rivers

Mount Wilhelm, Papua New Guinea 14,762 ft (4,500 m)
Mount Victoria, Papua New Guinea 13,363 ft (4,073 m)
Mount Cook, New Zealand 12,349 ft (3,764 m)
Mount Tasman, New Zealand 11,475 ft (3,498 m)
Mount Balbi, Papua New Guinea 8,999 ft (2,743 m)
Mount Kosciuszko, Australia 7,310 ft (2,228 m)

Murray-Darling 2,330 miles (3,750 km)
Darling 1,905 miles (3,070 km)
Murray 1,600 miles (2,575 km)
Murrumbidgee 1,050 miles (1,690 km)
Lachlan 922 miles (1,484 km)
Sepik 600 miles (965 km)

Political Map

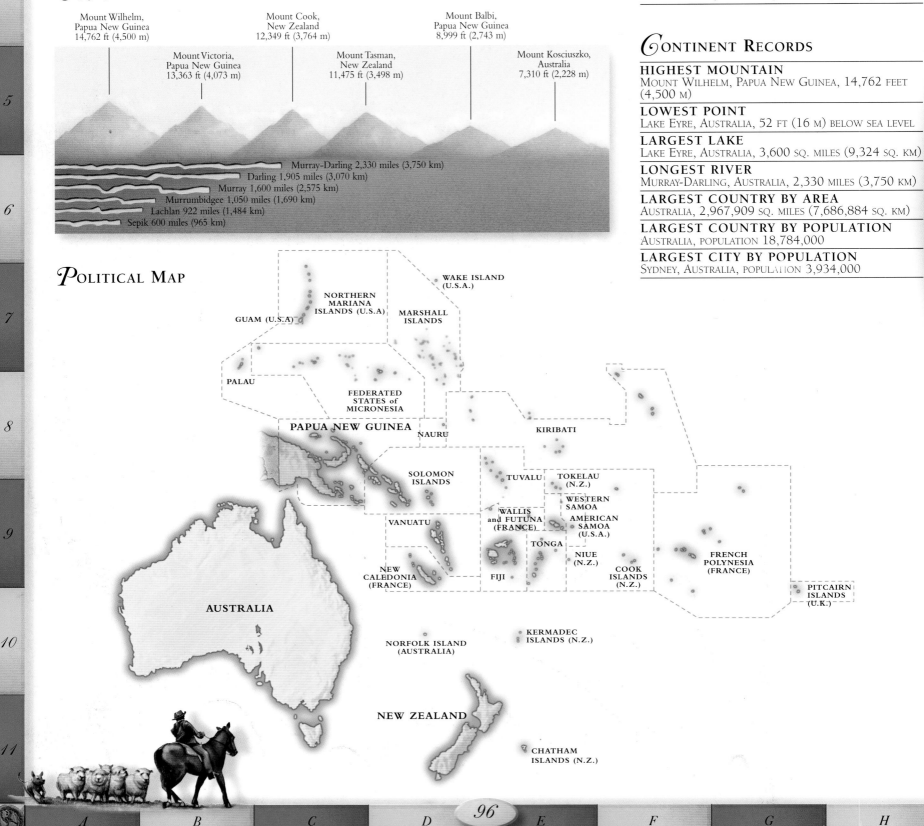

WAKE ISLAND (U.S.A.)
NORTHERN MARIANA ISLANDS (U.S.A.)
GUAM (U.S.A)
MARSHALL ISLANDS
PALAU
FEDERATED STATES of MICRONESIA
PAPUA NEW GUINEA
NAURU
KIRIBATI
SOLOMON ISLANDS
TUVALU
TOKELAU (N.Z.)
WESTERN SAMOA
WALLIS and FUTUNA (FRANCE)
AMERICAN SAMOA (U.S.A.)
VANUATU
TONGA
NIUE (N.Z.)
COOK ISLANDS (N.Z.)
FRENCH POLYNESIA (FRANCE)
NEW CALEDONIA (FRANCE)
FIJI
PITCAIRN ISLANDS (U.K.)
AUSTRALIA
KERMADEC ISLANDS (N.Z.)
NORFOLK ISLAND (AUSTRALIA)
NEW ZEALAND
CHATHAM ISLANDS (N.Z.)

AUSTRALIA AND OCEANIA

PHYSICAL MAP

ASIA

NORTH AMERICA

Arctic Circle

PACIFIC OCEAN

Tropic of Cancer

HAWAIIAN
ISLANDS

MARIANA
ISLANDS

MICRONESIA

MARSHALL
ISLANDS

CAROLINE ISLANDS

LINE ISLANDS

GILBERT
ISLANDS

MELANESIA

Equator

Nauru

PHOENIX
ISLANDS

New
Guinea   Sepik
          New
Mt.   Britain
Wilhelm   Mt.
                Balbi   SOLOMON ISLANDS

MARQUESAS
ISLANDS

Tokelau

POLYNESIA

Arafura
Sea

Torres Strait
CAPE
YORK
PENINSULA

Mt.
Victoria

Tuvalu

COOK ISLANDS

TUAMOTU
ARCHIPELAGO

GREAT
SANDY
DESERT

Great Barrier Reef

GREAT DIVIDING RANGE

Coral Sea

Vanuatu

FIJI
ISLANDS

SAMOA ISLANDS

SOCIETY
ISLANDS

MACDONNELL
RANGES

Australia

New
Caledonia

Tonga

PITCAIRN
ISLANDS

GREAT
VICTORIA
DESERT

Lake
Eyre

Fraser
Island

Tropic of Capricorn

Great
Australian
Bight

Darling

Lachlan
Murrumbidgee
Murray

Lord Howe
Island

Norfolk
Island

KERMADEC
ISLANDS

Mt.
Kosciuszko

Tasman
Sea

New
Zealand

North
Island

Tasmania

Mt.
Tasman

Mt. Cook

South
Island

CHATHAM
ISLANDS

Stewart
Island

Macquarie
Island

Australia and Papua New Guinea

AUSTRALIA IS AS BIG AS the United States mainland but has a smaller population than Texas. The vast, dry interior, known as the outback, consists mainly of deserts and grasslands. It contains mineral reserves and is used for grazing huge numbers of sheep and cattle, but few people live there. Most Australians live in or near cities along the east, southeast and southwest coasts, where the climate is temperate and the land fertile. The far northeast is tropical, with areas of dense rain forest. The southeast is cooler, and mountain snowfalls are common. Most of Australia's native peoples, the Aborigines, live in towns and cities, but some still follow old traditions in the outback. Aborigines originally came to Australia more than 40,000 years ago, having crossed over from the island of New Guinea when it was still attached to Australia. Papua New Guinea, an Australian territory until 1975, is made up of several island chains and half the island of New Guinea. This main island is covered in jungle and surrounded by swampy plains. Most people live in small villages, where they grow food in gardens and raise animals. Many communities have little contact with the outside world and have retained their own traditions and languages. Papua New Guinea has over 700 languages—more than any other country in the world.

AUSTRALIA
POPULATION: 18,784,000 ✳ CAPITAL: CANBERRA
PAPUA NEW GUINEA
POPULATION: 4,705,000 ✳ CAPITAL: PORT MORESBY

PAPUA NEW GUINEA

BISMARCK ARCHIPELAGO

Spirit house
Bismarck Sea
Manus
New Hanover
New Ireland
Tree kangaroo
Warrior in mud mask
INDONESIA
Madang
New Britain
Copper
Mt. Wilhelm 14,762 ft (4,500 m)
Lae
Timber
Bougainville
Solomon Sea
SOLOMON ISLANDS
Fly
Traditional dancer
PORT MORESBY
Clown fish
Coral Sea

MILES
0   100   200   300
0   200   400
KILOMETERS

Map labels (main map)

INDONESIA
EAST TIMOR
Timor Sea
Melvi... Isla...
Pineapple fish
KIMBERLEY PLATEAU
Bungle B...
SCALE
MILES
0   100   200   300
0   100   200   300   400   500
KILOMETERS
Broome
Derby
Baobab tree
Fitzroy
Wolfe Creek meteorite crater
Pearl farming
Bottle-nosed dolphin
GREAT SANDY DESERT
Port Hedland
Red kangaroo
Iron ore
Aboriginal dancers
GIBSON DESERT
Thorny devil
Grass trees
Emu
Boomerang
Blue-tongued lizards
Galahs
WESTERN AUSTRALIA
A
GREAT VICTORIA DESERT
Leafy seadragon
Pinnacles (rock formation)
Shearing sheep
NULLAR...
Geraldton
Budgerigars
Gold
Black swan
Kalgoorlie-Boulder
PERTH
DARLING RANGE
Cricket
Great white sha...
Wheat
Bunbury
Echidna
Wine
Albany
Great A...
Southern right whale
INDIAN OCEAN

TRADITIONAL DANCER
In Papua New Guinea, local tribes hold festivals of dancing, singing and feasting known as sing-sings. Tribe members wear headdresses and colorful body and face paint.

AUSTRALIA AND PAPUA NEW GUINEA *See World Fact File page 118*

INDONESIA PAPUA NEW GUINEA

Arafura Sea

Torres Strait

Dugongs

Bauxite (aluminum)

Harlequin fish

DARWIN

ARNHEM LAND

Saltwater crocodile

Groote Island

Gulf of Carpentaria

CAPE YORK PENINSULA

Scuba diving

Coral reef

Playing the didgeridoo

Tourism

NORTHERN TERRITORY

Giant termite mound

Cassowary

Cairns

Dingo

Road train

Carpet snake

Pineapples

GREAT BARRIER REEF

Townsville

Copper

Wallaby

Devil's Marbles (rock formation)

Mount Isa

Sugarcane

Mackay

led ard

School of the Air (school by radio)

Royal Flying Doctor Service

Coal

GREAT DIVIDING RANGE

Sulfur-crested cockatoo

Rockhampton

Blue-ringed octopus

MCDONNELL RANGES

Alice Springs

Hot-air ballooning

QUEENSLAND

Gum tree

Homestead

Rugby league

Fraser Island

Maryborough

Jluru (Ayers Rock)

Brumbies (wild horses)

Magpie

SIMPSON DESERT

STRALIA

Herding sheep

Gray kangaroo

Toowoomba

BRISBANE
Gold Coast

Camel

Opals

Lake Eyre

Tourism

SOUTH AUSTRALIA

Windmill

Merino sheep

Koala

Platypus

PACIFIC OCEAN

IN

Lake Gairdner

Lake Torrens

Kookaburra

Coal

Steelworker

Surf-lifesavers

Iron and steel

Port Augusta

Darling

NEW SOUTH WALES

Newcastle

Whyalla

Zinc

Wine

Broken Hill

Australian Rules football

Wombat

SYDNEY

Opera House and Harbour Bridge

lian Bight

Wheat

CANBERRA

Wollongong

ADELAIDE

Murray

AUSTRALIAN CAPITAL TERRITORY

Kangaroo Island

Surfing

VICTORIA

MELBOURNE

Mt. Kosciuszko 7,310 ft (2,228 m)

Sailing

Ballarat

Geelong

Tram

Bass Strait

King Island

Flinders Island

Twelve Apostles (rock formation)

Launceston

Tasmanian devil

TASMANIA

Apples

Port Arthur historic site

HOBART

◆ PROJECT: *Boomerang* ◆

Boomerangs are traditional Aboriginal throwing sticks. Some were used as weapons for hunting. Others were thrown for fun and were designed to return to the thrower. Traditional boomerangs are made from wood, but you can make one type out of a foam food tray.

❶ Cut two 1½-inch (4-cm) wide strips from the foam food tray.

❷ Use the strips to make an X, with one piece curving up and the other piece curving down. Staple them together.

❸ Now you just need to practice throwing your boomerang!

LOCATION

◆ AMAZING FACT ◆

The Great Barrier Reef, a coral reef that stretches 1,260 miles (2,025 km) down the northeast coast of Australia, is the largest natural structure in the world. It is so large that astronauts were able to see it from the Moon.

RED KANGAROO
Kangaroos are such specialized hoppers that they can no longer walk! The red kangaroo, the largest of these marsupials, can leap 40 feet (12 m) in one bound.

New Zealand and the Southwestern Pacific

SCATTERED ACROSS A VAST EXPANSE of ocean and separated from each other by great distances, the islands of the southwestern Pacific are among the most isolated places on Earth. The largest and most southerly group is New Zealand, consisting of two large islands—the North Island and the South Island—and several smaller islands. New Zealand is a modern, industrialized country. About 70 percent of the population live on the North Island, which has several active volcanoes. Lake Taupo, New Zealand's largest lake, lies in a crater that formed when a volcano exploded. The nearby volcanoes, Ruapehu and Ngauruhoe, have erupted several times in recent years. The Southern Alps form the "backbone" of the South Island. On their western side, temperate rain forests have grown up around a line of mighty glaciers that run down to the coast. More than half of New Zealand is used for growing crops and grazing animals—there are 20 sheep for every New Zealander! The country's original inhabitants, the Maori people, make up one-sixth of the population. Most other New Zealanders are descendants of British immigrants. Thousands of tropical islands lie to the north and east of New Zealand. Tourism is a growing industry in countries such as Fiji and Vanuatu. Some islands have developing towns with new businesses, but most islanders live in small villages. They fish for crabs, lobsters, turtles and tuna, and grow sweet potatoes and bananas. One of the most important export products is copra (dried coconut meat), which is used in making soap and candles.

FIJI
POPULATION: 813,000 * CAPITAL: SUVA

NEW ZEALAND
POPULATION: 3,663,000 * CAPITAL: WELLINGTON

SOLOMON ISLANDS
POPULATION: 455,500 * CAPITAL: HONIARA

TONGA
POPULATION: 109,100 * CAPITAL: NUKU'ALOFA

VANUATU
POPULATION: 189,100 * CAPITAL: PORT VILA

WESTERN SAMOA
POPULATION: 230,000 * CAPITAL: APIA

Barracuda
Kauri tree
Whangarei
North Island
Rugby
Great Barrier Island
Chemicals
Tuatara
Auckland
Sailing
Kiwi fruit
Waikato
Bay of Plenty
Hamilton
Geyser
Rotorua
Dairy cattle
Kiwi
Natural gas
Lake Taupo
New Plymouth
Traditional Maori war dance
Mt. Egmont (Taranaki) 8,260 ft (2,518 m)
Ruapehu 9,175 ft (2,796 m)
Wanganui
Napier
Oil rig
Gar
Wanganui
Hastings
Sheep
Giant tree fern
Snapper
Palmerston North
Lower Hutt
Cook Strait
Parliament House
Nelson
Timber
WELLINGTON
NEW ZEALAND
Tasman Sea
Greymouth
Sheep
South Island
Sperm whale
SOUTHERN ALPS
Skiing
Christchurch Cathedral
Mount Cook lily
Christchurch
Milford Sound
Mt. Cook 12,349 ft (3,764 m)
Textiles
Timaru
Hydroelectricity
Shrimp
Waitaki
Queenstown
Lake Wakatipu
Kea
Clutha
PACIFIC OCEAN
E Takahe
Hiking
Dunedin
Invercargill
Foveaux Strait
Albatross colony
Oyster fishing boat
E Blue whales
Stewart Island

N
W — E
S

MAORI WAR DANCE
Before going to battle, Maori warriors performed a war dance known as a *haka*. During the dance they would stick out their tongues and make fearsome faces.

WHALE SHARK
The whale shark is the largest living fish. It feeds by swimming along with its mouth wide open. It eats only plankton and small fish, and is harmless to humans.

The Polar Regions

THE REGIONS THAT SURROUND the North and South poles are the coldest and windiest parts of our planet. Both are permanently covered in snow and ice, and during winter months there is little or no daylight. Antarctica is a frozen continent surrounded by ocean. The Arctic is an area of frozen ocean surrounded by continents. In winter, the Arctic ice spreads southward, reaching North America, Europe and Asia. The northern fringes of these continents are home to native peoples who have adapted to Arctic life. They include the Saami (Lapps) of Scandinavia and the Inuit of Canada, Alaska, Greenland and Russia. A Danish territory, Greenland is the world's largest island. Most of it lies under a thick sheet of ice. Antarctica is the only continent with

no permanent population. Scientists spend part of the year at research stations, but many leave Antarctica before the cold, dark winter sets in. The continent is covered by a vast ice sheet which is two miles (3 km) thick in some places. Along the coast, the ice sheet forms huge ice shelves over the ocean. Giant blocks of ice break off and float away as icebergs. Some icebergs are as large as small countries and take years to melt. There is little life in the Antarctic interior, but whales, seals and fish swim just offshore, and during the summer enormous colonies of seabirds nest along the coast and on nearby islands.

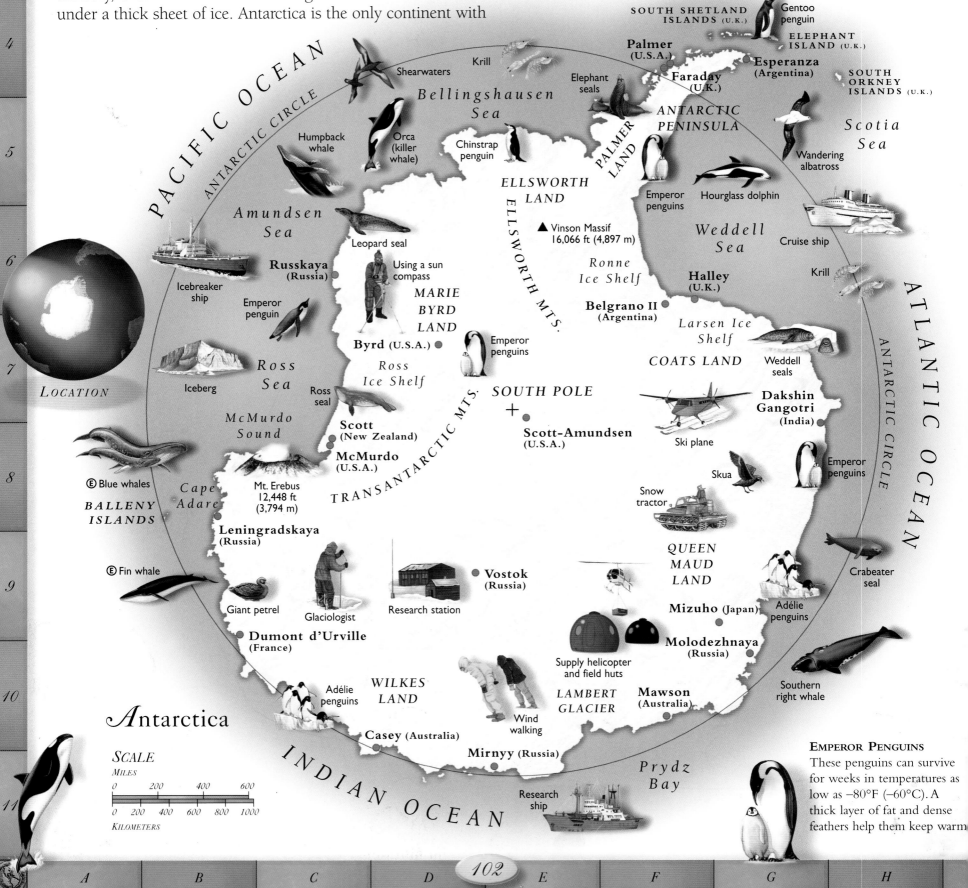

LOCATION

Antarctica

SCALE
MILES
0   200   400   600

0   200   400   600   800   1000
KILOMETERS

EMPEROR PENGUINS
These penguins can survive for weeks in temperatures as low as −80°F (−60°C). A thick layer of fat and dense feathers help them keep warm.

The Arctic

SCALE
MILES

| 0 | 200 | 400 | 600 |

| 0 | 200 | 400 | 600 | 800 | 1000 |

KILOMETERS

Icebreaker ship

Bering Strait

Reindeer

Chukchi hunter

ALASKA (U.S.A.)

Arctic hare

Oil

Chukchi Sea

Wrangel Island

Pevek

Ambarchik

ARCTIC CIRCLE

CANADA

Barrow

Prudhoe Bay

East Siberian Sea

NEW SIBERIAN ISLANDS

Walrus

Narwhal

Snow goose

Beaufort Sea

Arctic tern

Gray whale

Lena

Ptarmigan

Yakut woman and children

RUSSIA

Musk-ox

Banks Island

Zinc and lead

Skua

Polar bears

Laptev Sea

Nordvik

Kittiwake

Wolf

Snowmobile

Victoria Island

QUEEN ELIZABETH ISLANDS

Snowy owl

Walrus

ARCTIC OCEAN

NORTH POLE
+

SEVERNAYA ZEMLYA

Arctic fox

ARCTIC CIRCLE

Resolute

ⓔ Beluga whale

Dudinka

udson Bay

Baffin Island

Ellesmere Island

Kara Sea

FRANZ JOSEF LAND

Natural gas

LOCATION

Inuit fishing through ice

Thule

Walrus tusk carvings

Harp seals

NOVAYA ZEMLYA

CANADA

Baffin Bay

Jakobshavn houses

Hooded seal

Svalbard reindeer

Haddock

Tourism

Upernavik

GREENLAND (DENMARK)

Inuit hunter

SVALBARD (NORWAY)

Longyearbyen

Barents Sea

Nenet woman

Nar'yan-Mar

Musk-ox

Spitsbergen

Harbor seals

Snowmobile

Bowhead whale

Nuuk

Cod

Orca (killer whale)

NORTH CAPE

Murmansk

Iceberg

Tourism

Mt. Gunnbjørn 12,139 ft (3,700 m)

Jan Mayen Island (NORWAY)

Hammerfest

Julianehåb

Denmark Strait

Norwegian Sea

Sami (Lapp) man

FINLAND

CAPE FAREWELL

Puffins

SWEDEN

ICELAND

NORWAY

Davis Strait

Musk-ox

CHUKCHI HUNTER
Traditionally, Chukchi people hunted seals, walruses and whales from kayaks, using ivory-tipped harpoons. Now most hunters use rifles and travel in motorboats.

REINDEER
Huge herds of reindeer roam over the tundra in search of food. Their large hooves prevent them from sinking into the snow and help them dig through to reach plants and lichens.

World Fact File

NORTH AMERICA

CANADA

PRONUNCIATION: KA-nuh-duh
AREA: 3,851,809 sq. miles
(9,976,185 sq. km)
POPULATION: 31,007,000
CAPITAL: Ottawa
CURRENCY: 100 cents = 1 Canadian dollar (Can$)
OFFICIAL LANGUAGES: English, French
MAIN RELIGION: Christianity 72%
EXPORTS: Newsprint, wood pulp, timber, crude petroleum, machinery, natural gas, aluminum, motor vehicles and parts, telecommunications equipment

UNITED STATES OF AMERICA

PRONUNCIATION: yoo-NEYE-tuhd STAYTS of uh-MEHR-uh-kuh
AREA: 3,619,969 sq. miles (9,375,720 sq. km)
POPULATION: 274,088,480
CAPITAL: Washington, D.C.
CURRENCY: 100 cents = 1 United States dollar (US$)
OFFICIAL LANGUAGE: English
OTHER LANGUAGE: Spanish
MAIN RELIGIONS: Christianity 86%, Judaism 2%
EXPORTS: Motor vehicles, raw materials, consumer goods, agricultural products

MEXICO

PRONUNCIATION: MEK-si-koh
AREA: 761,600 sq. miles
(1,972,544 sq. km)
POPULATION: 100,295,000
CAPITAL: Mexico City
CURRENCY: 100 centavos = 1 Mexican peso (Mex$)
OFFICIAL LANGUAGE: Spanish
OTHER LANGUAGES: Regional languages
MAIN RELIGION: Christianity 95%
EXPORTS: Crude oil, oil products, coffee, silver, engines, motor vehicles, cotton, electronic goods

GUATEMALA

PRONUNCIATION: gwah-tuh-MAH-luh
AREA: 42,042 sq. miles (108,889 sq. km)
POPULATION: 12,336,000
CAPITAL: Guatemala
CURRENCY: 100 centavos = 1 Guatemalan quetzal (Q)
OFFICIAL LANGUAGE: Spanish
OTHER LANGUAGES: Quiche, Cakchiquel, Kekchi, and other regional languages
MAIN RELIGIONS: Christianity 99%, traditional Mayan religions
EXPORTS: Coffee, bananas, cotton, sugar, minerals, textiles

BELIZE

PRONUNCIATION: buh-LEEZ
AREA: 8,867 sq. miles
(22,966 sq. km)
POPULATION: 235,800
CAPITAL: Belmopan
CURRENCY: 100 cents = 1 Belizean dollar (Bz$)
OFFICIAL LANGUAGE: English
OTHER LANGUAGES: Spanish, Maya, Garifuna
MAIN RELIGION: Christianity 92%
EXPORTS: Sugar, molasses, citrus fruit, bananas, clothing, fish products, timber

HONDURAS

PRONUNCIATION: hahn-DER-uhs
AREA: 43,277 sq. miles
(112,087 sq. km)
POPULATION: 5,998,000
CAPITAL: Tegucigalpa
CURRENCY: 100 centavos = 1 lempira (L)
OFFICIAL LANGUAGE: Spanish
OTHER LANGUAGES: Regional languages
MAIN RELIGION: Christianity 97%
EXPORTS: Bananas, coffee, shrimp, lobsters, minerals, meat, timber

EL SALVADOR

PRONUNCIATION: el SAL-vuh-dor
AREA: 8,260 sq. miles
(21,393 sq. km)
POPULATION: 5,840,000
CAPITAL: San Salvador
CURRENCY: 100 centavos = 1 Salvadoran colón (C)
OFFICIAL LANGUAGE: Spanish
OTHER LANGUAGE: Nahua
MAIN RELIGION: Christianity 92%
EXPORTS: Coffee, sugarcane, shrimp

NICARAGUA

PRONUNCIATION: ni-kuh-RAH-gwuh
AREA: 49,579 sq. miles
(128,410 sq. km)
POPULATION: 4,718,000
CAPITAL: Managua
CURRENCY: 100 centavos = 1 gold cordoba (C$)
OFFICIAL LANGUAGE: Spanish
OTHER LANGUAGES: English, Indian
MAIN RELIGION: Christianity 100%
EXPORTS: Meat, coffee, cotton, sugar, bananas, seafood, gold

COSTA RICA

PRONUNCIATION: kaws-tuh REE-kuh
AREA: 19,652 sq. miles
(50,899 sq. km)
POPULATION: 3,675,000
CAPITAL: San José
CURRENCY: 100 centimos = 1 Costa Rican colón (C)
OFFICIAL LANGUAGE: Spanish
OTHER LANGUAGE: English
MAIN RELIGION: Christianity 95%
EXPORTS: Coffee, bananas, sugar, textiles

PANAMA

PRONUNCIATION: PA-nuh-mah
AREA: 33,659 sq. miles
(87,177 sq. km)
POPULATION: 2,779,000
CAPITAL: Panama
CURRENCY: 100 centesimos = 1 balboa (B)

PRONUNCIATION KEY

"a" sounds		"i" sounds		"u" sounds		zh	as in measure
a	as in pat	i	as in pit	uh	as in but	s	as in set
ah	as in father	eye	as in bite		and comma	ch	as in chase
ar	as in dark	ihr	as in hear	u	as in put	j	as in jug
ay	as in bay				and book	g	as in game
air	as in pair	"o" sounds		oo	as in boot	ng	as in sing
		o	as in pot	yoo	as in music		
"e" sounds		oh	as in boat				
		aw	as in paw			Emphasize the part
e	as in pet	or	as in poor	other sounds		of the word that
ee	as in feet	ow	as in how	th	as in thin	is written in
er	as in pert	oy	as in boy		and then	**BOLD CAPITAL**
ehr	as in Sierra			sh	as in show	**LETTERS**

OFFICIAL LANGUAGE: Spanish
OTHER LANGUAGES: English, regional languages
MAIN RELIGION: Christianity 100%
EXPORTS: Bananas, shrimp, sugar, coffee, clothing

THE BAHAMAS

PRONUNCIATION: the buh-HAH-muhz
AREA: 5,386 sq. miles (13,950 sq. km)
POPULATION: 284,800
CAPITAL: Nassau
CURRENCY: 100 cents = 1 Bahamian dollar (B$)
OFFICIAL LANGUAGE: English
OTHER LANGUAGE: Bahamian creole
MAIN RELIGION: Christianity 95%
EXPORTS: Pharmaceuticals, cement, rum, crayfish, refined petroleum products

CUBA

PRONUNCIATION: KYOO-buh
AREA: 42,804 sq. miles (110,862 sq. km)
POPULATION: 11,097,000
CAPITAL: Havana
CURRENCY: 100 centavos = 1 Cuban peso (Cu$)
OFFICIAL LANGUAGE: Spanish
MAIN RELIGION: Christianity 85%
EXPORTS: Sugar, shellfish, citrus fruit, coffee, tobacco, nickel, medical products

JAMAICA

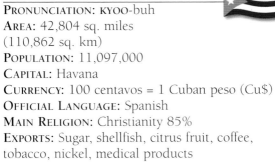

PRONUNCIATION: juh-MAY-kuh
AREA: 4,471 sq. miles (11,580 sq. km)
POPULATION: 2,653,000
CAPITAL: Kingston
CURRENCY: 100 cents = 1 Jamaican dollar (J$)
OFFICIAL LANGUAGE: English
OTHER LANGUAGE: Jamaican creole
MAIN RELIGION: Christianity 65%
EXPORTS: Bauxite, sugar, bananas, rum

HAITI

PRONUNCIATION: HAY-tee
AREA: 10,714 sq. miles (27,749 sq. km)
POPULATION: 6,885,000
CAPITAL: Port-au-Prince
CURRENCY: 100 centimes = 1 gourde (G)
OFFICIAL LANGUAGE: French
OTHER LANGUAGE: Haitian creole
MAIN RELIGION: Christianity 96%
EXPORTS: Clothing, coffee, sugar

DOMINICAN REPUBLIC

PRONUNCIATION: duh-MI-ni-kuhn ri-PUH-blik
AREA: 18,657 sq. miles (48,322 sq. km)
POPULATION: 8,130,000
CAPITAL: Santo Domingo
CURRENCY: 100 centavos = 1 Dominican peso (RD$)
OFFICIAL LANGUAGE: Spanish
MAIN RELIGION: Christianity 95%
EXPORTS: Minerals, sugar, coffee, cocoa, gold

ANTIGUA AND BARBUDA

PRONUNCIATION: an-TEE-guh and bar-BOO-duh
AREA: 171 sq. miles (443 sq. km)
POPULATION: 64,300
CAPITAL: St. John's
CURRENCY: 100 cents = 1 East Caribbean dollar (EC$)
OFFICIAL LANGUAGE: English
OTHER LANGUAGES: Regional languages
MAIN RELIGIONS: Christianity 97%, indigenous religions 3%
EXPORTS: Petroleum products, manufactured goods, machinery and transportation equipment, food and livestock

ST. KITTS–NEVIS

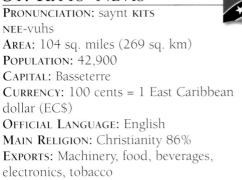

PRONUNCIATION: saynt KITS NEE-vuhs
AREA: 104 sq. miles (269 sq. km)
POPULATION: 42,900
CAPITAL: Basseterre
CURRENCY: 100 cents = 1 East Caribbean dollar (EC$)
OFFICIAL LANGUAGE: English
MAIN RELIGION: Christianity 86%
EXPORTS: Machinery, food, beverages, electronics, tobacco

DOMINICA

PRONUNCIATION: dah-muh-NEE-kuh
AREA: 289 sq. miles (749 sq. km)
POPULATION: 64,900
CAPITAL: Roseau
CURRENCY: 100 cents = 1 East Caribbean dollar (EC$)
OFFICIAL LANGUAGE: English
OTHER LANGUAGE: French patois
MAIN RELIGION: Christianity 92%
EXPORTS: Bananas, grapefruit, oranges, vegetables, soap, bay oil

ST. LUCIA

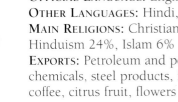

PRONUNCIATION: saynt LOO-shuh
AREA: 238 sq. miles (616 sq. km)
POPULATION: 154,100
CAPITAL: Castries
CURRENCY: 100 cents = 1 East Caribbean dollar (EC$)
OFFICIAL LANGUAGE: English
OTHER LANGUAGE: French patois
MAIN RELIGION: Christianity 100%
EXPORTS: Bananas, clothing, cocoa, fruit and vegetables, coconut oil

BARBADOS

PRONUNCIATION: bar-BAY-dohs
AREA: 166 sq. miles (430 sq. km)
POPULATION: 259,200
CAPITAL: Bridgetown
CURRENCY: 100 cents = 1 Barbadian dollar (Bds$)
OFFICIAL LANGUAGE: English
OTHER LANGUAGE: Barbadian creole
MAIN RELIGION: Christianity 71%
EXPORTS: Sugar, molasses, rum, other foods and beverages, chemicals, electrical components, clothing

ST. VINCENT AND THE GRENADINES

PRONUNCIATION: saynt VIN-suhnt and the gren-uh-DEENZ
AREA: 150 sq. miles (389 sq. km)
POPULATION: 120,600
CAPITAL: Kingstown
CURRENCY: 100 cents = 1 East Caribbean dollar (EC$)
OFFICIAL LANGUAGE: English
OTHER LANGUAGE: French patois
MAIN RELIGION: Christianity 75%
EXPORTS: Bananas, taro, tennis rackets

GRENADA

PRONUNCIATION: gruh-NAY-duh
AREA: 133 sq. miles (344 sq. km)
POPULATION: 97,100
CAPITAL: St. George's
CURRENCY: 100 cents = 1 East Caribbean dollar (EC$)
OFFICIAL LANGUAGE: English
OTHER LANGUAGE: French patois
MAIN RELIGION: Christianity 85%
EXPORTS: Bananas, cocoa, nutmeg, fruit and vegetables, clothing, mace

TRINIDAD AND TOBAGO

PRONUNCIATION: TRI-nuh-dad and tuh-BAY-goh
AREA: 1,980 sq. miles (5,128 sq. km)
POPULATION: 1,103,000
CAPITAL: Port-of-Spain
CURRENCY: 100 cents = 1 Trinidad and Tobago dollar (TT$)
OFFICIAL LANGUAGE: English
OTHER LANGUAGES: Hindi, French, Spanish
MAIN RELIGIONS: Christianity 60%, Hinduism 24%, Islam 6%
EXPORTS: Petroleum and petroleum products, chemicals, steel products, fertilizer, sugar, cocoa, coffee, citrus fruit, flowers

SOUTH AMERICA

COLOMBIA
PRONUNCIATION: kuh-LUHM-bee-uh
AREA: 439,735 sq. miles
(1,138,914 sq. km)
POPULATION: 39,310,000
CAPITAL: Bogotá
CURRENCY: 100 centavos = 1 Colombian
peso (Col$)
OFFICIAL LANGUAGE: Spanish
MAIN RELIGION: Christianity 95%
EXPORTS: Petroleum, coffee, coal, bananas, flowers

VENEZUELA
PRONUNCIATION: ve-nuh-ZWAY-luh
AREA: 352,143 sq. miles
(912,050 sq. km)
POPULATION: 23,204,000
CAPITAL: Caracas
CURRENCY: 100 centimos = 1 bolivar (Bs)
OFFICIAL LANGUAGE: Spanish
OTHER LANGUAGES: Regional languages
MAIN RELIGION: Christianity 98%
EXPORTS: Petroleum, bauxite and aluminum,
steel, chemicals, agricultural products,
manufactured goods

GUYANA
PRONUNCIATION: geye-AH-nuh
AREA: 83,000 sq. miles
(214,970 sq. km)
POPULATION: 705,200
CAPITAL: Georgetown
CURRENCY: 100 cents = 1 Guyanese dollar (G$)
OFFICIAL LANGUAGE: English
OTHER LANGUAGES: Regional languages
MAIN RELIGIONS: Christianity 57%,
Hinduism 33%, Islam 9%
EXPORTS: Sugar, molasses, bauxite, rice, shrimp

SURINAME
PRONUNCIATION: SUR-uh-nah-muh
AREA: 63,251 sq. miles
(163,820 sq. km)
POPULATION: 431,200
CAPITAL: Paramaribo
CURRENCY: 100 cents = 1 Surinamese guilder or
florin (Sf)
OFFICIAL LANGUAGE: Dutch
OTHER LANGUAGES: English, Sranang Tongo,
Hindustani, Javanese
MAIN RELIGIONS: Christianity 48%,
Hinduism 27%, Islam 20%, regional religions 5%
EXPORTS: Aluminum,
shrimp, fish, rice,
bananas

ECUADOR
PRONUNCIATION: E-kwuh-dor
AREA: 109,483 sq. miles
(283,561 sq. km)
POPULATION: 12,563,000
CAPITAL: Quito
CURRENCY: 100 centavos = 1 sucre (S/.)
OFFICIAL LANGUAGE: Spanish
OTHER LANGUAGES: Quechua, other regional
languages
MAIN RELIGION: Christianity 95%
EXPORTS: Petroleum, bananas, shrimp,
cocoa, coffee

PERU
PRONUNCIATION: puh-ROO
AREA: 496,222 sq. miles
(1,285,215 sq. km)
POPULATION: 26,625,000
CAPITAL: Lima
CURRENCY: 100 centimos = 1 nuevo sol (S/.)
OFFICIAL LANGUAGES: Spanish, Quechua
OTHER LANGUAGE: Aymara
MAIN RELIGION: Christianity 90%
EXPORTS: Copper, zinc, petroleum and petroleum
products, lead, refined silver, coffee, cotton

BRAZIL
PRONUNCIATION: bruh-ZIL
AREA: 3,284,426 sq. miles
(8,506,663 sq. km)
POPULATION: 171,854,000
CAPITAL: Brasília
CURRENCY: 100 centavos = 1 real (R$)
OFFICIAL LANGUAGE: Portuguese
OTHER LANGUAGES: Spanish, English, French
MAIN RELIGION: Christianity 70%
EXPORTS: Iron ore, soybean bran, bananas, orange
juice, shoes, coffee, motor vehicle parts

BOLIVIA
PRONUNCIATION: buh-LI-vee-uh
AREA: 424,162 sq. miles
(1,098,579 sq. km)
POPULATION: 7,983,000
CAPITALS: La Paz (seat of government),
Sucre (legal and judicial)
CURRENCY: 100 centavos = 1 boliviano ($B)
OFFICIAL LANGUAGES: Spanish, Quechua, Aymara
MAIN RELIGION: Christianity 100%
EXPORTS: Metals, natural gas, soybeans,
jewelry, timber

CHILE
PRONUNCIATION: CHI-lee
AREA: 292,257 sq. miles
(756,946 sq. km)
POPULATION: 14,974,000
CAPITAL: Santiago
CURRENCY: 100 centavos = 1 Chilean peso (Ch$)
OFFICIAL LANGUAGE: Spanish
OTHER LANGUAGES: Regional languages
MAIN RELIGION: Christianity 99%
EXPORTS: Copper, other metals and minerals,
timber products, fish, fruit

PARAGUAY
PRONUNCIATION: PAR-uh-gweye
AREA: 157,043 sq. miles
(406,741 sq. km)
POPULATION: 5,435,000
CAPITAL: Asunción
CURRENCY: 100 centimos = 1 guarani (G)
OFFICIAL LANGUAGE: Spanish
OTHER LANGUAGE: Guarani
MAIN RELIGION: Christianity 97%
EXPORTS: Cotton, soybeans, timber, vegetable oils,
meat products, coffee

ARGENTINA
PRONUNCIATION: ar-juhn-TEE-nuh
AREA: 1,072,156 sq. miles
(2,776,884 sq. km)
POPULATION: 36,738,000
CAPITAL: Buenos Aires
CURRENCY: 100 centavos = 1 peso
OFFICIAL LANGUAGE: Spanish
OTHER LANGUAGES: English, Italian,
German, French
MAIN RELIGIONS: Christianity 94%, Judaism 2%
EXPORTS: Manufactured goods, meat, wheat,
corn, oilseed

URUGUAY
PRONUNCIATION: OOR-uh-gweye
AREA: 68,039 sq. miles
(176,221 sq. km)
POPULATION: 3,309,000
CAPITAL: Montevideo
CURRENCY: 100 centesimos = 1 Uruguayan
peso ($Ur)
OFFICIAL LANGUAGE: Spanish
MAIN RELIGIONS: Christianity 68%, Judaism 2%
EXPORTS: Wool, textiles, beef and other animal
products, leather, rice

EUROPE

UNITED KINGDOM
PRONUNCIATION: yoo-NEYE-tuhd KING-duhm
AREA: 94,251 sq. miles (244,110 sq. km)
POPULATION: 59,114,000
CAPITAL: London
CURRENCY: 100 pence = 1 British pound (£)
OFFICIAL LANGUAGE: English
OTHER LANGUAGES: Welsh, Scottish Gaelic, Irish Gaelic
MAIN RELIGIONS: Christianity 90%, Islam 3%, Sikh 1%, Hinduism 1%, Judaism 1%
EXPORTS: Manufactured goods, machinery, fuels, chemicals, transportation equipment

IRELAND
PRONUNCIATION: EYER-luhnd
AREA: 26,600 sq. miles (68,894 sq. km)
POPULATION: 3,633,000
CAPITAL: Dublin
CURRENCY: 100 pence = 1 Irish pound (£Ir)
OFFICIAL LANGUAGES: English, Irish (Gaelic)
MAIN RELIGION: Christianity 96%
EXPORTS: Chemicals, data processing equipment, industrial machinery, livestock, animal products

PORTUGAL
PRONUNCIATION: POR-chi-guhl
AREA: 35,383 sq. miles (91,642 sq. km)
POPULATION: 9,919,000
CAPITAL: Lisbon
CURRENCY: 100 centavos = 1 Portuguese escudo (Esc)
OFFICIAL LANGUAGE: Portuguese
MAIN RELIGION: Christianity 98%
EXPORTS: Clothing, shoes, machinery, cork, paper products, animal skins

SPAIN
PRONUNCIATION: spayn
AREA: 194,881 sq. miles (504,742 sq. km)
POPULATION: 39,168,000
CAPITAL: Madrid
CURRENCY: 100 centimos = 1 peseta (Pta)
OFFICIAL LANGUAGE: Castilian Spanish
OTHER LANGUAGES: Catalan, Galician, Basque
MAIN RELIGION: Christianity 99%
EXPORTS: Motor vehicles, manufactured goods, food, machinery

ANDORRA
PRONUNCIATION: an-DOR-uh
AREA: 180 sq. miles (482 sq. km)
POPULATION: 66,000
CAPITAL: Andorra
CURRENCIES: 100 centimes = 1 French franc (F), 100 centimos = 1 peseta (Pta)
OFFICIAL LANGUAGE: Catalan
OTHER LANGUAGES: French, Spanish
MAIN RELIGION: Christianity 95%
EXPORTS: Electricity, tobacco products, furniture

FRANCE
PRONUNCIATION: frans
AREA: 212,918 sq. miles (551,458 sq. km)
POPULATION: 58,979,000
CAPITAL: Paris
CURRENCY: 100 centimes = 1 French franc (F)
OFFICIAL LANGUAGE: French
OTHER LANGUAGES: Occitan, German, Breton, Catalan, Arabic
MAIN RELIGIONS: Christianity 92%, Judaism 1%, Islam 1%
EXPORTS: Machinery and transportation equipment, chemicals, food, agricultural products, iron and steel products, textiles, clothing

MONACO
PRONUNCIATION: MAH-nuh-koh
AREA: 0.58 sq. miles (1.5 sq. km)
POPULATION: 32,200
CAPITAL: Monaco
CURRENCY: 100 centimes = 1 French franc (F)
OFFICIAL LANGUAGE: French
OTHER LANGUAGES: English, Italian, Monégasque
MAIN RELIGION: Christianity 95%
EXPORTS: Pharmaceuticals, perfumes, clothing

THE NETHERLANDS
PRONUNCIATION: the NE-ther-luhndz
AREA: 16,033 sq. miles (41,525 sq. km)
POPULATION: 15,808,000
CAPITALS: Amsterdam; The Hague (judicial)
CURRENCY: 100 cents = 1 Netherlands florin (f)
OFFICIAL LANGUAGE: Dutch
MAIN RELIGIONS: Christianity 59%, Islam 3%
EXPORTS: Metal products, chemicals, processed food, tobacco, agricultural products

BELGIUM
PRONUNCIATION: BEL-juhm
AREA: 11,781 sq. miles (30,513 sq. km)
POPULATION: 10,183,000
CAPITAL: Brussels
CURRENCY: 100 centimes = 1 Belgian franc (BF)
OFFICIAL LANGUAGES: Dutch (Flemish), French
OTHER LANGUAGE: German
MAIN RELIGION: Christianity 100%
EXPORTS: Iron and steel, transportation equipment, tractors, diamonds, petroleum products

LUXEMBOURG
PRONUNCIATION: LUK-suhm-berg
AREA: 999 sq. miles (2,587 sq. km)
POPULATION: 429,100
CAPITAL: Luxembourg
CURRENCY: 100 centimes = 1 Luxembourg franc (LuxF)
OFFICIAL LANGUAGES: Letzeburgesh, German, French
OTHER LANGUAGE: English
MAIN RELIGIONS: Christianity 99%, Judaism 1%
EXPORTS: Steel products, chemicals, rubber products, glass, aluminum

GERMANY
PRONUNCIATION: JER-muh-nee
AREA: 137,735 sq. miles (356,734 sq. km)
POPULATION: 82,088,000
CAPITAL: Berlin
CURRENCY: 100 pfennig = 1 deutsche mark (DM)
OFFICIAL LANGUAGE: German
MAIN RELIGIONS: Christianity 72%, Islam 2%
EXPORTS: Machines and machine tools, chemicals, motor vehicles, iron and steel products, agricultural products, raw materials, fuels

SWITZERLAND
PRONUNCIATION: SWIT-suhr-luhnd
AREA: 15,941 sq. miles (41,287 sq. km)
POPULATION: 7,276,000
CAPITAL: Bern
CURRENCY: 100 centimes = 1 Swiss franc (SFR)
OFFICIAL LANGUAGES: German, French, Italian, Romansch
MAIN RELIGION: Christianity 86%
EXPORTS: Machinery, precision instruments, metal products, food, textiles

LIECHTENSTEIN

PRONUNCIATION: LIK-tuhn-shteyen
AREA: 62 sq. miles (161 sq. km)
POPULATION: 32,100
CAPITAL: Vaduz
CURRENCY: 100 centimes = 1 Swiss franc (SwF)
OFFICIAL LANGUAGE: German
MAIN RELIGION: Christianity 88%
EXPORTS: Machinery, dental products, stamps, hardware, pottery

AUSTRIA

PRONUNCIATION: AWS-tree-uh
AREA: 32,375 sq. miles
(83,851 sq. km)
POPULATION: 8,140,000
CAPITAL: Vienna
CURRENCY: 100 groschen = 1 Austrian
schilling (AS)
OFFICIAL LANGUAGE: German
MAIN RELIGION: Christianity 83%
EXPORTS: Machinery, electrical equipment,
iron and steel, lumber, textiles, paper
products, chemicals

ITALY

PRONUNCIATION: IT-uh-lee
AREA: 116,313 sq. miles
(301,251 sq. km)
POPULATION: 56,736,000
CAPITAL: Rome
CURRENCY: 100 centesimi = 1 Italian lira (Lit)
OFFICIAL LANGUAGE: Italian
OTHER LANGUAGES: German, French, Slovene
MAIN RELIGION: Christianity 98%
EXPORTS: Metals, textiles, clothing, machinery,
motor vehicles, transportation equipment,
chemicals

SAN MARINO

PRONUNCIATION: san muh-REE-noh
AREA: 24 sq. miles (62 sq. km)
POPULATION: 25,100
CAPITAL: San Marino
CURRENCY: 100 centesimi = 1 Italian lira (Lit)
OFFICIAL LANGUAGE: Italian
MAIN RELIGION: Christianity 95%
EXPORTS: Building stone, lime, timber, chestnuts,
wheat, wine, baked goods, animal skins, ceramics

VATICAN CITY

PRONUNCIATION: VA-ti-kuhn city
AREA: 0.17 sq. miles (0.44 sq. km)
POPULATION: 870
CAPITAL: Vatican City
CURRENCY: Vatican lira (VLit)
OFFICIAL LANGUAGES: Italian, Latin
MAIN RELIGION: Christianity 100%
EXPORTS: None

MALTA

PRONUNCIATION: MAWL-tuh
AREA: 122 sq. miles (316 sq. km)
POPULATION: 381,700
CAPITAL: Valletta
CURRENCY: 100 cents = 1 Maltese lira (LM)
OFFICIAL LANGUAGES: Maltese, English
MAIN RELIGION: Christianity 98%
EXPORTS: Machinery and transportation
equipment, clothing, shoes, printed matter

SLOVENIA

PRONUNCIATION: sloh-VEE-nee-uh
AREA: 7,819 sq. miles (20,251 sq. km)
POPULATION: 1,971,000
CAPITAL: Ljubljana
CURRENCY: 100 stotins = 1 tolar (SlT)
OFFICIAL LANGUAGE: Slovenian
OTHER LANGUAGE: Serbo-Croatian
MAIN RELIGIONS: Christianity 96%, Islam 1%
EXPORTS: Motor vehicles, furniture, machinery,
manufactured goods, chemicals, textiles, food,
raw materials

CROATIA

PRONUNCIATION: kroh-AY-shuh
AREA: 21,829 sq. miles
(56,537 sq. km)
POPULATION: 4,677,000
CAPITAL: Zagreb
CURRENCY: 100 lipas = 1 Croatian kuna (HRK)
OFFICIAL LANGUAGE: Serbo-Croatian
MAIN RELIGIONS: Christianity 88%, Islam 1%
EXPORTS: Machinery and transportation
equipment, other manufactured goods,
chemicals, food, livestock, raw materials,
fuels and lubricants

BOSNIA AND HERZEGOVINA

PRONUNCIATION: BAHZ-nee-uh and
hert-suh-goh-VEE-nuh
AREA: 19,904 sq. miles (51,750 sq. km)
POPULATION: 3,483,000
CAPITAL: Sarajevo
CURRENCY: 100 pfenniga = 1 marka (KM)
OFFICIAL LANGUAGE: Serbo-Croatian
MAIN RELIGIONS: Christianity 50%, Islam 40%
EXPORTS: Timber, furniture

YUGOSLAVIA

PRONUNCIATION: yoo-goh-SLAH-vee-uh
AREA: 39,449 sq. miles (102,173 sq. km)
POPULATION: 11,207,000
CAPITAL: Belgrade
CURRENCY: 100 paras = 1 Yugoslav new dinar (YD)
OFFICIAL LANGUAGE: Serbo-Croatian
OTHER LANGUAGES: Albanian, Hungarian
MAIN RELIGIONS: Christianity 70%, Islam 19%
EXPORTS: Textiles, leather goods, machinery

ROMANIA

PRONUNCIATION: roh-MAY-nee-uh
AREA: 91,699 sq. miles (237,500 sq. km)
POPULATION: 22,335,000
CAPITAL: Bucharest
CURRENCY: 100 bani = 1 leu (L)
OFFICIAL LANGUAGE: Romanian
OTHER LANGUAGES: Hungarian, German
MAIN RELIGION: Christianity 82%
EXPORTS: Metals and metal products, mineral
products, textiles, electrical equipment,
transportation equipment

BULGARIA

PRONUNCIATION: buhl-GAIR-ee-uh
AREA: 42,823 sq. miles
(110,912 sq. km)
POPULATION: 8,195,000
CAPITAL: Sofia
CURRENCY: 100 stotinki = 1 lev (Lv)
OFFICIAL LANGUAGE: Bulgarian
MAIN RELIGIONS: Christianity 85%, Islam 13%,
Judaism 1%
EXPORTS: Machinery, manufactured goods, fuels,
minerals, raw materials, metals

ALBANIA

PRONUNCIATION: al-BAY-nee-uh
AREA: 11,100 sq. miles
(28,749 sq. km)
POPULATION: 3,365,000
CAPITAL: Tiranë
CURRENCY: 100 qintars = 1 lek (L)
OFFICIAL LANGUAGE: Albanian
OTHER LANGUAGE: Greek
MAIN RELIGIONS: Islam 70%, Christianity 30%
EXPORTS: Asphalt, metals and metallic ores,
electricity, crude oil, fruit and vegetables, tobacco

MACEDONIA

PRONUNCIATION: ma-suh-DOH-nee-uh
AREA: 9,928 sq. miles (25,714 sq. km)
POPULATION: 2,023,000
CAPITAL: Skopje
CURRENCY: 100 deni = 1 Macedonian denar (MKD)
OFFICIAL LANGUAGE: Macedonian
OTHER LANGUAGES: Albanian, Turkish,
Serbo-Croatian
MAIN RELIGIONS: Christianity 67%, Islam 30%
EXPORTS: Manufactured goods, machinery and
transportation equipment, food,beverages,
tobacco, chemicals

GREECE

PRONUNCIATION: grees
AREA: 50,944 sq. miles
(131,945 sq. km)
POPULATION: 10,708,000
CAPITAL: Athens
CURRENCY: 100 lepta = 1 drachma (Dr)
OFFICIAL LANGUAGE: Greek
OTHER LANGUAGES: English, French
MAIN RELIGIONS: Christianity 98%, Islam 1%
EXPORTS: Manufactured goods, food, fuels

ESTONIA

PRONUNCIATION: e-STOH-nee-uh
AREA: 17,413 sq. miles
(45,100 sq. km)
POPULATION: 1,409,000
CAPITAL: Tallinn
CURRENCY: 100 cents = 1 Estonian kroon (EEK)
OFFICIAL LANGUAGE: Estonian
OTHER LANGUAGES: Russian, Ukrainian, English
MAIN RELIGION: Christianity 100%
EXPORTS: Textiles, food, motor vehicles, metals

LATVIA

PRONUNCIATION: LAT-vee-uh
AREA: 24,595 sq. miles
(63,701 sq. km)
POPULATION: 2,354,000
CAPITAL: Riga
CURRENCY: 100 santims = 1 Latvian lat (LVL)
OFFICIAL LANGUAGE: Lettish
OTHER LANGUAGES: Lithuanian, Russian
MAIN RELIGION: Christianity 100%
EXPORTS: Oil products, timber, metals, dairy products, furniture, textiles

LITHUANIA

PRONUNCIATION: li-thuh-WAY-nee-uh
AREA: 25,174 sq. miles
(65,201 sq. km)
POPULATION: 3,585,000
CAPITAL: Vilnius
CURRENCY: 100 centas = 1 Lithuan litas (Lt)
OFFICIAL LANGUAGE: Lithuanian
OTHER LANGUAGES: Polish, Russian
MAIN RELIGION: Christianity 100%
EXPORTS: Electronics, petroleum products, food, chemicals

BELARUS

PRONUNCIATION: be-luh-ROOS
AREA: 80,154 sq. miles
(207,599 sq. km)
POPULATION: 10,402,000
CAPITAL: Minsk
CURRENCY: Belarusian rubel (BR)
OFFICIAL LANGUAGE: Belarusian
OTHER LANGUAGE: Russian
MAIN RELIGION: Christianity 68%
EXPORTS: Machinery and transportation equipment, chemicals, food

POLAND

PRONUNCIATION: POH-luhnd
AREA: 120,756 sq. miles
(312,758 sq. km)
POPULATION: 38,609,000
CAPITAL: Warsaw
CURRENCY: 100 groszy = 1 zloty (Zl)
OFFICIAL LANGUAGE: Polish
MAIN RELIGION: Christianity 95%
EXPORTS: Machinery and transportation equipment, manufactured goods, food, fuels

CZECH REPUBLIC

PRONUNCIATION: chek ri-PUH-blik
AREA: 30,450 sq. miles
(78,866 sq. km)
POPULATION: 10,281,000
CAPITAL: Prague
CURRENCY: 100 haleru = 1 koruna (Kc)
OFFICIAL LANGUAGE: Czech
OTHER LANGUAGE: Slovak
MAIN RELIGION: Christianity 47%
EXPORTS: Manufactured goods, machinery and transportation equipment, chemicals, fuels, minerals, metals, agricultural products

SLOVAKIA

PRONUNCIATION: sloh-VAH-kee-uh
AREA: 18,923 sq. miles (49,011 sq. km)
POPULATION: 5,397,000
CAPITAL: Bratislava
CURRENCY: 100 halierov = 1 koruna (Sk)
OFFICIAL LANGUAGE: Slovak
OTHER LANGUAGE: Hungarian
MAIN RELIGION: Christianity 72%
EXPORTS: Machinery and transportation equipment, chemicals, fuels, minerals and metals, agricultural products

UKRAINE

PRONUNCIATION: yoo-KRAYN
AREA: 233,089 sq. miles
(603,701 sq. km)
POPULATION: 49,812,000
CAPITAL: Kiev
CURRENCY: 100 kopiykas = 1 hryvna
OFFICIAL LANGUAGE: Ukrainian
OTHER LANGUAGES: Russian, Romanian, Polish, Hungarian
MAIN RELIGIONS: Christianity 90%, Judaism 2%
EXPORTS: Coal, electricity, metals, chemicals, machinery and transportation equipment, grain, meat

HUNGARY

PRONUNCIATION: HUHNG-uh-ree
AREA: 35,919 sq. miles
(93,030 sq. km)
POPULATION: 10,187,000
CAPITAL: Budapest
CURRENCY: 100 filler = 1 forint (Ft)
OFFICIAL LANGUAGE: Hungarian
MAIN RELIGION: Christianity 92%
EXPORTS: Raw materials, machinery and transportation equipment, manufactured goods, food, agriculture, fuels, energy

MOLDOVA

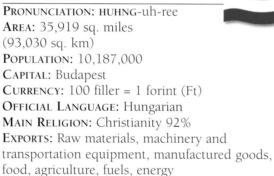

PRONUNCIATION: mawl-DOH-vuh
AREA: 13,012 sq. miles
(33,701 sq. km)
POPULATION: 4,461,000
CAPITAL: Chişinău
CURRENCY: Leu (L)
OFFICIAL LANGUAGE: Moldovian
OTHER LANGUAGES: Russian, Gagauz
MAIN RELIGIONS: Christianity 99%, Judaism 1%
EXPORTS: Food, wine, tobacco, textiles, shoes, machinery, chemicals

ICELAND

PRONUNCIATION: EYES-luhnd
AREA: 39,702 sq. miles
(102,828 sq. km)
POPULATION: 272,600
CAPITAL: Reykjavík
CURRENCY: 100 aurar = 1 Icelandic krona (IKr)

OFFICIAL LANGUAGE: Icelandic
MAIN RELIGION: Christianity 99%
EXPORTS: Fish and fish products, animal products, minerals

NORWAY

PRONUNCIATION: NOR-way
AREA: 154,790 sq. miles
(400,906 sq. km)
POPULATION: 4,439,000
CAPITAL: Oslo
CURRENCY: 100 oere = 1 Norwegian krone (NKr)
OFFICIAL LANGUAGE: Norwegian
OTHER LANGUAGES: Lapp, Finnish
MAIN RELIGION: Christianity 91%
EXPORTS: Petroleum and petroleum products, metals and metal products, fish and fish products, chemicals, natural gas, ships

SWEDEN

PRONUNCIATION: SWEE-duhn
AREA: 173,665 sq. miles
(449,792 sq. km)
POPULATION: 8,912,000
CAPITAL: Stockholm
CURRENCY: 100 oere = 1 Swedish krona (SKr)
OFFICIAL LANGUAGE: Swedish
OTHER LANGUAGES: Lapp, Finnish
MAIN RELIGION: Christianity 96%
EXPORTS: Machinery, motor vehicles, paper products, pulp and wood, iron and steel products, chemicals, petroleum and petroleum products

FINLAND

PRONUNCIATION: FIN-luhnd
AREA: 130,128 sq. miles
(337,032 sq. km)
POPULATION: 5,159,000
CAPITAL: Helsinki
CURRENCY: 100 pennia = 1 markka (FMk)
OFFICIAL LANGUAGES: Finnish, Swedish
OTHER LANGUAGES: Lapp, Russian
MAIN RELIGION: Christianity 90%
EXPORTS: Paper and pulp, machinery, chemicals, metals, timber

DENMARK

PRONUNCIATION: DEN-mark
AREA: 16,629 sq. miles
(43,069 sq. km)
POPULATION: 5,357,000
CAPITAL: Copenhagen
CURRENCY: 100 ore = 1 Danish krone (DKr)
OFFICIAL LANGUAGE: Danish
OTHER LANGUAGES: Faroese, Greenlandic, German
MAIN RELIGION: Christianity 93%
EXPORTS: Meat and meat products, dairy products, transportation equipment, ships, fish, chemicals, industrial machinery

ASIA

RUSSIA

PRONUNCIATION: RUH-shuh
AREA: 6,592,812 sq. miles
(17,075,383 sq. km)
POPULATION: 146,394,000
CAPITAL: Moscow
CURRENCY: 100 kopecks = 1 ruble (R)
OFFICIAL LANGUAGE: Russian
MAIN RELIGIONS: Christianity 75%, Islam,
Buddhism
EXPORTS: Petroleum and petroleum products,
natural gas, timber and timber products, metals,
chemicals, manufactured goods

TURKEY

PRONUNCIATION: TER-kee
AREA: 301,380 sq. miles
(780,574 sq. km)
POPULATION: 65,600,000
CAPITAL: Ankara
CURRENCY: Turkish lira (TL)
OFFICIAL LANGUAGE: Turkish
OTHER LANGUAGES: Kurdish, Arabic
MAIN RELIGION: Islam 99%
EXPORTS: Manufactured goods, food,
mining products

CYPRUS

PRONUNCIATION: SEYE-pruhs
AREA: 3,572 sq. miles (9,251 sq. km)
POPULATION: 754,100
CAPITAL: Nicosia
CURRENCY: 100 cents = 1 Cypriot pound (£C);
100 kurus = 1 Turkish lira (TL)
OFFICIAL LANGUAGES: Greek, Turkish
OTHER LANGUAGE: English
MAIN RELIGIONS: Christianity 78%, Islam 18%
EXPORTS: Citrus fruit, potatoes, grapes, wine,
cement, clothing, shoes

GEORGIA

PRONUNCIATION: JOR-juh
AREA: 26,911 sq. miles
(69,699 sq. km)
POPULATION: 5,067,000
CAPITAL: Tbilisi
CURRENCY: Lari
OFFICIAL LANGUAGE: Georgian
OTHER LANGUAGES: Russian, Armenian, Azeri
MAIN RELIGIONS: Christianity 83%, Islam 11%
EXPORTS: Citrus fruit, tea, wine, machinery,
metals, textiles, chemicals, fuel re-exports

ARMENIA

PRONUNCIATION: ar-MEE-nee-uh
AREA: 11,506 sq. miles
(29,800 sq. km)
POPULATION: 3,410,000
CAPITAL: Yerevan
CURRENCY: 100 luma = 1 dram
OFFICIAL LANGUAGE: Armenian
OTHER LANGUAGE: Russian
MAIN RELIGION: Christianity 94%
EXPORTS: Gold and jewelry, aluminum,
transportation equipment, electrical equipment

AZERBAIJAN

PRONUNCIATION: a-zuhr-beye-ZHAHN
AREA: 33,436 sq. miles
(86,599 sq. km)
POPULATION: 7,909,000
CAPITAL: Baku
CURRENCY: 100 gopiks = 1 manat
OFFICIAL LANGUAGE: Azerbaijani
OTHER LANGUAGES: Russian, Armenian
MAIN RELIGIONS: Islam 94%, Christianity 5%
EXPORTS: Oil, gas, chemicals, oil field equipment,
textiles, cotton

KAZAKSTAN

PRONUNCIATION: kuh-zahk-STAHN
AREA: 1,048,300 sq. miles
(2,715,097 sq. km)
POPULATION: 16,825,000
CAPITAL: Astana
CURRENCY: 100 tiyn = 1 tenge
OFFICIAL LANGUAGE: Kazak
OTHER LANGUAGE: Russian
MAIN RELIGIONS: Islam 47%, Christianity 46%
EXPORTS: Oil, metals, chemicals, grain, wool,
meat, coal

UZBEKISTAN

PRONUNCIATION: uz-be-ki-STAN
AREA: 173,591 sq. miles
(449,601 sq. km)
POPULATION: 24,103,000
CAPITAL: Tashkent
CURRENCY: Som (UKS)
OFFICIAL LANGUAGE: Uzbek
OTHER LANGUAGES: Russian, Tajik
MAIN RELIGIONS: Islam 88%, Christianity 9%
EXPORTS: Cotton, gold, natural gas, mineral
fertilizer, metals, textiles, food

TURKMENISTAN

PRONUNCIATION: terk-me-nuh-STAN
AREA: 188,455 sq. miles
(488,098 sq. km)
POPULATION: 4,367,000
CAPITAL: Ashkhabad
CURRENCY: 100 tenesi = 1 manat
OFFICIAL LANGUAGE: Turkmen
OTHER LANGUAGES: Russian, Uzbek
MAIN RELIGIONS: Islam 89%, Christianity 9%
EXPORTS: Natural gas, cotton, petroleum products,
electricity, textiles, carpets

KYRGYZSTAN

PRONUNCIATION: kihr-gi-STAN
AREA: 76,641 sq. miles
(198,500 sq. km)
POPULATION: 4,547,000
CAPITAL: Bishkek
CURRENCY: 100 tyiyn = 1 Kyrgyzstani som (KGS)
OFFICIAL LANGUAGE: Kyrgyz
OTHER LANGUAGE: Russian
MAIN RELIGIONS: Islam 75%, Christianity 20%
EXPORTS: Wool, chemicals, cotton, metals, shoes,
machinery, tobacco

TAJIKISTAN

PRONUNCIATION: tah-ji-ki-STAN
AREA: 55,251 sq. miles
(143,100 sq. km)
POPULATION: 6,103,000
CAPITAL: Dushanbe
CURRENCY: 100 tanga = 1 Tajikistani ruble (TR)
OFFICIAL LANGUAGE: Tajik
OTHER LANGUAGE: Russian
MAIN RELIGION: Islam 85%
EXPORTS: Cotton, aluminum, fruit and
vegetables, textiles

SYRIA

PRONUNCIATION: SIHR-ee-uh
AREA: 71,498 sq. miles
(185,180 sq. km)
POPULATION: 17,214,000
CAPITAL: Damascus
CURRENCY: 100 piastres = 1 Syrian pound (£S)
OFFICIAL LANGUAGE: Arabic
OTHER LANGUAGES: Kurdish, Armenian, Aramaic,
Circassian, French
MAIN RELIGIONS: Islam 90%, Christianity 10%
EXPORTS: Petroleum, textiles, cotton, fruit and
vegetables, wheat, barley, chickens

IRAQ

PRONUNCIATION: i-RAHK
AREA: 168,927 sq. miles
(437,521 sq. km)
POPULATION: 22,428,000
CAPITAL: Baghdad
CURRENCY: 1,000 fils = 1 Iraqi dinar (ID)
OFFICIAL LANGUAGES: Arabic, Kurdish (in
Kurdish regions)
OTHER LANGUAGES: Assyrian, Armenian
MAIN RELIGIONS: Islam 97%, Christianity 3%
EXPORTS: Crude oil and refined products,
fertilizer, sulfur

IRAN

PRONUNCIATION: i-RAHN
AREA: 635,932 sq. miles
(1,647,064 sq. km)
POPULATION: 65,180,000
CAPITAL: Tehran
CURRENCY: 100 dinars = 1 rial (R)
OFFICIAL LANGUAGE: Farsi (Persian)
OTHER LANGUAGES: Turkic, Kurdish
MAIN RELIGION: Islam 99%
EXPORTS: Petroleum, carpets, fruit, nuts,
animal skins

LEBANON

PRONUNCIATION: LE-buh-nuhn
AREA: 3,949 sq. miles (10,228 sq. km)
POPULATION: 3,563,000
CAPITAL: Beirut
CURRENCY: 100 piastres = 1 Lebanese pound (£L)
OFFICIAL LANGUAGES: Arabic, French
OTHER LANGUAGES: Armenian, English
MAIN RELIGIONS: Islam 70%, Christianity 30%
EXPORTS: Agricultural products, chemicals,
textiles, metals, jewelry

ISRAEL

PRONUNCIATION: IZ-ray-uhl
AREA: 7,992 sq. miles (20,699 sq. km)
POPULATION: 5,750,000
CAPITAL: Jerusalem
CURRENCY: 100 new agorot = 1 new Israeli
shekel (NIS)
OFFICIAL LANGUAGES: Hebrew, Arabic
OTHER LANGUAGE: English
MAIN RELIGIONS: Judaism 80%, Islam 15%,
Christianity 2%
EXPORTS: Machinery, cut diamonds, chemicals,
textiles, agricultural products, metals

JORDAN

PRONUNCIATION: JOR-duhn
AREA: 34,575 sq. miles
(89,549 sq. km)
POPULATION: 4,562,000
CAPITAL: Amman
CURRENCY: 1,000 fils = 1 Jordanian dinar (JD)
OFFICIAL LANGUAGE: Arabic
OTHER LANGUAGE: English
MAIN RELIGIONS: Islam 96%, Christianity 4%
EXPORTS: Phosphates, fertilizer, potash,
agricultural products, manufactured goods

SAUDI ARABIA

PRONUNCIATION: SOW-dee
uh-RAY-bee-uh
AREA: 865,000 sq. miles (2,240,350 sq. km)
POPULATION: 21,505,000
CAPITAL: Riyadh
CURRENCY: 100 halalas = 1 Saudi riyal (SR)
OFFICIAL LANGUAGE: Arabic
MAIN RELIGION: Islam 100%
EXPORTS: Petroleum and petroleum products

KUWAIT

PRONUNCIATION: koo-WAYT
AREA: 6,880 sq. miles (17,819 sq. km)
POPULATION: 1,992,000
CAPITAL: Kuwait
CURRENCY: 1,000 fils = 1 Kuwaiti dinar (KD)
OFFICIAL LANGUAGE: Arabic
OTHER LANGUAGE: English
MAIN RELIGIONS: Islam 85%, Christianity 8%,
Hinduism and Parsi 2%
EXPORTS: Oil

BAHRAIN

PRONUNCIATION: bah-RAYN
AREA: 255 sq. miles (661 sq. km)
POPULATION: 629,100
CAPITAL: Manama
CURRENCY: 1,000 fils = 1 Bahraini dinar (BD)
OFFICIAL LANGUAGE: Arabic
OTHER LANGUAGES: English, Farsi, Urdu
MAIN RELIGION: Islam 100%
EXPORTS: Petroleum and petroleum
products, aluminum

QATAR

PRONUNCIATION: KAH-tuhr
AREA: 4,400 sq. miles (11,395 sq. km)
POPULATION: 723,600
CAPITAL: Doha
CURRENCY: 100 dirhams = 1 Qatari riyal (QR)
OFFICIAL LANGUAGE: Arabic
OTHER LANGUAGE: English
MAIN RELIGION: Islam 95%
EXPORTS: Petroleum products, steel, fertilizer

UNITED ARAB EMIRATES

PRONUNCIATION: yoo-NEYE-tuhd
A-ruhb EM-uh-ruhts
AREA: 30,000 sq. miles (77,701 sq. km)
POPULATION: 2,345,000
CAPITAL: Abu Dhabi
CURRENCY: 100 fils = 1 Emirian dirham (Dh)
OFFICIAL LANGUAGE: Arabic
OTHER LANGUAGES: Persian, English, Hindi, Urdu
MAIN RELIGION: Islam 96%
EXPORTS: Crude oil, natural gas, dried fish, dates

OMAN

PRONUNCIATION: oh-MAHN
AREA: 82,000 sq. miles
(212,380 sq. km)
POPULATION: 2,447,000
CAPITAL: Muscat
CURRENCY: 1,000 baiza = 1 Omani rial (RO)
OFFICIAL LANGUAGE: Arabic
OTHER LANGUAGES: English, Baluchi, Urdu,
Indian languages
MAIN RELIGIONS: Islam 86%, Hinduism 13%
EXPORTS: Petroleum, fish, copper, textiles

YEMEN

PRONUNCIATION: YE-muhn
AREA: 203,849 sq. miles
(527,969 sq. km)
POPULATION: 16,943,000
CAPITAL: Sanaa
CURRENCY: Yemeni rial (YRI)
OFFICIAL LANGUAGE: Arabic
MAIN RELIGION: Islam 99%
EXPORTS: Crude oil, cotton, coffee, animal skins,
vegetables, dried and salted fish

AFGHANISTAN

PRONUNCIATION: af-GA-nuh-stan
AREA: 250,775 sq. miles
(649,507 sq. km)
POPULATION: 25,825,000
CAPITAL: Kabul
CURRENCY: 100 puls = 1 afghani (AF)
OFFICIAL LANGUAGES: Afghan, Persian, Pashto
OTHER LANGUAGES: Uzbek, Turkmen
MAIN RELIGIONS: Islam 99%, Hinduism and Judaism 1%
EXPORTS: Fruit, nuts, handwoven carpets, wool, cotton, animal skins, precious and semiprecious gemstones

PAKISTAN

PRONUNCIATION: pa-ki-STAN
AREA: 310,403 sq. miles
(803,944 sq. km)
POPULATION: 138,124,000
CAPITAL: Islamabad
CURRENCY: 100 paisa = 1 Pakistani rupee (PRe)
OFFICIAL LANGUAGES: Urdu, English
OTHER LANGUAGES: Punjabi, Sindhi, Pashto, Baluchi
MAIN RELIGION: Islam 97%
EXPORTS: Cotton, textiles, clothing, rice, leather, carpets

INDIA

PRONUNCIATION: IN-dee-uh
AREA: 1,195,063 sq. miles
(3,095,472 sq. km)
POPULATION: 1,000,849,000
CAPITAL: New Delhi
CURRENCY: 100 paise = 1 Indian rupee (Re)
OFFICIAL LANGUAGES: Hindi, English
OTHER LANGUAGES: Hindustani, Bengali, Telugu, Marathi, Tamil, Urdu, Gujarati, Malayalam, Kannada, Oriya, Punjabi, Assamese, Kashmiri, Rajasthani, Sindhi, Sanskrit
MAIN RELIGIONS: Hinduism 80%, Islam 14%, Christianity 3%
EXPORTS: Clothing, gemstones and jewelry, engineering equipment, chemicals, leather goods, cotton yarn, fabric

NEPAL

PRONUNCIATION: nuh-PAHL
AREA: 54,362 sq. miles
(140,798 sq. km)
POPULATION: 24,303,000
CAPITAL: Kathmandu
CURRENCY: 100 paisa = 1 Nepalese rupee (NR)
OFFICIAL LANGUAGE: Nepali
MAIN RELIGIONS: Hinduism 90%, Buddhism 5%, Islam 3%
EXPORTS: Carpets, clothing, leather goods, jute goods, grain

BHUTAN

PRONUNCIATION: boo-TAHN
AREA: 16,000 sq. miles
(41,440 sq. km)
POPULATION: 1,952,000
CAPITAL: Thimphu
CURRENCY: 100 chetrums = 1 ngultrum (Nu); Indian currency is also legal tender
OFFICIAL LANGUAGE: Dzongkha
OTHER LANGUAGES: Tibetan and Nepali
MAIN RELIGIONS: Buddhism 75%, Hinduism 25%
EXPORTS: Timber, handicrafts, cement, fruit, electricity, gemstones, spices

BANGLADESH

PRONUNCIATION: bahng-gluh-DESH
AREA: 55,126 sq. miles
(142,776 sq. km)
POPULATION: 127,118,000
CAPITAL: Dhaka
CURRENCY: 100 paisa = 1 taka (Tk)
OFFICIAL LANGUAGE: Bengali
OTHER LANGUAGE: English
MAIN RELIGIONS: Islam 88%, Hinduism 11%, Buddhism and Christianity 1%
EXPORTS: Garments, jute and jute goods, leather, shrimp

MALDIVES

PRONUNCIATION: MAWL-deevz
AREA: 115 sq. miles (298 sq. km)
POPULATION: 300,300
CAPITAL: Male
CURRENCY: 100 laari = 1 rufiyaa (Rf)
OFFICIAL LANGUAGE: Divehi (Maldivian)
OTHER LANGUAGE: English
MAIN RELIGION: Islam 100%
EXPORTS: Fish, clothing

SRI LANKA

PRONUNCIATION: sree LAHNG-kuh
AREA: 25,332 sq. miles
(65,610 sq. km)
POPULATION: 19,145,000
CAPITAL: Colombo
CURRENCY: 100 cents = 1 Sri Lankan rupee (SLRe)
OFFICIAL LANGUAGES: Sinhala, Tamil
OTHER LANGUAGE: English

MAIN RELIGIONS: Buddhism 69%, Hinduism 15%, Christianity 8%, Islam 8%
EXPORTS: Textiles, tea, diamonds and other precious gemstones, petroleum products, rubber products, agricultural products, marine products

MYANMAR (BURMA)

PRONUNCIATION: MYAHN-mar
(BER-muh)
AREA: 261,789 sq. miles
(678,034 sq. km)
POPULATION: 48,082,000
CAPITAL: Yangon (Rangoon)
CURRENCY: 100 pyas = 1 kyat (K)
OFFICIAL LANGUAGE: Burmese
MAIN RELIGIONS: Buddhism 89%, Christianity 4%, Islam 4%
EXPORTS: Pulses and beans, rice, timber

LAOS

PRONUNCIATION: lows
AREA: 91,428 sq. miles
(236,799 sq. km)
POPULATION: 5,408,000
CAPITAL: Vientiane
CURRENCY: 100 at = 1 new kip (NK)
OFFICIAL LANGUAGE: Lao
OTHER LANGUAGES: French, English
MAIN RELIGIONS: Buddhism 60%, animism 34%, Christianity 2%
EXPORTS: Electricity, timber products, coffee, tin, textiles

VIETNAM

PRONUNCIATION: vee-et-NAHM
AREA: 130,468 sq. miles
(337,912 sq. km)
POPULATION: 77,312,000
CAPITAL: Hanoi
CURRENCY: 100 xu = 1 new dong (D)
OFFICIAL LANGUAGE: Vietnamese
OTHER LANGUAGES: French, Chinese, English, Khmer, tribal languages
MAIN RELIGIONS: Buddhism 55%, Christianity 7%, Taoism, indigenous religions, Islam
EXPORTS: Petroleum, rice, agricultural products, marine products, coffee

THAILAND

PRONUNCIATION: TEYE-land
AREA: 198,455 sq. miles
(513,998 sq. km)
POPULATION: 60,609,000
CAPITAL: Bangkok
CURRENCY: 100 satang = 1 baht (B)
OFFICIAL LANGUAGE: Thai
OTHER LANGUAGES: English, Chinese, Malay
MAIN RELIGIONS: Buddhism 95%, Islam 4%
EXPORTS: Machinery, manufactured goods, agricultural products, fish

CAMBODIA

PRONUNCIATION: kam-BOH-dee-uh
AREA: 69,898 sq. miles
(181,036 sq. km)
POPULATION: 11,627,000
CAPITAL: Phnom Penh
CURRENCY: 100 sen = 1 new riel (CR)
OFFICIAL LANGUAGE: Khmer
OTHER LANGUAGE: French
MAIN RELIGIONS: Buddhism 95%, Islam 2%
EXPORTS: Timber, rubber, soybeans, sesame

MALAYSIA

PRONUNCIATION: muh-LAY-zhuh
AREA: 128,727 sq. miles
(333,403 sq. km)
POPULATION: 21,376,000
CAPITAL: Kuala Lumpur
CURRENCY: 100 sen = 1 ringgit (M$)
OFFICIAL LANGUAGE: Malay
OTHER LANGUAGES: English, Chinese languages,
Tamil, Teluga, regional languages
MAIN RELIGIONS: Islam 53%, Buddhism 17%,
Confucianism 12%, Christianity 9%,
Hinduism 7%
EXPORTS: Electronic equipment, petroleum and
petroleum products, palm oil, timber and timber
products, rubber, textiles

PHILIPPINES

PRONUNCIATION: FI-luh-peenz
AREA: 115,651 sq. miles
(299,536 sq. km)
POPULATION: 79,346,000
CAPITAL: Manila
CURRENCY: 100 centavos = 1 Philippine peso (P)
OFFICIAL LANGUAGES: Pilipino, English
OTHER LANGUAGES: Regional languages
MAIN RELIGIONS: Christianity 92%, Islam 5%,
Buddhism 3%
EXPORTS: Electronics, textiles, coconut products,
copper, fish

SINGAPORE

PRONUNCIATION: SING-uh-por
AREA: 225 sq. miles (583 sq. km)
POPULATION: 3,532,000
CAPITAL: Singapore
CURRENCY: 100 cents = 1 Singapore dollar (S$)
OFFICIAL LANGUAGES: Chinese, Malay, Tamil,
English
MAIN RELIGIONS: Buddhism 28%, Islam 15%,
Christianity 13%, Taoism 13%, Hinduism 5%
EXPORTS: Computer equipment, rubber and
rubber products, petroleum products,
telecommunications equipment

BRUNEI

PRONUNCIATION: broo-NEYE
AREA: 2,226 sq. miles
(5,765 sq. km)
POPULATION: 323,000
CAPITAL: Bandar Seri Begawan
CURRENCY: 100 cents = 1 Bruneian dollar (B$)
OFFICIAL LANGUAGE: Malay
OTHER LANGUAGES: English, Chinese
MAIN RELIGIONS: Islam 63%, Buddhist 14%,
Christianity 8%, indigenous religions
EXPORTS: Crude oil, liquefied natural gas,
petroleum products

INDONESIA

PRONUNCIATION: in-duh-NEE-zhuh
AREA: 779,675 sq. miles
(2,019,358 sq. km)
POPULATION: 216,109,000
CAPITAL: Jakarta
CURRENCY: 100 sen = 1 Indonesian rupiah (Rp)
OFFICIAL LANGUAGE: Bahasa Indonesia
OTHER LANGUAGES: English, Dutch, Javanese,
regional languages
MAIN RELIGIONS: Islam 88%, Christianity 9%,
Hinduism 2%, Buddhism 1%
EXPORTS: Manufactured goods, fuels, food,
raw materials

EAST TIMOR

PRONUNCIATION: EEST TEE-MAW
AREA: 7,000 sq. miles (19,000 sq.km)
POPULATION: 650,000
CAPITAL: Dili
CURRENCY: 100 sen = 1 rupiah (Rp)
OFFICIAL LANGUAGE: Bahasa Indonesia
OTHER LANGUAGES: Tetum, Portuguese
MAIN RELIGION: Christianity 90%
EXPORTS: Oil, minerals, coffee

CHINA

PRONUNCIATION: CHEYE-nuh
AREA: 3,700,000 sq. miles
(9,583,000 sq. km)
POPULATION: 1,246,872,000
CAPITAL: Beijing
CURRENCY: 10 jiao = 1 yuan (Y)
OFFICIAL LANGUAGE: Mandarin
OTHER LANGUAGES: Cantonese, Shanghainese,
Fuzhou, Hokkien-Taiwanese
MAIN RELIGIONS: Daoism (Taoism) 20%,
Buddhism 6%, Islam 3%, Christianity 1%
EXPORTS: Textiles, clothing, shoes, toys,
machinery, weapons

MONGOLIA

PRONUNCIATION: mahn-GOHL-yuh
AREA: 604,247 sq. miles
(1,565,000 sq. km)
POPULATION: 2,618,000
CAPITAL: Ulaanbaatar
CURRENCY: 100 mongos = 1 tughrik (Tug)
OFFICIAL LANGUAGE: Khalkha Mongol
OTHER LANGUAGES: Turkic, Russian, Chinese

MAIN RELIGIONS: Buddhism 95%, Islam 4%
EXPORTS: Copper, livestock, animal products,
cashmere, wool, animal skins, metals

NORTH KOREA

PRONUNCIATION: north kuh-REE-uh
AREA: 46,609 sq. miles
(120,717 sq. km)
POPULATION: 21,386,000
CAPITAL: P'yŏngyang
CURRENCY: 100 chon = 1 North Korean
won (KW)
OFFICIAL LANGUAGE: Korean
MAIN RELIGIONS: Chondogya 14%, Buddhism 2%,
Christianity 1%
EXPORTS: Minerals, metal products, agricultural
and fishery products, manufactured goods

SOUTH KOREA

PRONUNCIATION: sowth kuh-REE-uh
AREA: 38,022 sq. miles
(98,477 sq. km)
POPULATION: 46,885,000
CAPITAL: Seoul
CURRENCY: 100 chon = 1 South Korean won (W)
OFFICIAL LANGUAGE: Korean
OTHER LANGUAGE: English
MAIN RELIGIONS: Christianity 49%, Buddhism
47%, Confucianism 3%
EXPORTS: Electronic and electrical equipment,
machinery, steel, motor vehicles, ships, textiles,
clothing, shoes, fish

TAIWAN

PRONUNCIATION: TEYE-WAHN
AREA: 13,887 sq. miles
(35,967 sq. km)
POPULATION: 22,113,000
CAPITAL: Taipei
CURRENCY: 100 cents = 1 New Taiwan dollar
(NT$)
OFFICIAL LANGUAGE: Mandarin
OTHER LANGUAGES: Taiwanese, Hakka
MAIN RELIGIONS: Buddhism 43%, Daoism
(Taoism) 21%, Christianity 7%, Confucianism
EXPORTS: Electrical machinery, electronic goods,
textiles, shoes, food, timber products

JAPAN

PRONUNCIATION: juh-PAN
AREA: 143,619 sq. miles
(371,973 sq. km)
POPULATION: 126,182,000
CAPITAL: Tokyo
CURRENCY: 100 sen = 1 yen (¥)
OFFICIAL LANGUAGE: Japanese
MAIN RELIGIONS: Shinto and Buddhism 84%
EXPORTS: Machinery, motor vehicles,
consumer electronics

AFRICA

MOROCCO

PRONUNCIATION: muh-RAH-koh
AREA: 172,413 sq. miles
(446,550 sq. km)
POPULATION: 29,662,000
CAPITAL: Rabat
CURRENCY: 100 centimes = 1 Moroccan
dirham (DH)
OFFICIAL LANGUAGE: Arabic
OTHER LANGUAGES: Berber, French
MAIN RELIGIONS: Islam 99%, Christianity 1%
EXPORTS: Food, beverages, consumer goods,
phosphates

ALGERIA

PRONUNCIATION: al-JIHR-ee-uh
AREA: 918,497 sq. miles
(2,378,907 sq. km)
POPULATION: 31,134,000
CAPITAL: Algiers
CURRENCY: 100 centimes = 1 Algerian dinar (DA)
OFFICIAL LANGUAGE: Arabic
OTHER LANGUAGES: French, Berber
MAIN RELIGIONS: Islam 99%, Christianity and
Judaism 1%
EXPORTS: Petroleum, natural gas

TUNISIA

PRONUNCIATION: too-NEE-zhuh
AREA: 63,378 sq. miles
(164,149 sq. km)
POPULATION: 9,514,000
CAPITAL: Tunis
CURRENCY: 1,000 millimes = 1 Tunisian
dinar (TD)
OFFICIAL LANGUAGE: Arabic
OTHER LANGUAGE: French
MAIN RELIGIONS: Islam 98%, Christianity 1%,
Judaism 1%
EXPORTS: Agricultural products, chemicals

LIBYA

PRONUNCIATION: LI-bee-uh
AREA: 679,360 sq. miles
(1,759,540 sq. km)
POPULATION: 4,993,000
CAPITAL: Tripoli

CURRENCY: 1,000 dirhams =
1 Libyan dinar (LD)
OFFICIAL LANGUAGE: Arabic
OTHER LANGUAGES: Italian,
English
MAIN RELIGION: Islam 97%
EXPORTS: Crude oil, refined
petroleum products, natural gas

CAPE VERDE ISLANDS

PRONUNCIATION: kayp VAIRD islands
AREA: 1,557 sq. miles (4,033 sq. km)
POPULATION: 405,800
CAPITAL: Praia
CURRENCY: 100 centavos = 1 Cape Verdean
escudo (CVEsc)
OFFICIAL LANGUAGE: Portuguese
OTHER LANGUAGE: Cape Verde creole
MAIN RELIGION: Christianity 97%
EXPORTS: Fish, bananas, animal skins

EGYPT

PRONUNCIATION: EE-juhpt
AREA: 386,900 sq. miles
(1,002,071 sq. km)
POPULATION: 67,274,000
CAPITAL: Cairo
CURRENCY: 100 piasters = 1 Egyptian pound (£E)
OFFICIAL LANGUAGE: Arabic
OTHER LANGUAGES: English, French
MAIN RELIGIONS: Islam 94%, Christianity 6%
EXPORTS: Crude oil and petroleum products,
cotton, textiles, metal products, chemicals

MAURITANIA

PRONUNCIATION: maw-ruh-TAY-nee-uh
AREA: 397,955 sq. miles
(1,030,807 sq. km)
POPULATION: 2,582,000
CAPITAL: Nouakchott
CURRENCY: 5 khoums = 1 ouguiya (UM)
OFFICIAL LANGUAGES: Hasaniya Arabic, Wolof
OTHER LANGUAGES: French, Pular, Soninke
MAIN RELIGION: Islam 100%
EXPORTS: Iron ore, fish, fish products

MALI

PRONUNCIATION: MAH-lee
AREA: 478,652 sq. miles
(1,239,709 sq. km)
POPULATION: 10,429,000
CAPITAL: Bamako
CURRENCY: 100 centimes = 1 CFA
franc (CFAF)
OFFICIAL LANGUAGE: French
OTHER LANGUAGES: Regional
languages
MAIN RELIGIONS: Islam 90%,
indigenous religions 9%,
Christianity 1%
EXPORTS: Cotton, livestock, gold

BURKINA FASO

PRONUNCIATION: ber-KEE-nuh FAH-soh
AREA: 105,869 sq. miles
(274,201 sq. km)
POPULATION: 11,576,000
CAPITAL: Ouagadougou
CURRENCY: 100 centimes = 1 CFA franc (CFAF)
OFFICIAL LANGUAGE: French
OTHER LANGUAGES: Tribal languages
MAIN RELIGIONS: Islam 50%, indigenous religions
40%, Christianity 10%
EXPORTS: Cotton, gold, animal products

NIGER

PRONUNCIATION: NEYE-juhr
AREA: 459,073 sq. miles
(1,188,999 sq. km)
POPULATION: 9,963,000
CAPITAL: Niamey
CURRENCY: 100 centimes = 1 CFA franc (CFAF)
OFFICIAL LANGUAGE: French
OTHER LANGUAGES: Hausa, Djerma
MAIN RELIGIONS: Islam 80%, indigenous
religions 14%, Christianity 1%
EXPORTS: Uranium ore, livestock, cowpeas, onions

CHAD

PRONUNCIATION: chad
AREA: 495,752 sq. miles
(1,283,998 sq. km)
POPULATION: 7,558,000
CAPITAL: N'Djamena
CURRENCY: 100 centimes = 1 CFA franc (CFAF)
OFFICIAL LANGUAGES: French, Arabic
OTHER LANGUAGES: Sara, Sango
MAIN RELIGIONS: Islam 50%, Christianity 25%,
indigenous religions and animism 25%
EXPORTS: Cotton, cattle, textiles, fish

SUDAN

PRONUNCIATION: soo-DAN
AREA: 967,500 sq. miles
(2,505,825 sq. km)
POPULATION: 34,476,000
CAPITAL: Khartoum
CURRENCY: 100 piastres = 1 Sudanese pound (£Sd)
OFFICIAL LANGUAGE: Arabic
OTHER LANGUAGES: Nubian, Ta Bedawie, Nilotic,
Nilo-Hamitic, regional languages, English
MAIN RELIGIONS: Islam 70%, indigenous
religions 25%, Christianity 5%
EXPORTS: Gum, livestock, cotton, sesame, peanuts

ERITREA

PRONUNCIATION: ehr-uh-TREE-uh
AREA: 45,405 sq. miles
(117,599 sq. km)
POPULATION: 3,985,000
CAPITAL: Asmara
CURRENCY: 100 cents = 1 nafka
OFFICIAL LANGUAGES: Arabic, Tigrinya, Tigre
OTHER LANGUAGES: African languages
MAIN RELIGIONS: Islam 50%, Christianity 50%
EXPORTS: Salt, animal skins, oilseed

ETHIOPIA

PRONUNCIATION: ee-thee-OH-pee-uh
AREA: 471,775 sq. miles
(1,221,897 sq. km)
POPULATION: 59,681,000
CAPITAL: Addis Ababa
CURRENCY: 100 cents = 1 birr (Br)
OFFICIAL LANGUAGE: Amharic
OTHER LANGUAGES: African languages,
Arabic, English
MAIN RELIGIONS: Islam 50%, Christianity 40%,
animism 10%
EXPORTS: Coffee, leather products, gold

DJIBOUTI

PRONUNCIATION: ji-BOO-tee
AREA: 8,880 sq. miles
(22,999 sq. km)
POPULATION: 447,500
CAPITAL: Djibouti
CURRENCY: 100 centimes = 1 Djiboutian
franc (DF)
OFFICIAL LANGUAGES: French, Arabic
OTHER LANGUAGES: Somali, Afar
MAIN RELIGIONS: Islam 94%, Christianity 6%
EXPORTS: Animal skins, coffee

SOMALIA

PRONUNCIATION: soh-MAH-lee-uh
AREA: 246,154 sq. miles
(637,539 sq. km)
POPULATION: 7,141,000
CAPITAL: Mogadishu
CURRENCY: 100 cents = 1 Somali shilling (So.Sh.)
OFFICIAL LANGUAGE: Somali
OTHER LANGUAGES: Arabic, Italian, English
MAIN RELIGION: Islam 99%
EXPORTS: Bananas, livestock, fish, animal skins

SENEGAL

PRONUNCIATION: sen-i-GAWL
AREA: 76,124 sq. miles
(197,161 sq. km)
POPULATION: 10,052,000
CAPITAL: Dakar
CURRENCY: 100 centimes = 1 CFA franc (CFAF)
OFFICIAL LANGUAGE: French
OTHER LANGUAGES: Regional languages
MAIN RELIGIONS: Islam 92%, indigenous
religions 6%, Christianity 2%
EXPORTS: Fish, peanuts, petroleum products,
phosphates, cotton

GAMBIA

PRONUNCIATION: GAM-bee-uh
AREA: 4,003 sq. miles (10,368 sq. km)
POPULATION: 1,337,000
CAPITAL: Banjul
CURRENCY: 100 bututs = 1 dalasi (D)
OFFICIAL LANGUAGE: English
OTHER LANGUAGES: African languages
MAIN RELIGIONS: Islam 90%, Christianity 9%,
indigenous religions 1%
EXPORTS: Peanuts, fish, palm kernels

GUINEA-BISSAU

PRONUNCIATION: gi-nee-bi-SOW
AREA: 13,948 sq. miles
(36,125 sq. km)
POPULATION: 1,235,000
CAPITAL: Bissau
CURRENCY: 100 centimes = 1 CFA franc (CFAF)
OFFICIAL LANGUAGE: Portuguese
OTHER LANGUAGES: Criolo, African languages
MAIN RELIGIONS: Indigenous religions 50%,
Islam 45%, Christianity 5%
EXPORTS: Cashews, fish, peanuts, palm kernels,
timber

GUINEA

PRONUNCIATION: GI-nee
AREA: 94,925 sq. miles
(245,856 sq. km)
POPULATION: 7,539,000
CAPITAL: Conakry
CURRENCY: 100 centimes = 1 Guinean franc (FG)
OFFICIAL LANGUAGE: French
OTHER LANGUAGES: Tribal languages
MAIN RELIGIONS: Islam 85%, Christianity 8%,
indigenous religions 7%
EXPORTS: Bauxite, alumina, diamonds, gold,
coffee, pineapples, bananas, palm kernels

SIERRA LEONE

PRONUNCIATION: see-EHR-uh lee-OHN
AREA: 27,699 sq. miles
(71,740 sq. km)
POPULATION: 5,297,000
CAPITAL: Freetown
CURRENCY: 100 cents = 1 leone (Le)
OFFICIAL LANGUAGE: English
OTHER LANGUAGES: Mende, Temne, Krio
MAIN RELIGIONS: Islam 60%, indigenous
religions 30%, Christianity 10%
EXPORTS: Diamonds and other minerals, coffee,
cocoa, fish

LIBERIA

PRONUNCIATION: leye-BIHR-ee-uh
AREA: 43,000 sq. miles
(111,370 sq. km)
POPULATION: 2,924,000
CAPITAL: Monrovia
CURRENCY: 100 cents = 1 Liberian dollar (L$)
OFFICIAL LANGUAGE: English
OTHER LANGUAGES: Niger-Congo languages
MAIN RELIGIONS: Indigenous religions 70%,
Islam 20%, Christianity 10%
EXPORTS: Iron ore, rubber, timber, coffee

CÔTE D'IVOIRE
(IVORY COAST)

PRONUNCIATION: koht dee-VWAR
AREA: 124,503 sq. miles
(322,463 sq. km)
POPULATION: 15,818,000
CAPITALS: Abidjan (seat of government),
Yamoussoukro (official)
CURRENCY: 100 centimes = 1 CFA franc (CFAF)
OFFICIAL LANGUAGE: French
OTHER LANGUAGES: Regional languages
MAIN RELIGIONS: Islam 60%, Christianity 22%,
indigenous religions 18%
EXPORTS: Cocoa, coffee, timber, petroleum, cotton,
bananas, pineapples, palm oil

GHANA

PRONUNCIATION: GAH-nuh
AREA: 92,100 sq. miles
(238,539 sq. km)
POPULATION: 18,888,000
CAPITAL: Accra
CURRENCY: 100 pesewas = 1 new cedi (₵)
OFFICIAL LANGUAGE: English
OTHER LANGUAGES: African languages
MAIN RELIGIONS: Indigenous religions 38%, Islam
30%, Christianity 24%
EXPORTS: Cocoa, gold, timber, tuna, bauxite,
aluminum

TOGO

PRONUNCIATION: TOH-goh
AREA: 21,853 sq. miles
(56,599 sq. km)
POPULATION: 5,082,000
CAPITAL: Lomé
CURRENCY: 100 centimes = 1 CFA franc (CFAF)
OFFICIAL LANGUAGE: French
OTHER LANGUAGES: Regional languages
MAIN RELIGIONS: Indigenous religions 70%,
Christianity 20%, Islam 10%
EXPORTS: Phosphates, cotton, cocoa, coffee

BENIN

PRONUNCIATION: buh-NEEN
AREA: 43,483 sq. miles
(112,621 sq. km)
POPULATION: 6,306,000
CAPITALS: Cotonou (de facto), Porto-Novo (legal)
CURRENCY: 100 centimes = 1 CFA franc (CFAF)
OFFICIAL LANGUAGE: French
OTHER LANGUAGES: Fon, Yoruba, regional languages
MAIN RELIGIONS: Indigenous religions 70%, Islam 15%, Christianity 15%
EXPORTS: Cotton, crude oil, palm products, cocoa

NIGERIA

PRONUNCIATION: neye-JIHR-ee-uh
AREA: 356,669 sq. miles
(923,773 sq. km)
POPULATION: 113,829,000
CAPITAL: Abuja
CURRENCY: 100 kobo = 1 naira (₦)
OFFICIAL LANGUAGE: English
OTHER LANGUAGES: Regional languages
MAIN RELIGIONS: Islam 50%, Christianity 40%, indigenous religions 10%
EXPORTS: Oil, cocoa, rubber

CAMEROON

PRONUNCIATION: ka-muh-ROON
AREA: 183,591 sq. miles
(475,501 sq. km)
POPULATION: 15,456,000
CAPITAL: Yaoundé
CURRENCY: 100 centimes = 1 CFA franc (CFAF)
OFFICIAL LANGUAGES: English, French
OTHER LANGUAGES: African languages
MAIN RELIGIONS: Indigenous religions 51%, Christianity 33%, Islam 16%
EXPORTS: Petroleum products, timber, cocoa beans, aluminum, coffee, cotton

EQUATORIAL GUINEA

PRONUNCIATION: e-kwuh-TOR-ee-uhl GI-nee
AREA: 10,825 sq. miles (28,037 sq. km)
POPULATION: 465,800
CAPITAL: Malabo
CURRENCY: 100 centimes = 1 CFA franc (CFAF)
OFFICIAL LANGUAGES: Spanish, French
OTHER LANGUAGES: Pidgin English, regional languages
MAIN RELIGION: Christianity 85%
EXPORTS: Coffee, timber, cocoa

CENTRAL AFRICAN REPUBLIC

PRONUNCIATION: SEN-truhl AF-ri-kuhn ri-PUH-blik
AREA: 240,376 sq. miles (622,374 sq. km)
POPULATION: 3,445,000
CAPITAL: Bangui
CURRENCY: 100 centimes = 1 CFA franc (CFAF)
OFFICIAL LANGUAGE: French
OTHER LANGUAGES: Sangho, Arabic, Hunsa, Swahili
MAIN RELIGIONS: Christianity 50%, indigenous religions 24%, Islam 15%
EXPORTS: Diamonds, timber, cotton, coffee, tobacco

SÃO TOMÉ AND PRÍNCIPE

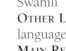

PRONUNCIATION: sow tuh-MAY and PRIN-suh-pee
AREA: 372 sq. miles (963 sq. km)
POPULATION: 154,900
CAPITAL: São Tomé
CURRENCY: 100 centimos = 1 dobra (Db)
OFFICIAL LANGUAGE: Portuguese
MAIN RELIGION: Christianity 100%
EXPORTS: Cocoa, copra, coffee, palm oil

GABON

PRONUNCIATION: ga-BOHN
AREA: 102,317 sq. miles
(265,001 sq. km)
POPULATION: 1,226,000
CAPITAL: Libreville
CURRENCY: 100 centimes = 1 CFA franc (CFAF)
OFFICIAL LANGUAGE: French
OTHER LANGUAGES: African languages
MAIN RELIGIONS: Christianity 60%, animism 40%, Islam 1%
EXPORTS: Crude oil, timber, manganese, uranium

CONGO

PRONUNCIATION: KAHN-goh
AREA: 132,047 sq. miles
(342,002 sq. km)
POPULATION: 2,717,000
CAPITAL: Brazzaville
CURRENCY: 100 centimes = 1 CFA franc (CFAF)
OFFICIAL LANGUAGE: French
OTHER LANGUAGES: African languages
MAIN RELIGIONS: Christianity 50%, animism 48%, Islam 2%
EXPORTS: Crude oil, timber, sugar, cocoa, coffee, diamonds

DEMOCRATIC REPUBLIC OF THE CONGO (ZAIRE)

PRONUNCIATION: de-muh-KRA-tik ri-PUH-blik of the KAHN-goh
AREA: 905,356 sq. miles
(2,344,872 sq. km)
POPULATION: 50,482,000
CAPITAL: Kinshasa
CURRENCY: Congolese franc (CF)
OFFICIAL LANGUAGE: French
OTHER LANGUAGES: Lingala, Swahili, Kingwana, Kikongo, Tshiluba
MAIN RELIGIONS: Christianity 70%, Kimbanguism 10%, Islam 10%
EXPORTS: Copper, coffee, diamonds, crude oil

UGANDA

PRONUNCIATION: yoo-GAN-duh
AREA: 91,134 sq. miles
(236,037 sq. km)
POPULATION: 22,805,000
CAPITAL: Kampala
CURRENCY: 100 cents = 1 Ugandan shilling (USh)
OFFICIAL LANGUAGE: English
OTHER LANGUAGES: Luganda, Swahili, Bantu and other regional languages
MAIN RELIGIONS: Christianity 66%, indigenous religions 18%, Islam 16%
EXPORTS: Coffee, cotton, tea

KENYA

PRONUNCIATION: ken-yuh
AREA: 224,960 sq. miles
(582,646 sq. km)
POPULATION: 28,809,000
CAPITAL: Nairobi
CURRENCY: 100 cents = 1 Kenyan shilling (KSh)
OFFICIAL LANGUAGES: English, Swahili
OTHER LANGUAGES: Indigenous languages
MAIN RELIGIONS: Christianity 66%, indigenous religions 26%, Islam 7%
EXPORTS: Tea, coffee, petroleum products

RWANDA

PRONUNCIATION: ruh-WAHN-duh
AREA: 10,169 sq. miles (26,338 sq. km)
POPULATION: 8,155,000
CAPITAL: Kigali
CURRENCY: 100 centimes = 1 Rwandan franc (RF)
OFFICIAL LANGUAGES: Kinyarwanda, French, English
OTHER LANGUAGE: Kiswahili
MAIN RELIGIONS: Christianity 74%, indigenous religions 25%, Islam 1%
EXPORTS: Coffee, tea, minerals

BURUNDI

PRONUNCIATION: boo-RUN-dee
AREA: 10,759 sq. miles (27,866 sq. km)
POPULATION: 5,736,000
CAPITAL: Bujumbura
CURRENCY: 100 centimes = 1 Burundi franc (FBu)
OFFICIAL LANGUAGES: Kirundi, French
OTHER LANGUAGE: Swahili
MAIN RELIGIONS: Christianity 67%, indigenous religions 32%, Islam 1%
EXPORTS: Coffee, tea, cotton, animal skins

TANZANIA

PRONUNCIATION: tan-zuh-NEE-uh
AREA: 364,900 sq. miles (945,091 sq. km)
POPULATION: 31,271,000
CAPITALS: Dar es Salaam (seat of government), Dodoma (official)

CURRENCY: 100 cents = 1 Tanzanian shilling (TSh)
OFFICIAL LANGUAGES: Swahili, English
MAIN RELIGIONS: Christianity 45%, Islam 35%, indigenous religions 20%
EXPORTS: Coffee, cotton, tobacco, tea, cashew nuts, sisal (fiber)

ANGOLA

PRONUNCIATION: ang-GOH-luh
AREA: 481,351 sq. miles (1,246,699 sq. km)
POPULATION: 11,178,000
CAPITAL: Luanda
CURRENCY: 100 lwei = 1 kwanza (NKz)
OFFICIAL LANGUAGE: Portuguese
OTHER LANGUAGES: Bantu and other African languages
MAIN RELIGIONS: Christianity 53%, indigenous religions 47%
EXPORTS: Oil, diamonds, refined petroleum products, gas, coffee, sisal (fiber), fish and fish products, timber, cotton

ZAMBIA
PRONUNCIATION: zam-bee-uh
AREA: 290,585 sq. miles (752,615 sq. km)
POPULATION: 9,664,000
CAPITAL: Lusaka
CURRENCY: 100 ngwee = 1 Zambian kwacha (ZK)
OFFICIAL LANGUAGE: English
OTHER LANGUAGES: Regional languages
MAIN RELIGIONS: Christianity 75%, Islam and Hinduism 24%, indigenous religions 1%
EXPORTS: Copper, zinc, cobalt, lead, tobacco

ZIMBABWE
PRONUNCIATION: zim-BAH-bway
AREA: 150,820 sq. miles (390,624 sq. km)
POPULATION: 11,164,000
CAPITAL: Harare
CURRENCY: 100 cents = 1 Zimbabwean dollar (Z$)
OFFICIAL LANGUAGE: English
OTHER LANGUAGES: Regional languages
MAIN RELIGIONS: Syncretic (part Christianity, part indigenous religions) 50%, Christianity 25%, indigenous religions 24%
EXPORTS: Tobacco, manufactured goods, gold, textiles

MALAWI
PRONUNCIATION: muh-LAH-wee
AREA: 45,747 sq. miles (118,485 sq. km)
POPULATION: 10,001,000
CAPITAL: Lilongwe
CURRENCY: 100 tambala = 1 Malawian kwacha (MK)
OFFICIAL LANGUAGES: English, Chichewa
OTHER LANGUAGES: Regional languages
MAIN RELIGIONS: Christianity 75%, Islam 20%, indigenous religions 5%
EXPORTS: Tobacco, tea, sugar, coffee, peanuts, timber products

MOZAMBIQUE

PRONUNCIATION: moh-zahm-BEEK
AREA: 297,846 sq. miles (771,421 sq. km)
POPULATION: 19,125,000
CAPITAL: Maputo
CURRENCY: 100 centavos = 1 metical (Mt)
OFFICIAL LANGUAGE: Portuguese
OTHER LANGUAGES: Regional languages
MAIN RELIGIONS: Indigenous religions 50%, Christianity 30%, Islam 20%
EXPORTS: Shrimp, cashews, cotton, sugar, copra, citrus fruit

NAMIBIA
PRONUNCIATION: nuh-MI-bee-uh
AREA: 318,321 sq. miles (824,451 sq. km)
POPULATION: 1,649,000
CAPITAL: Windhoek
CURRENCY: 100 cents = 1 Namibian dollar (N$)
OFFICIAL LANGUAGE: English
OTHER LANGUAGES: Afrikaans, German, regional languages
MAIN RELIGION: Christianity 90%
EXPORTS: Diamonds, copper, gold, zinc, lead, uranium, cattle, processed fish

BOTSWANA
PRONUNCIATION: bawt-SWAH-nuh
AREA: 219,916 sq. miles (569,582 sq. km)
POPULATION: 1,465,000
CAPITAL: Gaborone
CURRENCY: 100 thebe = 1 pula (P)
OFFICIAL LANGUAGE: English
OTHER LANGUAGE: Setswana
MAIN RELIGIONS: Indigenous religions 50%, Christianity 50%
EXPORTS: Diamonds, copper and nickel, meat

SOUTH AFRICA
PRONUNCIATION: sowth AF-ri-kuh
AREA: 471,445 sq. miles (1,221,043 sq. km)
POPULATION: 43,427,000
CAPITALS: Bloemfontein (judicial), Cape Town (legislative), Pretoria (administrative)
CURRENCY: 100 cents = 1 rand (R)
OFFICIAL LANGUAGES: Afrikaans, English, Xhosa, Zulu and other regional languages
MAIN RELIGIONS: Christianity 68%, Hinduism, Islam
EXPORTS: Gold, diamonds and other minerals and metals, food, chemicals

SWAZILAND

PRONUNCIATION: swah-zee-land
AREA: 6,705 sq. miles (17,366 sq. km)
POPULATION: 986,000
CAPITAL: Mbabane, Lobamba (legislative)
CURRENCY: 100 cents = 1 lilangeni (E)
OFFICIAL LANGUAGES: English, Swazi
MAIN RELIGIONS: Christianity 60%, indigenous religions 40%
EXPORTS: Sugar, wood pulp, cotton, asbestos

LESOTHO

PRONUNCIATION: luh-SOH-toh
AREA: 11,716 sq. miles (30,344 sq. km)
POPULATION: 2,129,000
CAPITAL: Maseru
CURRENCY: 100 licente = 1 loti (L)
OFFICIAL LANGUAGES: English, Sesotho
OTHER LANGUAGES: Zulu, Xhosa
MAIN RELIGIONS: Christianity 80%, indigenous religions 20%
EXPORTS: Wool, mohair, wheat, cattle, peas, beans, corn, animal skins, baskets

COMOROS
PRONUNCIATION: KAH-muh-rohz
AREA: 719 sq. miles (1,862 sq. km)
POPULATION: 562,800
CAPITAL: Moroni
CURRENCY: 100 centimes = 1 Comoran franc (CF)
OFFICIAL LANGUAGES: Arabic, French
OTHER LANGUAGE: Comoran
MAIN RELIGIONS: Islam 86%, Christianity 14%
EXPORTS: Vanilla, cloves, perfume oil, copra

MADAGASCAR
PRONUNCIATION: ma-duh-GAS-kuhr
AREA: 226,657 sq. miles (587,042 sq. km)
POPULATION: 14,874,000
CAPITAL: Antananarivo
CURRENCY: 100 centimes = 1 Malagasy franc (FMG)
OFFICIAL LANGUAGES: French, Malagasy
MAIN RELIGIONS: Indigenous religions 52%, Christianity 41%, Islam 7%
EXPORTS: Coffee, vanilla, cloves, shellfish, sugar, petroleum products

SEYCHELLES
PRONUNCIATION: say-SHELZ
AREA: 107 sq. miles (277 sq. km)
POPULATION: 79,200
CAPITAL: Victoria
CURRENCY: 100 cents = 1 Seychelles rupee (SRe)
OFFICIAL LANGUAGES: English, French
OTHER LANGUAGE: Seychelles creole
MAIN RELIGION: Christianity 98%
EXPORTS: Fish, cinnamon, copra, petroleum products

MAURITIUS
PRONUNCIATION: maw-RI-shuhs
AREA: 720 sq. miles (1,865 sq. km)
POPULATION: 1,183,000
CAPITAL: Port Louis
CURRENCY: 100 cents = 1 Mauritian rupee (MauR)
OFFICIAL LANGUAGE: English
OTHER LANGUAGES: Mauritian creole, French, Hindi, Urdu, Hakka, Bojpoori
MAIN RELIGIONS: Hinduism 52%, Christianity 28%, Islam 17%
EXPORTS: Textiles, sugar, light manufactured goods

Australia and Oceania

Australia

Pronunciation: aw-STRAYL-yuh
Area: 2,967,909 sq. miles (7,686,884 sq. km)
Population: 18,784,000
Capital: Canberra
Currency: 100 cents =1 Australian dollar ($A)
Official Language: English
Other Languages: Aboriginal languages
Main Religion: Christianity 76%
Exports: Coal, gold, meat, wool, wheat, machinery and transportation equipment

Papua New Guinea

Pronunciation: PA-pyoo-uh noo GI-nee
Area: 178,260 sq. miles (461,693 sq. km)
Population: 4,705,000
Capital: Port Moresby
Currency: 100 toea = 1 kina (K)
Official Languages: English, pidgin English, Motu
Other Languages: Regional languages
Main Religions: Christianity 66%, indigenous religions 34%
Exports: Gold, copper ore, oil, lumber, palm oil, coffee, cocoa, lobster

New Zealand

Pronunciation: noo ZEE-luhnd
Area: 103,736 sq. miles (268,676 sq. km)
Population: 3,663,000
Capital: Wellington
Currency: 100 cents = 1 New Zealand dollar (NZ$)
Official Language: English
Other Language: Maori
Main Religion: Christianity 67%
Exports: Wool, lamb, mutton, beef, fish, cheese, chemicals, forestry products, fruit and vegetables, manufactured goods

Solomon Islands

Pronunciation: SAH-luh-muhn islands
Area: 11,500 sq. miles (29,785 sq. km)
Population: 455,500
Capital: Honiara
Currency: 100 cents = 1 Solomon Islands dollar (SI$)
Official Language: English
Other Language: Melanesian pidgin
Main Religions: Christianity 96%, indigenous religions 4%
Exports: Fish, timber, palm oil, cocoa, copra

Western Samoa

Pronunciation: WEST-ern suh-MOH-uh
Area: 1,100 sq. miles (2,850 sq. km)
Population: 230,000
Capital: Apia
Currency: 100 sene = 1 tala (WS$)
Official Languages: Samoan (Polynesian), English
Main Religion: Christianity 99%
Exports: Coconut oil and cream, taro, copra, cocoa

Vanuatu

Pronunciation: van-wah-TOO
Area: 5,700 sq. miles (14,763 sq. km)
Population: 189,100
Capital: Port Vila
Currency: 100 centimes = 1 vatu (VT)
Official Languages: English, French
Other Language: Bislama
Main Religions: Christianity 77%, indigenous religions 8%
Exports: Copra, beef, cocoa, timber, coffee

Fiji

Pronunciation: FEE-jee
Area: 7,055 sq. miles (18,272 sq. km)
Population: 813,000
Capital: Suva
Currency: 100 cents = 1 Fijian dollar (F$)
Official Language: English
Other Languages: Fijian, Hindustani
Main Religions: Christianity 52%, Hinduism 38%, Islam 8%
Exports: Sugar, clothing, gold, processed fish, timber

Tonga

Pronunciation: TAHNG-guh
Area: 270 sq. miles (699 sq. km)
Population: 109,100
Capital: Nuku'alofa
Currency: 100 seniti = 1 pa'anga (T$)
Official Languages: Tongan, English
Main Religion: Christianity 70%
Exports: Squash, vanilla, fish, root crops, coconut oil

Kiribati

Pronunciation: kihr-uh-BAH-tee
Area: 277 sq. miles (717 sq. km)
Population: 85,500
Capital: Tarawa
Currency: 100 cents = 1 Australian dollar ($A)
Official Language: English
Other Language: Gilbertese
Main Religion: Christianity 94%
Exports: Copra, seaweed, fish

Marshall Islands

Pronunciation: MAR-shuhl islands
Area: 70 sq. miles (181 sq. km)
Population: 65,500
Capital: Majuro
Currency: 100 cents = 1 United States dollar (US$)
Official Language: English
Other Languages: Marshallese, Japanese
Main Religion: Christianity 98%
Exports: Coconut oil, fish, livestock, coffee

Federated States of Micronesia

Pronunciation: FE-der-ayt-ed STAYTS of meye-kruh-NEE-zhuh
Area: 266 sq. miles (689 sq. km)
Population: 131,500
Capital: Palikir
Currency: 100 cents = 1 United States dollar (US$)
Official Language: English
Other Languages: Regional languages
Main Religion: Christianity 97%
Exports: Fish, copra, bananas, black pepper

Nauru

Pronunciation: nah-OO-roo
Area: 8.5 sq. miles (22 sq. km)
Population: 10,600
Capital: None. Government offices in Yaren district
Currency: 100 cents = 1 Australian dollar ($A)
Official Language: Nauruan
Other Language: English
Main Religion: Christianity 100%
Export: Phosphates

Palau

Pronunciation: puh-LOW
Area: 191 sq. miles (495 sq. km)
Population: 18,500
Capital: Koror
Currency: 100 cents = 1 United States dollar (US$)
Official Language: English
Other Languages: Palauan, Sonsorolese, Angaur, Japanese, Tobi
Main Religions: Christianity 67%, Modekngei religion 33%
Exports: Shellfish, tuna, copra, handicrafts

Tuvalu

Pronunciation: too-VAH-loo
Area: 9 sq. miles (23 sq. km)
Population: 10,600
Capital: Funafuti Island
Currency: 100 cents = 1 Tuvaluan dollar ($T) or 1 Australian dollar ($A)
Official Languages: Tuvaluan, English
Main Religion: Christianity 98%
Exports: Copra

*T*erritories and Dependencies

THE COUNTRIES LISTED BELOW govern land outside their national borders. These areas of land are known as territories or dependencies. Some territories are governed directly by the country to which they belong. Others receive only protection and financial assistance, and have their own governments and laws.

UNITED STATES OF AMERICA

AMERICAN SAMOA: South Pacific Ocean; 76 sq. miles (197 sq. km); population 63,800
GUAM: Western Pacific Ocean; 209 sq. miles (541 sq. km); population 151,800
MIDWAY: Central Pacific Ocean; 2 sq. miles (5 sq. km); no permanent population
NORTHERN MARIANA ISLANDS: North Pacific Ocean; 184 sq. miles (477 sq. km); population 69,400
PUERTO RICO: Caribbean Sea; 70 sq. miles (113 sq. km); population 3,888,000
VIRGIN ISLANDS OF THE UNITED STATES: Caribbean Sea; 133 sq. miles (345 sq. km); population 119,900
WAKE ISLAND: North Pacific Ocean; 3 sq. miles (7.7 sq. km); population 126

UNITED KINGDOM

ANGUILLA: Caribbean Sea; 35 sq. miles (91 sq. km); population 11,600
BERMUDA: North Atlantic Ocean; 20 sq. miles (52 sq. km); population 62,500
BRITISH INDIAN OCEAN TERRITORY: Indian Ocean; 23 sq. miles (60 sq. km); no permanent population
BRITISH VIRGIN ISLANDS: Caribbean Sea; 59 sq. miles (153 sq. km); population 19,200
CAYMAN ISLANDS: Caribbean Sea; 118 sq. miles (306 sq. km); population 39,400
FALKLAND ISLANDS AND DEPENDENCIES (SOUTH GEORGIA AND SOUTH SANDWICH ISLANDS): South Atlantic Ocean; 6,270 sq. miles (16,240 sq. km); population 2,800
GIBRALTAR: Southern Spain; 2.25 sq. miles (6 sq. km); population 29,200
GUERNSEY: English Channel; 30 sq. miles (78 sq. km); population 65,400
ISLE OF MAN: Irish Sea; 221 sq. miles (572 sq. km); population 75,700
JERSEY: English Channel; 45 sq. miles (116 sq. km); population 89,730
MONTSERRAT: Caribbean Sea; 40 sq. miles (104 sq. km); population 12,860

PITCAIRN ISLANDS: South Pacific Ocean; 18 sq. miles (47 sq. km); population 50
ST. HELENA AND DEPENDENCIES (ASCENSION ISLAND AND TRISTAN DA CUNHA): South Atlantic Ocean; 119 sq. miles (308 sq. km); population 7,150
TURKS AND CAICOS ISLANDS: Caribbean Sea; 166 sq. miles (430 sq. km); population 16,900

FRANCE

FRENCH GUIANA: Northern South America; 35,126 sq. miles (90,976 sq. km); population 168,000
FRENCH POLYNESIA: South Pacific Ocean; 1,261 sq. miles (3,266 sq. km); population 242,100
GUADELOUPE: Caribbean Sea; 582 sq. miles (1,507 sq. km); population 421,000
MARTINIQUE: Caribbean Sea; 425 sq. miles (1,101 sq. km); population 411,600
MAYOTTE: Mozambique Channel, Africa; 144 sq. miles (373 sq. km); population 149,400
NEW CALEDONIA: South Pacific Ocean; 7,367 sq. miles (19,081 sq. km); population 197,400
RÉUNION: Indian Ocean; 969 sq. miles (2,510 sq. km); population 717,800
ST-PIERRE AND MIQUELON: North Atlantic Ocean; 93 sq. miles (241 sq. km); population 7,000
WALLIS AND FUTUNA ISLANDS: South Pacific Ocean; 106 sq. miles (275 sq. km); population 15,200

THE NETHERLANDS

ARUBA: Caribbean Sea; 69 sq. miles (179 sq. km); population 68,700
NETHERLANDS ANTILLES: Caribbean Sea; 371 sq. miles (961 sq. km); population 207,900

NORWAY

JAN MAYEN ISLAND: North Atlantic Ocean; 144 sq. miles (373 sq. km); no permanent population
SVALBARD: Arctic Ocean; 23,958 sq. miles (62,052 sq. km); population 2,505

DENMARK

FAEROE ISLANDS: North Atlantic Ocean; 540 sq. miles (1,399 sq. km); population 41,100
GREENLAND: North Atlantic Ocean; 840,000 sq. miles (2,175,000 sq. km); population 59,900

AUSTRALIA

CHRISTMAS ISLAND: Indian Ocean; 52 sq. miles (135 sq. km); population 2,380
COCOS (KEELING) ISLANDS: Indian Ocean; 9 sq. miles (23 sq. km); population 636
HEARD AND MCDONALD ISLANDS: Indian Ocean; 113 sq. miles (293 sq. km); no permanent population
NORFOLK ISLAND: South Pacific Ocean; 13 sq. miles (34 sq. km); population 1,905

NEW ZEALAND

COOK ISLANDS: South Pacific Ocean; 92 sq. miles (238 sq. km); population 20,200
NIUE: South Pacific Ocean; 100 sq. miles (259 sq. km); population 2,105
TOKELAU: South Pacific Ocean; 4 sq. miles (10 sq. km); population 1,475

DISPUTED TERRITORIES

GAZA STRIP (PALESTINE): Middle East; disputed by Israel and Palestine, Palestinian interim self-government; 146 sq. miles (378 sq. km); population 1,113,000
KASHMIR: Southern Asia; disputed by India and Pakistan; 53,665 sq. miles (138,992 sq. km); population 7,718,700
TURKISH FEDERATED STATE OF CYPRUS: Mediterranean Sea; disputed by Turkey and Cyprus; 1,322 sq. miles (3,424 sq. km); population 177,120
WEST BANK (PALESTINE): Middle East; disputed by Israel and Palestine, Palestinian interim self-government; 2,100 sq. miles (5,640 sq. km); population 1,612,000
WESTERN SAHARA: Northwestern Africa; disputed by Morocco and separatist movement; 102,703 sq. miles (266,001 sq. km); population 239,400

Glossary

acid rain ~ Rain that has combined with pollution in the atmosphere to form an acid. Acid rain can kill plants and damage buildings.

adaptation ~ A change that occurs in a plant's structure or in an animal's body or behavior to allow it to cope better with its environment.

agriculture ~ The use of the land to grow crops and raise animals. Agriculture is another word for farming.

altitude ~ The height of a place or object above sea level.

ancestor ~ A member of a person's family who lived a long time ago.

Antarctic Circle ~ A line of latitude at 66.5° south which marks the boundary of Earth's southern polar region. South of this line there is continuous daylight in midsummer and continuous darkness in midwinter.

archipelago ~ A large group of islands.

Arctic Circle ~ A line of latitude at 66.5° north that marks the boundary of Earth's northern polar region. North of this line there is continuous daylight in midsummer and continuous darkness in midwinter.

arid ~ Having low rainfall and, as a result, little vegetation. Very arid areas are called deserts.

atoll ~ A low, ring-shaped, sandy island enclosing a lagoon. An atoll is usually formed by the growth of a coral reef on top of an undersea mountain.

axis ~ An imaginary line through the center of Earth around which the planet is constantly rotating.

basin ~ 1. A wide, bowl-shaped depression in the landscape. 2. An area of land that is drained by a river and its tributaries.

bay ~ A body of water partly enclosed by land.

bight ~ A recess in a stretch of coastline which forms a large bay.

border ~ A line that separates one country from another.

canal ~ An artificial waterway, normally created by digging a large ditch to carry water to an irrigation area or to create a transportation route for shipping.

canyon ~ A deep, steep-sided valley formed by a river.

cape ~ A piece of land that juts out into a lake or sea.

capital ~ The city where a state or country's government is located. Sometimes a country has more than one capital because parts of its government are located in different cities.

cartographer ~ A person who makes maps. The science of making maps is known as cartography.

channel ~ A narrow stretch of water between two landmasses.

climate ~ The pattern of weather that occurs in a place over an extended period of time. Earth can be divided into a number of climate zones.

compass ~ 1. A device that contains a magnetic needle which indicates the direction of north. 2. An arrow or similar icon that indicates the direction of north on a map.

coniferous ~ Coniferous trees are evergreen trees that produce seeds inside cones and usually have thin, needle-shaped or scaly leaves.

continent ~ One of Earth's seven major landmasses: Europe, Asia, Africa, North America, South America, Australia and Antarctica.

coral ~ A hard, rocky material formed by the skeletons of tiny creatures called coral polyps.

crop ~ A plant that is grown in large quantities by farmers. Crops include foods such as cereals and vegetables as well as other plants such as cotton and tobacco.

crust ~ The hard, thin rocky layer that covers the surface of Earth. The crust is broken into segments called plates.

culture ~ The shared traditions and way of life of a people.

currency ~ The kind of money used in a country.

dam ~ A wall-like barrier built to hold back the water of a river and create an artificial lake called a reservoir.

deciduous ~ Deciduous trees shed their leaves every year, usually in fall. The tree remains bare during winter but grows new leaves in spring.

deforestation ~ The cutting down of forest trees for timber, or to clear land for farming or building.

delta ~ A fan-shaped area of land formed by silt deposited by rivers where they empty into the sea.

dependency ~ A region or landmass governed by another country.

descendants ~ The offspring of a person, including his or her children, children's children, and so on.

desert ~ A dry area with low rainfall and sparse vegetation that is adapted to withstand drought.

earthquake ~ A shaking of the ground caused by the sudden movement of part of Earth's crust.

ecosystem ~ A community of plants and animals and the environment to which they are adapted.

endangered ~ An animal or plant species that is in danger of becoming extinct.

environment ~ The natural surroundings of a community of plants and animals, particularly the shape of the land, the climate and the soil.

equator ~ An imaginary line that circles the globe midway between the North and South poles. The equator divides the world into the Northern and Southern hemispheres.

ethnic group ~ A group of people sharing the same origin, language, nationality and lifestyle.

evergreen ~ An evergreen tree is a tree that does not shed its leaves in winter.

evolution ~ A process of gradual change, especially in living things.

exports ~ Goods that are sold to other countries.

extinct ~ An extinct species of animal or plant is one that no longer exists because all the individual animals or plants died.

federation ~ A union, by mutual agreement, of states or territories to form one country.

fertile ~ Fertile land is land with good soil. Plants grow well in fertile land if there is good rainfall or irrigation.

fjord ~ A deep, steep-sided valley gouged out by a glacier and later flooded by the sea to form a narrow inlet.

forestry ~ The science of making use of and managing forest resources.

fossil ~ The remains or traces of a prehistoric plant or animal, normally found between layers of rock.

fossil fuel ~ Fuel found deep underground which formed from the decayed remains of prehistoric plants and animals. The most common fossil fuels are coal, oil and natural gas.

gazetteer ~ An index of place names.

geyser ~ A spring that boils and emits hot water and steam.

glacier ~ A large mass of ice that moves slowly down the side of a mountain or along a valley, and is constantly replenished by snowfall at the top of the mountain.

gorge ~ A deep, steep-sided, rocky valley.

grassland ~ A large area of land covered with grass plants.

Greenwich meridian ~ An imaginary line that extends from the North Pole to the South Pole through Greenwich, England, and that marks 0° longitude.

gulf ~ A large bay.

hemisphere ~ One half of the world. Earth is divided into Northern and Southern hemispheres by the equator, and into Eastern and Western hemispheres by the Greenwich meridian (0°) and 180° line.

high-tech industries ~ Industries that produce electronic goods such as computers.

hydroelectricity ~ Electricity produced using the power of running water.

iceberg ~ A large block of ice floating in the sea. Icebergs break off the ends of glaciers and ice sheets. The part of an iceberg under the surface of the sea is usually eight times as large as the part above the surface.

ice cap ~ A sheet of ice and snow that covers an area permanently. Ice caps are found in polar regions and on some high mountaintops.

immigrant ~ A person who has come from one country to live in another.

independent ~ Not governed by another country.

inlet ~ A narrow bay.

irrigation ~ The process of providing water to farmland by artificial means, such as pumping water from rivers, lakes and dams, or diverting water through channels and pipes.

island ~ An area of land surrounded by water.

kingdom ~ A country whose ruler or head of state is a king or queen.

lagoon ~ 1. A shallow area of salt water separated from the sea by a strip of land. 2. Inland bodies of water that were previously part of a river.

landmass ~ A large area of land not covered by water.

latitude ~ Distance north or south of the equator measured in degrees.

livestock ~ Animals, such as cattle or sheep, raised by farmers.

longitude ~ Distance east or west of the Greenwich meridian measured in degrees.

marsh ~ An area of wet land containing plants adapted to growth in water. Also called a swamp or wetland.

manufacturing ~ The making of useful products from raw materials.

migration ~ Movement of people or animals to another country or region. Many animals migrate to find food or avoid severe weather.

mineral ~ A substance occurring naturally in Earth's crust that is neither plant nor animal. Well-known minerals include chalk, clay and many metals.

native people ~ The original human inhabitants of a region or country.

nomad ~ A person who does not live in one place but continually moves around. Nomads often move in search of food and water for themselves and their animals.

North Pole ~ see pole

oasis ~ A patch of land in a desert where there is water and more vegetation than elsewhere.

peninsula ~ A long strip of land that extends outward from a larger landmass and is almost surrounded by water.

plain ~ An area of flat or rolling land with shallow river valleys.

plantation ~ A piece of land where a particular tree crop is grown. Such crops include forest trees, rubber and coconut palms.

plate ~ One of the segments of Earth's crust.

plateau ~ An area of flat or rolling land with deep river valleys, gorges and canyons.

pole ~ The points on Earth's surface representing the ends of the planet's axis, around which it is constantly rotating. The North Pole is Earth's most northern point. The South Pole is the most southern point. The regions around the poles are known as the polar regions.

population ~ 1. The people who live in a place. 2. The total number of people living in a place.

populous ~ A populous country is a country with a large population.

principality ~ A country whose ruler or head of state is a prince or princess.

radioactive ~ Radioactive materials emit high-energy particles in the form of invisible rays. Some natural substances, such as uranium, are radioactive.

rain forest ~ A type of dense forest that grows in regions of high rainfall.

range ~ 1. A chain of mountains. 2. An area of open grassland where animals graze.

raw materials ~ Natural substances which can be turned into useful products. Examples include timber, coal and coffee beans. Raw materials are also known as resources.

reef ~ A ridge of rock, sand or coral lying just below the surface of the sea.

republic ~ A country led by an elected representative called a president.

reservoir ~ An artificial lake, usually created by building a dam across a river.

resources ~ Substances or materials that occur naturally in a place and are of value to the area's inhabitants. Resources that can never be used up, such as water and waves, are called renewable resources. Resources that will eventually be used up, such as coal and other minerals, are known as nonrenewable resources.

river basin ~ An area of land drained by a river and its tributaries.

rural ~ Relating to the countryside. Rural industry means industry located in country areas.

savanna ~ A type of grassland with scattered trees. Most savannas occur in tropical areas that have a distinct summer wet season.

scale ~ An indication on a map of how distances on the map relate to actual distances.

scrub ~ An area of land covered with shrubs and low trees.

sea level ~ The average height of the surface of the sea, which is used as a base point for measuring altitude.

South Pole ~ see pole

species ~ Animals or plants of the same type.

steppe ~ A type of dry grassland that covers parts of eastern Europe and central Asia.

strait ~ A narrow strip of water that connects two larger bodies of water.

swamp ~ An area of wet land containing plants adapted to growth in water. Also called a marsh or wetland.

technology ~ The use of scientific knowledge to carry out certain tasks or solve certain problems. Using machines in industry is an example of technology.

temperate ~ Neither hot nor cold. Most of Earth's temperate regions are located between the tropics and the polar regions.

territory ~ 1. A large area of land. 2. All the land and sea governed by a country or state. 3. A region or landmass governed by a country that is located in another part of the world.

textiles ~ Woven or knitted fabrics.

time zone ~ A region in which everyone uses the same time. The world is divided into 24 time zones. The time in each zone is usually one hour earlier than the zone to its east.

trade ~ The buying and selling of goods.

tributary ~ A stream or river that flows into a larger stream or river.

Tropic of Cancer/Capricorn ~ see tropics

tropics ~ 1. The hot, wet regions of Earth that lie near the equator. 2. Either of two lines of latitude: the Tropic of Cancer at 23.5° north and the Tropic of Capricorn at 23.5° south. Because Earth is tilted at an angle of 23.5°, these lines mark the point at which the Sun is directly overhead in summer.

tundra ~ A cold, barren area where much of the soil is frozen and the vegetation consists of only mosses, lichens and other small plants adapted to withstanding intense cold. Tundra is found near the Arctic Circle and on mountaintops.

urban ~ Relating to cities. A country's urban population is the number of people that live in its cities.

valley ~ A long, narrow depression in the land along which a river usually flows.

vegetation ~ The community of plants that is characteristic of a particular region.

volcano ~ A mountain that has been built up from molten rock erupting through a hole in Earth's crust.

wetland ~ An area of wet land containing plants adapted to growth in water. Also called a swamp or marsh.

woodland ~ An area of land covered with widely spaced trees and shrubs.

Index and Gazetteer

Acknowledgments

Weldon Owen would like to thank the following people for their assistance in the production of this book:
Helen Bateman, Anthony Burton, Alastair Campbell, Jo Collard, Melanie Corfield, Simon Corfield, Sharon Dalgleish, Libby Frederico, Kathy Gammon, Kathy Gerrard, Janine Googan, Greg Hassall, Lynn Humphries, Chris Jackson, Megan Johnston, Ralph Kelly, Jennifer Le Gras, Rosemary McDonald, Kylie Mulquin, Nicholas Rowland, Rachel Smith, Julie Stanton, Dawn Titmus, Greg Tobin, Wendy van Buuren, Michael Wyatt

Cartographic sources: U.S. Central Intelligence Agency; International Boundaries Research Unit, Durham University, United Kingdom; U.S. Geographer General

Photographic credits: 14 bottom left, **David Weintraub**/The Photo Library—Sydney; 14 bottom center, **Stephen Wilkes**/The Image Bank; 14 bottom right, **Mats Wibe Lund**/Icelandic Photo; 15 center far right, **David Hardy**/SPL/The Photo Library—Sydney; 15 bottom left, **Francois Gohier**/Ardea London; 15 bottom center, **B. McDairmant**/Ardea London; 15 bottom right, **International Photo Library**; 16 top far right, **Robert Harding** Picture Library; 16 bottom, **David W. Hamilton**/The Image Bank; 17 top left, **Jeffrey C. Drewitz**/The Photo Library—Sydney; 17 top center left, **Sobel/Klonsky**/The Image Bank; 17 top center, **Horizon International**; 17 top center right, **Staffan Widstrand**/Bruce Coleman Limited; 17 top right, **Christer Fredriksson**/Bruce Coleman Limited; 19 top center, **Alain Compost**/Bruce Coleman Limited; 27 top, **Horizon International**; 27 center, **Shone/Gamma/Picturemedia**; 27 bottom, **Witt/Sipa Press**/The Photo Library—Sydney

The Polar Regions
102

Northern
Europe
72

North
Eur
7

The United
Kingdom and the
Republic of Ireland
56

The Low
Countrie
62

Western Canada
and Alaska
34

Western Central Europe

Eastern Canada
36

France 60

Central
United
States
42

Western
United States
44

38 Northeastern
United States

Spain and Portugal
58

Italy

Southern
United States
40

Mexico,
Central America
and the Caribbean
46

Northern
Africa
92

Northern
South America
50

Southern
South America
52